CONSTRUCTIVE SPIRIT
QUAKERS IN REVOLUTIONARY RUSSIA

Intentional Productions
PO Box 94814
Pasadena, California 91109

CONSTRUCTIVE SPIRIT
QUAKERS IN
REVOLUTIONARY RUSSIA

David McFadden and Claire Gorfinkel
With an overview by Sergei Nikitin

acknowledgments:

The authors gratefully acknowledge the assistance and support of many people and institutions without whose cooperation this book would not have been possible: the American Friends Service Committee, Irwin Abrams, Margaret Hope Bacon, Blue Mountain Center, Jane Bowles, Betsy Brown, Alyson Cafferky, Louise Carcusa, Steve Cary, Charles Cherry, A.O. Chubarian, Wendy Chmielewski, Nancy Cogsdale, Aaron Coles, Peter Dyson, Rebecca Elswit, Fairfield University Research Committee, Olga Filimonova, Terry Foss, J. William Frost, Lee Jones Hargedon, Mary Hoxie Jones, Thomas C. Kennedy, Emma Lapsansky, Larry Miller, Svetlana Morozova, Tatiana Pavlova, Diana Peterson, Katherine A.S. Siegel, Rosemary Shiras, Jack Sutters, Anna Tavis, Margaret Trott, Barbara Swann, Sergei Shilov, Larry Swink, the Archivists at the Hoover Institution on War, Revolution and Peace, Stanford University; and at the Buzuluk and Samara Archives, Josef Keith and Malcolm Thomas, Friends House London; Elaine Markinson of the Inn, West Branch, Iowa; Dale Moyer and Dwight Miller, Hoover Library, West Branch, Iowa; Norval and Joan Tucker and West Branch Friends Meeting; Librarian, South China Maine; The Tolstoy State Museum, and all the famine survivors and their relatives in the Buzuluk and "pro volshe" area who shared their stories with us.

Book and cover design by Anne Richardson-Daniel

© 2004
Intentional Productions
Pasadena, California
ISBN 0-9648042-5-5
Library of Congress Number 2003116972

For Carrie, Alex, and Annie:
may their lives be as blessed with friendship
and meaningful work as ours have been.

CONTENTS

pbotoGRapbs, iLLustRatioNs, (Dap

*We wanted to show our faith in action
and to show it in a way that would both
bring healing ... and at the same time
take us out of self and selfish aims
and carry us into the furnace where
others were suffering.*

Rufus Jones
A Service of Love in War Time

INTRODUCTION
A STORY THAT DESERVES TO BE TOLD

More than eighty years ago, Rufus Jones wrote *A Service of Love in War Time*. His goal was to interpret the founding of the American Friends Service Committee and its earliest attempts "to express their spirit of human love to a part of the world ... caught in the awful tangle of the tragedy"[1] of the First World War. He focused principally on the relief and reconstruction work in France, and the initial group of 100 volunteers known as the "Haverford Unit," who exemplified both the high ideals and the creativity of the earliest AFSC. As Jones notes, the Haverford Unit was not entirely composed of Quakers, but all were convinced that war was incompatible with their religious faith. As a matter of deeply held principle they felt compelled to seek exemption from military service. At the same time they wanted to express their love of country and their willingness to accept some personal risk through alternative service. It is a wonderful story with which Rufus Jones was intimately involved – one that could be told because it was largely completed – and he tells it in characteristically lucid prose.

The work in France – driving ambulances, reconstructing homes, roads and villages – was hard physical labor, only men were subject to the draft, and the Haverford Unit was made up entirely of men. However, in June 1917 the American Friends Service Committee had arranged for a small team to join English Friends in Buzuluk, Russia, where they were providing relief to tens of thousands of refugees who had fled from fighting between the German and the Russian armies. The "American Unit" consisted of six extraordinary women: Anna J. Haines, Lydia Lewis, Esther White, Emilie Bradbury, Nancy Babb and Amelia Fabriszewski. When Rufus Jones wrote *A Service of Love in War Time* their story was still unfolding. He recorded his hope "that persons of leisure will be found in the not distant future" who would write about those who

> have gone out with living faith and with efficient relief into some of
> the darkest regions of the suffering world, both in war-time and in the
> no less appalling period which has followed the armistice.[2]

In 1937, Mary Hoxie Jones (Rufus' daughter) resumed telling the history of the American Friends Service Committee's first twenty years. She devotes five pages of *Swords into Ploughshares* to the basic facts of war refugee and famine relief work in Russia, from 1916 to 1920. A skilled writer like her father, she also offers a sensitive composite portrait of the British and American women. Richenda Scott's 1964 volume *Quakers in Russia* tells of the British experience in comprehensive detail, starting in the 1700s. But her references to the roles of American Friends and the American government during the first part of the 20th Century are limited.

J. William Frost also took up the task of telling the AFSC's early history. Writing in 1992 for the 75th Anniversary of the organization, his article *"Our Deeds Carry Our Message"* concisely recaps the early formative years, the work in France and later in Germany, and the internal struggles over how best to express Quaker values. He neatly illuminates the lengthy controversy over feeding programs in Russia, "the [AFSC] Board had to convince the Soviet leaders that Friends were not part of a British and U.S. plot to undermine the Revolution and at the same time persuade a strongly anti-Communist American public to provide food and funds for Russian relief." [3] According to Frost:

> During its ten years in Russia, the AFSC fed children and nursing mothers with A.R.A. food, and, on its own, the entire population in the district of Buzuluk. It imported medical supplies, provided medical care and training programs for mothers and babies, ran orphanages and schools, imported horses, and taught modern farming methods while contending with sporadic harassments from the Soviets, Hoover, and the media. . . . [4]

Our initial challenge in this work was to take up Rufus Jones' call, to tell the stories of the courageous Americans, and especially the women who left us the most interesting and detailed records. Nancy Babb, for example, was in Russia off and on from the end of WWI through the Civil War, the early years of the socialist revolution and the worst phase of the famine. She said she went to be "a living testimony of justice, Christianity, and the spirit of Friends Service," yet she almost single-handedly mobilized 11,000 Russians, farmed 1,800 acres, started cottage industries and public works projects, oversaw 44 clinics and built a county hospital. Her unique and innovative "food for work" program allowed peasants to exchange their labor, rather than goods or (often non-existent) cash, for desperately needed commodities, basic foodstuffs and medicine. Thus, while saving lives, she also enabled the peasants to preserve their dignity and developed one of the guiding principles of "appropriate development" efforts to this day.

We were also drawn to other tasks: to explore the complex dilemmas of politics, religious witness and service, both from the vantage point of the relief workers themselves and the administrative leadership at home. Staff in the field anguished over how to express their faith amidst great suffering in a foreign land. Should they be explicit, providing written statements of religious principles, or would their convictions shine implicitly through the work? Did they have to choose between 'tracts' and tractors? Meanwhile, back in

Philadelphia, New York and Washington, the AFSC staff and committee leadership faced controversies over secular ideologies and their relationships with donors, the US government (particularly the American Relief Administration under the leadership of Herbert Hoover, himself a Quaker) Bolsheviks, labor unions and the left. We hope these historical precedents will help illuminate both the past, and the present work of the American Friends Service Committee.

The Politics of Service

A broad green lawn stretches out in front of the Honolulu Friends Meetinghouse. At the top of the driveway near the wide front stairs there's a water spigot with a drinking fountain attached. From a comfortable vantage point on the Meetinghouse porch one can observe the weekend joggers, high school running teams, would-be marathoners, and all kinds of people as they pause on their walks, their jogs, their morning runs, their afternoon workouts, to help themselves to a refreshing drink of water.

This passing procession offers a metaphor for the American Friends Service Committee's early mission of "offering a cool drink of water" to all victims of war and natural disasters, regardless of race or national origin, political affiliation or religious creed, and its evolution over almost ninety years. For example in 1969 AFSC's work in Vietnam was focused on serving the needs of "both sides" in the conflict. The hospital at Quang Ngai treated all victims of the war so long as they did not bring weapons into the compound. Medical supplies were conscientiously delivered to both North and South Vietnam, and the AFSC assumed substantial legal and financial risks for delivering aid to "the enemy." The AFSC publicly opposed the war starting in the mid-1960s, but in the 1970s it became clear that more was needed. Those who were truly concerned with relieving suffering must call attention to the American government's complicity and *responsibility* for the violence. They needed to stand with the oppressed, to be political, stage demonstrations – sit-ins, walkouts, blockades, boycotts, teach-ins, civil disobedience and other forms of nonviolent witness. It was not enough to help the victims; they needed to *stop the war*.

Individual and corporate roles in perpetuating oppression through privileges of class, race, gender and so forth became more apparent. Once it had been appropriate to send a delegation to rebuild a community center in a low-income neighborhood. Now the challenge was to provide the tools and the training, to "empower" the local community to make their own decisions about what would be repaired and then do the work themselves. Sending bales of clothing and truckloads of food was no longer a sufficient response to war or natural disaster. Communities needed supplies and tools to rebuild their own roads, bridges and schools, to replant their crops, equip their hospitals and clinics. Offering people a "cool drink of water" – whether they were refugees fleeing wars or natural disasters or folks running through the Honolulu neighborhood – was no longer sufficient. It was time to build dams and pipelines, to stop dumping pollutants in the streams, to test the water *and make sure that it was clean.*

Constructive Spirit

The stories of Anna Haines, Nancy Babb and the other Quakers who went to Russia to provide relief from war and famine during the first years of the AFSC demonstrate that complex issues of witness, politics and service have been present throughout its history. In 1917, the AFSC and the British Quaker International Service argued over the mission of "neutral" service, relief for its own sake and because children were starving. Some felt threatened by any association with the Bolsheviks, while others were enthusiastic partisans of their revolution. Some people felt that being identified with the *United States* government was problematic.

Some field staff wanted greater independence. They felt that the central offices shouldn't set directions or even policy. Neither Philadelphia nor London could possibly understand them, the contexts of their work or the hardships they alternately enjoyed and endured. They manifested profoundly different working styles, with varying degrees of harmony. Nancy Babb was fiercely independent, creative, self-motivated, driven, a consummate organizer with little inclination for analysis. Some found her hard to work with. Her one surviving journal (fifty undated pages of scrawled sentence fragments) is frustrating for what is *not* revealed. Anna Haines, by contrast, carefully typed long letters describing and analyzing everything she saw and did. In 1920, she was clearly thrilled by the Quakers' eight-pointed reconstruction star shining "in uncracked purity of line," guaranteeing the security of foodstuffs in the warehouse (see chapter 7). She was a team player who referred to herself as mere "ballast," even as she trudged through snowy Moscow streets to negotiate with Bolshevik authorities and search out the meanings of Quaker Service.

Meanwhile, supervisors back home had numerous, often conflicting, constituencies to consider. They dealt with funders and other relief organizations, Quakers and publicists, government officials and bureaucrats. They begged the field staff for more clarity, more reports and more photographs to help with "message work," garnering public sympathy and fundraising. In the distinct leadership styles of AFSC Chairman Rufus Jones and Executive Secretary Wilbur Thomas we see a creative dynamic that has persisted throughout AFSC's history as well. Jones, an academic, philosopher and writer, was a bridge-builder, attuned to the mystical potential of action and risk-taking. Ever conscious of his diverse Quaker constituency, even in his activism he focused on broad organizational goals, the big picture. Thomas, a Quaker Pastor from the Midwest, focused on getting the work done. His priority was the program in the field; his constituency was the staff and those whom they went to serve. His mission was to help the team achieve their objectives whether that meant amassing supplies, feeding children or confronting powerful government officials. His terms were more secular; his vision was more political. His investment was in affecting change. Both men played essential roles in advancing the organization and its work.

Why did they go to Russia? Were they missionaries intent on promoting their faith? Were they young people seeking adventure before "settling down?" Were they altruists committed to serving those less fortunate than they? Were they mystics who felt a "call?" Were they public servants with a mission to perform? Were they visionaries who wanted to experience the revolution? Was it Russia that called them? The answer is "all of the above" and "we don't know." Richenda Scott characterized the first contingent of twenty-six British Friends as "strangely assorted."

> There were women in early middle life, of tried solidity and worth, … people from … upper middle class comforts and conventions … with no specific qualifications; skilled doctors and surgeons; … keen young intellectuals … whose main … interests lay in … hammering out their own philosophy of life and attempting to apply it in action; enthusiastic idealists … willing to throw themselves headlong into the most humdrum and unpleasant tasks; slightly older people of more sober, practical outlook, lacking the fire of an overpowering idea – people of different gifts and varying limitations, from a wide range of social settings, religious allegiances and educational opportunities.

Our challenge is to look to the work itself and then we may conclude, as J. William Frost has so skillfully done, "Our deeds carry our message." As we approach the hundredth anniversary of the founding of the AFSC, there are many lessons to learn from its past. But first the stories deserve to be told.

1. A PERSONAL OVERVIEW
BY SERGEI NIKITIN

I heard about Quakers for the first time in 1991 when I was 34 years old, staying with my pen pal Tom Somerford, in England. It sounded like the perfect religion: listening to the Divine Spirit from within, no rituals, no priests. I borrowed some leaflets from a Quaker meetinghouse, and when I returned to Russia I wrote to Harvey Gillman, Outreach Secretary at Friends House in London. He sent me more literature and we exchanged letters and discussed Quaker theology.

Peter and Roswitha Jarman came to Russia in 1990 as the first "permanent" Quaker representatives since 1931 and I was glad to meet them. In 1993 I participated in a Quaker International Service Project (QISP), and visited Friends House in London. Bill Chadkirk, then head of QISP was the first person to tell me about British and American Friends who came to a very remote and small Russian town of Buzuluk in 1917 just on the eve of the Bolshevik revolution and the Civil War. He said they were warmly welcomed, even by the Soviet authorities. The brave foreigners stayed there, helped refugees and local peasants, suffered from cold, hunger and uncertainty, and hid themselves along with the local civilians in the cellars of houses during the Civil War fighting. Later they saved many lives during the years of the Great Famine.

I am not a historian. My English is far from perfect, but I was absolutely convinced that I should

Sergei Nikitin in front of Totskoye library, 1998

investigate the whole story. I thought it should be known in Russia, particularly in the town where the Quakers worked. I studied at Woodbrooke, and the Friends House library in London. I went to Buzuluk and Samara to see if there were people who remembered the Friends relief work or any documents in the archives. In 1997, as a Pendle Hill international student, I got an amazing opportunity to work in the AFSC archives. Every week during the term I went to the Friends Center to read the documents related to the period.

The more I read, the more I admired the Friends who worked in Russia long ago. I felt great sympathy towards them and some of them became my friends although of course I had never met them. I looked at the old photographs taken in Russia eighty years ago with great curiosity. It was a tremendous feeling to see the faces of those whose letters and diaries I was reading.

How did the Story Begin?

As a result of World War I, thousands and thousands of refugees had to leave Poland (which was then a part of the Russian Empire) Byelorussia (now Belarus) and the Baltic provinces, and move east with their families to places where nobody welcomed them. The worst situation was in the Samara district, beyond the Volga River, and the most appalling conditions were in the Buzuluk district, where about 26,000 refugees formed a quarter of the total population. They lacked clothing and food. They were not used to the cold winter climate. The Russian government gave them some money but scarcely enough to prevent starvation. The local peasants did not welcome the refugees because they did not have enough food for themselves. The refugees had nothing to do, and their idleness may have been the most depressing thing for them.

Russian Foreign Minister Sergei Sazonov (who was well known as an Anglophile in the Russian government) issued an appeal. It reached England in 1916, along with accounts of the terrible situation of the refugees from all the western fronts of Russia, prompting the Friends' War Victims Relief Committee (FWVRC) to send a mission from London to investigate. William Cadbury, Joseph Burtt, Robert Tatlock and Theodore Rigg arrived at Petrograd, the Russian capitol on April 19, 1916. [1]

Some recall that the Russian authorities warmly welcomed them, but I found a letter in the St. Petersburg archives from the Director of the Police Department to the Department of Religious Affairs "concerning the arrival of the English Quakers to Petrograd." It says, "A group of Quakers came to Petrograd and its intention is to organize aid to the Russian refugees and victims of the World War." His brief account of Quaker history includes, "Rigid discipline within the sect forbids its members to join the army and this fact requires our attention." The author says that George Fox, the leader of the Quaker sect, who died in 1915 (sic!), was a chairman of the "Society of the British-German Friendship" and Quakers were not sympathetic to the current war. He adds that Quakers were known for their intense desire to propagate their ideas, and that Russian sects consider Quakers very generous. "Therefore I dare to ask you whether I should put the visitors under police supervision and make further reports on those whom the Quakers will meet."[2]

The Quaker investigators went from Petrograd to Moscow where they learned that the worst situation was in Buzuluk, between Samara and Orenburg. William Cadbury returned to England with a report and the three other Friends went to Buzuluk to work out how to help the refugees. As a result, Friends decided to send a group of doctors, nurses and relief workers to the Buzuluk district.

The first team of relief workers and doctors arrived in August 1916, and by April 1917 there were about 35 workers in the Buzuluk area. They opened five work centers for refugees to clean, spin, and weave wool and an orphanage in Mogotovo for the refugee children whose fathers were fighting in the war and whose mothers had died. They established a hospital in Andreevka that ultimately served some 4,200 refugees. Theodore Rigg, a 28-year-old Quaker from New Zealand, who had experience with relief work in France, Monte Negro and Albania, became head of the Friends Unit.[3]

In June 1917, six American Friends – Nancy Babb, Emilie Bradbury, Anna Haines, Lydia Lewis, Esther White and Amelia Fabriszewski – left Philadelphia for Russia. Theodore Rigg wrote to Henry Cadbury (the chairman of the Young Friends Committee), "We are looking forward to the arrival of our American Friends and hope that they will not be delayed on their journey, as we are extremely understaffed at present and hope that our Friends will relieve the strain to which some of our workers have been subjected for some considerable time now." [4]

No one met the Americans when they arrived at the station in Buzuluk at 10 PM on August 26. None of the locals knew where the English Mission (as it was known in Buzuluk) was. Eventually Theodore Rigg found them. Emilie Bradbury noted in her diary that they went to bed at 2 AM. They soon divided up to work alongside the British Friends in different villages. Anna Haines reported back to Philadelphia, "We who are helping the refugees are none too popular with the native population, who are in many cases as poor as the refugees." [5]

Of course the small group of Friends could not help all the refugees, but they chose the most difficult place and they did their best to help those who suffered. One report said, "In the district where our relief work has been actively pursued, there are some 5,200 refugees, which is only about 12% of the [total population]. ... We have the satisfaction of feeling that we have helped the most needy refugees in the Buzuluk district." [6]

The Quaker team organized holidays for refugee children and work places for the adults. Emilie Bradbury described a Christmas party in Andreevka where they played games and had "tea, bread, some little hard cubes sweetened with a black kind of molasses, sunflowers seeds and sugar!" That was a delicious treat for the refugee children. One old woman who watched the merriment told Emily, "I am 60 years old, but I've never seen anything like that." It must have been a Christmas to remember, and something new for the Russians – to celebrate with the strange people who came from God knows where, and spoke an unfamiliar language but were so friendly to them![7]

One month after the Russian Revolution of November 1917, Bolshevik troops arrived in Buzuluk. The Friends reported, "We are treated with the utmost respect by the Bolshevik representatives here." But another letter stated, "During the last two weeks the Bolshevik Commissioners have carried out some drastic measures against the capitalistic and property owning class of Buzuluk. The position of the refugees at the present moment is exceedingly bad for the peasants are refusing to supply them with but the scantiest ration." [8]

As the village centers were closed down and local authorities took control of the hospital in Andreevka, the Quakers took responsibility for reorganizing and maintaining an orphanage in Buzuluk. Fortunately, more Russian doctors returned home at the end of the war and they were able to run the hospital.

The Quaker Unit needed money to purchase food for the refugees. Somehow the sum of 5,000 British pounds had been transferred to Russia from London, and in June 1918 Theodore Rigg traveled to Moscow to bring back the money in rubles. While he was in Moscow, the Czech occupation of Samara spread, and Rigg's return to Buzuluk required crossing both Czech and Bolshevik front lines. For a brief time the Quakers had to take refuge from the fighting in a basement. Emilie Bradbury wrote in her diary on June 28, 1918, "Great excitement talking over the bombardment – one girl's father killed but no one else seems to have suffered, though many of the landlords went to the basements." [9] Two additional soup kitchens for refugees were opened, along with a hostel and a workshop for boys, and despite the hardships, Rigg reported that the majority of the unit workers were prepared to stay on through another winter while anticipating the arrival of new workers from England and America.

The presence of the group of foreigners in the small town must have seemed very peculiar to locals but the Quaker example of working, rather than talking or preaching like missionaries, had considerable impact. A local Buzuluk newspaper praised the Friends' work saying that "real Russian citizens are educated here, not clodhoppers." He described his visit to a Quaker workshop for children:

> "Why do not we do as they do? Do not we see how poor we are? Do we still believe we can sit with our hand on our knees and build castles in the air? ... Some people may say they are too businesslike, energetic, cold and uninteresting. That is the common opinion about

English and American people in Russia. But if you had seen how simply and nicely they talked, how pleased they were with my interest in their work, I am sure you would not call them cold. ... And now let us learn from them, let us follow their example, quick-quick. It is better to have something good not our own than to have our own but bad." [10]

By the autumn of 1918, the situation in Buzuluk became rather unstable. Theodore Rigg and Esther White had gone to Moscow and then to Tambov to manage the three children's colonies which had been handed over to the Quakers by the Soviet authorities and the Tolstoyans (see chapter 3). They remained there until March 1919. Later that year they were married at the Coulter Street Friends Meeting in Germantown, Pennsylvania. In his memoirs, Rigg reflected that the selection of Esther White as his companion to work at the children's colonies "was splendid" for him. "I had already formed a very high opinion of her ability, enthusiasm and courage. I was confident that we could work happily together and that she should be a most reliable and helpful partner in the difficulties which were bound to occur." He said that their hazardous journeys and hardships led to a comradeship and esteem that remained with them throughout their married life.[11]

In his final report, written on his way home from Russia, Theodore Rigg made some very interesting observations about Russia, which I think are still true today.

All Russians, even the educated ones, are extraordinarily generous and friendly. They will give their money, their clothes, their hospitality almost to the limit of their resources, but one thing they do not give and that is the greatest gift of all – their lives in service to remedy the evils of their land. Their petty round of pleasure, their friends, the delights of the towns are too great for them – they cannot leave them. ... Some educated Russians are atheistic, but the vast majority do believe in God – a God however who is far removed from their lives. Their church gives them no conception of the humanity of Christ – Christ as a brother and friend. Their religion gives them no conception of that spiritual life and that inner communion which to Friends is their support and stay from day to day, and which enables them to face all things – imprisonment and even death – with calmness and peace. [12]

Theodore Rigg proposed establishing a "Quaker Embassy" in Russia, where a small group of people would help keep in touch with Russian life and contribute whatever good their training, their temperament, and their ideals enabled them to offer.

When the fighting made it impossible for them to remain in Buzuluk, the rest of the Quaker group went to Siberia where they worked with the American Red Cross and the YMCA helping prisoners of war and refugees until November 1919. As they were leaving, they received several farewell letters from the local peasants. One said, "We all the citizens of Vassileyevka decided to bring you our sincere gratitude for all the work you've done for us at this difficult time. Though you leave us, we strongly believe that you will remain our friends as before, and that you will give us the same help in the future (if it is possible)." [13] Very soon the Quakers came to aid the Russians in this region, who were dying of starvation.

Quakers never gave up the idea of coming back to Russia. In 1920 two British Friends obtained permission to bring food supplies for the children of Petrograd and Moscow. One of them, Gregory Welch, had been to Russia in 1917, and this time he was allowed to remain only one month, while Arthur Watts stayed in Soviet Russia for the rest of his life.

Friends hoped that the Revolution would provide an atmosphere of real freedom, that it would become easier to spread Quaker ideas. William Albright reported from Russia, "Two striking sayings are prominent in Moscow. One, recently put up, faces you as you enter Red Square, by the side of the Kremlin: "Religion is the opiate of the people." Another is still allowed to stand high on the corner of the University, "The light of Christ will enlighten everyone." In fact, the Soviet authorities were mostly opposed to the Russian Orthodox and Catholic Churches. But since other religious sects had suffered from the Orthodox Church, the Bolsheviks were initially rather friendly to the non-Orthodox Christians. In 1921, when the Dukhobors asked to visit Soviet Russia to discuss the possibility of the whole community's return from Canada, Lenin's response was, "We should allow them to come immediately and do it extremely kindly." [14]

Arthur Watts' reports were full of optimism and praise for the Bolsheviks. He described participating in the voluntary Saturday labour, "I was greatly impressed ... there was a great spirit of service ... and I saw no indication of any sort of compulsion." He visited a children's colony near Moscow and concluded, "In less than two minutes, I was one of the great big family. Here was real communal life, life full of promise. The great lack of material needs was obvious, but the spirit was all that one could desire." [15]

By contrast, Gregory Welch criticized Watts for taking "a rosy view" of the Soviet government. He wanted Friends to help Russia as Quaker ambassadors, by promoting spiritual values. He said that the need was so colossal that "what we can do will hardly be a drop in the bucket, and if they [Soviet Authorities] think we are doing any propaganda we would immediately be turned out." [16]

Thus, Friends were ambivalent about cooperating with the Soviet government to distribute humanitarian aid from abroad. Welch basically mistrusted the Soviets and opposed such cooperation. Herbert Sefton-Jones was a prominent British Friend who advocated British involvement in WWI and later supported the League of Nations. He had been involved in famine relief work in 1891, and he accused the Soviet government of confiscating some 700 million pounds in British investments along with another 300 million British pounds from Europe. Sefton-Jones wrote a letter in *The*

Friend. "In view of the fact that these confiscated revenues are ... being used for the subversion of civilized governments in the very countries to which the Soviet is appealing for charity is it right, in the view of our own people ... to take the children's bread and cast it to the Bolsheviks?" Ruth Fry, head of the Friends War Victims Relief Committee, did not answer the main point of the Sefton-Jones letter. However, she said she believed the Soviet government was doing all in their power to relieve the distress, and "using very large sums of its money for the purchase of food abroad. ... I do not believe that we as relief workers have the facts upon which any true judgment may be formed."[17]

Ultimately, Arthur Watts and Ruth Fry prevailed and the relief work continued. Many Friends and non-Friends donated funds to meet the needs of suffering Russians. However, Arthur Watts informed the Soviet government:

> We wish you to clearly understand our motive in sending supplies to Russia. Friends are always anxious to give material help wherever it is needed without attaching any conditions as to their being allowed to spread the religious views held by the Society of Friends. We feel, however, that honesty demands that you should know of our desire to come into religious fellowship with people in Russia who have views similar to our own. [18]

In 1921, a terrible famine broke out in Russia as a result of drought, very poor harvest and ruthless state policy towards those who had surplus grain. Peasants, knowing that their grain would be expropriated, had not seen any reason to sow their seeds. Some 20 million people were affected by the famine, and Soviet authorities had to rely on foreign organizations to feed starving people. The Quakers were already in Russia, and so they returned to the area where they had worked from 1916 to 1918. Food and clothing were shipped to Russia for them to distribute to save the dying.

A small group of Quaker relief workers arrived in Buzuluk in September and December 1921. Seven Americans were responsible for the eastern part of the county while fifteen British Friends covered the town of Buzuluk and the northern part of the county. They were immediately faced with difficult choices. Initially they focused on feeding children in orphanages, but people from nearby villages began abandoning their children at the orphanages in the hope that the Quakers would save them. So the Friends tried establishing soup kitchens for starving children in the villages. But they still had doubts, *Why children only?* Would it have been better to take care of young people from 15 – 25 years of age, so they could later propagate the race? Some Friends asked, "Did we save children, only to let the Bolsheviks teach them communism with no parental restraints?"

It was a dark, sad experience. Friends were forced to choose whom to feed and whom to reject, therefore sentencing some to death. Murray Kenworthy, the head of the American unit, questioned whether it was wise to feed a hundred and run out of food, or feed fifty who might then be able to survive the winter. Then they realized that if you do not feed mothers, small children would become orphans, so the feeding program was expanded to provide food for mothers as well. The relief workers also found feeding themselves raised ethical dilemmas, but they had to eat enough to keep themselves healthy and to be able to feed the others dying from starvation. They had to draw the curtains while they ate in their dining room to keep the crowd of starving people from gathering and looking in to see them. The door of the office was always barred and unbarred as the workers came and went. One Friend wrote in his letter, "the shadows that drift by our office windows and some whispering at our door wring our hearts, one feels an utter brute to turn from them, but what can one do?" [19]

The situation was appalling. People ate grass and leaves. They were too weak to bury the bodies lying on the streets. When winter came, the heap of frozen corpses was piled in the cemetery. Yet the numbers of people being fed increased steadily until by spring 1922, thirty-three British and fourteen Americans Quakers were feeding most of them. Friends were also involved in distributing food from the organization formed by Fridtjof Nansen, the famous Norwegian diplomat and polar explorer. At least eight other foreign agencies were feeding Russians in the Samara region, but in the Buzuluk area, the Friends took the lead.

In spring 1922 the Friends decided to distribute dry rations instead of running a soup kitchen. Food was shipped to Reval, Estonia, by sea, and sent from there to Moscow by train. Friends in Moscow forwarded it to Buzuluk where it was stored at the railway station warehouses. Under Quaker supervision, representatives from villages collected the food for soup kitchens and distribution as dry rations. Many relief workers became ill with typhus, and some died.

Although they witnessed some cannibalism, Friends said that they marveled at the courage with which the Russian people met the terrible conditions thrust upon them by the famine. Conditions slowly improved, but even after the 1922 harvest, people were still supplementing the donated food

Murray Kenworthy in Russia, 1921 or 1922

with grass and weeds. The Quakers decided to stay and turn from food relief to providing industries, agriculture and other reconstruction work. They decided to buy both horses and tractors so that the peasants and the homes for children could plough their fields.

Several Friends gave intriguing descriptions of meeting "Russian Quakers" during the years of the relief work. Beulah Hurley wrote that several visitors came to call in July 1922, saying their families had been members of The Society of Friends ever since it was founded in Russia some 150 years earlier! They invited the American Friends to their meeting for worship. The sole person who knew both Russian and English was a chauffeur named Sam. According to Beulah Hurley, someone rose and spoke, long and eloquently. As he sat down one Friend whispered: "Sam, what did he say?" Sam condensed it graphically in one sentence: "by God, we love peace!" Sam translated the next speaker: "By Jesus Christ, you're right!" [20]

In October 1922, Friends concluded a new agreement with the Soviet government for the period October 1922 through July 1923. The Quakers promised to feed about 200,000 people, to purchase horses for peasants, to establish weaving and spinning industries for the manufacture of clothing, and to carry on medical work. But as the US government (ARA) programs increased, it was more difficult to raise funds in the US and Britain. Appeals for contributions said, "less than 5 cents a day, one dollar a month, will save a life. [21]

Wilbur Thomas, the AFSC executive secretary, visited Russia in 1923. His rather naïve report stated "there is no religious persecution here" and he accused Arthur Watts of being a communist, although he acknowledged that Watts was good at the pioneer work he was doing at a time when no other person could have been of such service to Russia. [22]

Although I do not think that the Friends' work was known farther than Samara, it was greatly admired by Russians, and many local people were curious about the Quakers who came to help. In the AFSC archives, I found one letter by a mechanic in charge of a water pump at Novo-Sergeevka railway station. He said he had heard about Quakers from "Uncle Tom's Cabin" but that information was not sufficient for him. He said had heard different explanations for why the Friends were feeding hungry Russians. Some people thought they were to be compensated in gold, or Russia would have to give up Kamchaatka to America. Others thought we were helped just by such workers as we ourselves are. Edwin Vail, an American Quaker working in Gamaleyevka, replied "Quakers are simply trying to put in practice the way of living which Jesus taught," and he affirmed that Friends received no money from the Soviet government and received no salary for their work. [23]

In 1923, Karl Lander, the Soviet Representative for Foreign Relief Organizations, wrote to the Friends' office in Moscow, informing them that the Soviets would no longer underwrite the costs of rents, railway tickets, and transport for the relief organizations. As of August 1, they should send money rather than workers, purchase food in Russia and pay for their own expenses. Thanks to long-standing relationships, AFSC was able to secure some exceptions to the new rules.

Friends invented new ways of making people busy and feeding children, especially by helping the famine sufferers help themselves. 5,000 children were fed and their widowed mothers worked spinning, weaving and sewing to pay for their rations. 970 women were similarly employed in Sorochinskoye. Elderly people from that area still recall the unique quality of the wool they received from abroad!

In 1924 Friends branched out in industrial work, repairing bridges and digging deep wells and canals to drain marshland. They proposed opening a Technical and Agricultural School for orphans and poorest families' children at Oomnovka, but by that time the Soviet education system was actively opposing any religious instruction in the schools and the plan was abandoned. But the main focus became medical relief. In June both a prenatal clinic and a day camp for tubercular children were opened in Sorochinskoye.

By 1925 some Friends favored opening an International Center in Moscow to promote good will and reconciliation, while others continued to emphasize relief and service opportunities, and advocated opening a model health clinic. But changing Soviet priorities and financial difficulties forced cutbacks, rather than expansion of the Moscow work. In 1927 British Friends considered closing the Moscow office for a few months to save money, while American Friends explored the possibility of opening a nurses' training school. Dorice White, the last Quaker worker in Moscow supported herself by teaching English and renting out some rooms. She knew that it would be impossible for Friends to return if the Moscow office were officially closed. By 1927 it was clear that no more Quaker proposals would reach fruition. Still, Quakers were in the Soviet Union longer than any other non-governmental foreign religious organization. The Friends Center in Moscow provided a meeting place for like-minded people, a place for some foreign visitors to stay, and an opportunity for engagement with sympathetic Tolstoyans (see glossary).

In 1930 Dorice White went to Ireland for a holiday and was denied permission to return to Moscow. In 1931 she was allowed to collect her things, but that was the end of Friends' presence in Russia that began in 1916. Various delegations and work projects visited in 1930, 1948, 1949 and 1955. Then, in 1995, Friends House Moscow* was established. I had the privilege of serving on the staff there for three years. With an international Quaker governing board, today Friends House Moscow is an expression of Friends faith and practice, striving to encourage the development of civil society based on mutual trust and community cooperation. It provides services to refugees and other underprivileged people, and promotes interethnic and inter-religious understanding, conflict resolution and Alternatives to Violence, environmental awareness, and alternatives to military service. Perhaps in the 21st Century Friends are finally fulfilling the mission of 20th Century Friends who sought a permanent Quaker presence in Russia.

* From the Friends House Moscow mission statement: Friends House Moscow ... seeks to encourage spiritual growth and the development of a civil society based on mutual trust and community cooperation. We aim to provide a stable and visible presence in the face of rapidly changing conditions as we express the unique faith and practice of the Religious Society of Friends ... by working for social justice based on our fundamental belief in the presence of God in each individual.

2. "WHAT IF THE EMPEROR OF RUSSIA SHOULD WANT A PERSON"
QUAKERS IN RUSSIA BEFORE WWI

Quakers in Russia, by Richenda Scott, provides a detailed report on the Quaker experience in Russia from the founding of the Society of Friends until her book was published in 1964. In addition to her sensitive exploration of Friends' faith and social witness, she has included a comprehensive, if necessarily brief, overview of Russian history which puts the Quaker work in context. Because *Quakers in Russia* is no longer in print, we take the liberty of quoting from it extensively below. (For additional background, see also Stephen Frick's articles in the *Journal of the Friends Historical Society* and *Quaker Peace Testimony* by Peter Brock.)

Quaker outreach to Russia is as old as the Society of Friends. While the text of his letters is lost, it is clear that the earliest Quaker, George Fox, wrote to Tsar Alexis I, in 1656 and 1661, perhaps seeking opportunities to promote his new-found faith, perhaps to call the Tsar's attention to famines in Poland. The first well-documented encounter between Friends and Russians began in 1697 when Peter the Great visited London "to learn what he could ... of the science of shipbuilding in the Thames dockyards." [1] Two young Friends arranged to personally present him with copies of Robert Barclay's *Apology* (in Latin) along with a description of their own religious values (in translation). The Tsar (and his interpreter) followed up by attending Gracechurch Friends Meeting. When they learned that the Tsar also spoke German, Friends sent additional books to him and arranged a meeting with William Penn, who – overcoming the language barrier – evidently had a lasting impact. The Tsar attended Deptford Friends Meeting several times, and according to Richenda Scott:

> The hours of stillness in the austere meeting house at Deptford ... must have made some impression on the enigmatic, brutal personality of Peter the Great. ... In 1712, in the course of the Great Northern War against Sweden, Peter entered the town of Friedrichstadt in Holstein and suddenly asked the Burogmeister if there were any Quakers among the inhabitants. He was told that there were a few, and learned also that an officer had billeted thirty of his soldiers in the meeting house. The Tsar sent an order that the men and their baggage were to be turned out immediately, and asked that Friends would call together a meeting for worship which he could attend. 'And the place being made ready, they had their meeting ... to which the Tsar came and brought ... several ...

great men,' ... [after which he] turned back to the prosecution of his plans for the war. ... His path did not again cross the by-ways of the Quakers. [2]

Friends may have gone to Russia for many reasons, but Richenda Scott describes the breadth and depth of some Quakers' personal and religious witness, their willingness to follow a 'leading' from God, and their commitment to humanitarian service – along with a great sense of adventure.

In the early 18th century, smallpox was among the most dreaded diseases, killing one out of six who contracted it. By 1718, some doctors had begun to explore the science of inoculation to prevent the disease or at least minimize its devastation. As smallpox was particularly severe in Russia, the Empress, Catherine the Great, sought out the most experienced British doctor and offered herself as a "test case" for the new science. Thomas Dimsdale (1712 – 1800) was a Quaker medical doctor, who was said to be so skillful that he could inoculate children in their sleep without waking them. At Catherine's invitation, Dimsdale set out for St. Petersburg in July 1768. He was accompanied by his son Nathaniel who was a medical student.

Known for her strong political will, Catherine graciously received the British doctor and he began inoculating several children in order to provide the fluid that would eventually be injected in the Empress. According to Scott:

> She desired that her inoculation should be carried out in the strictest secrecy, and refused to have any other doctors in attendance. When Catherine felt ready to undergo the operation, she sent a carriage for Dimsdale late at night and without warning. He had only time to lift from his bed the child selected to provide the pus, throw a pelisse around the boy and carry him out to the carriage. Then the doctor was driving through the chill night, his mind filled with apprehension at the responsibility laid upon him. For five days no word of the inoculation was allowed to be published or whispered, and tradition has it that a series of fast post horses was maintained in readiness, at Catherine's behest, in case the injection proved fatal, so that the doctor could be conveyed swiftly out of the country and away from any ill consequences to himself. Within three weeks she had fully recovered, and there were great rejoicings in the capital. [3]

During his year in Russia, Dr. Dimsdale also inoculated the Empress' fourteen-year-old son, the Grand Duke, and members of many prominent households in both St. Petersburg and Moscow, before returning home. In 1781, Catherine called him to Russia a second time, to inoculate her two young grandsons. On that journey he was accompanied by his wife who helped nurse the princes during their recovery, for which she became known as their "English Mamma."

Tsar Alexander I was one of Catherine's two grandsons whom Dimsdale inoculated. Known as "one of the most interesting, contradictory and baffling characters in the long list of Russian rulers," he began his reign in 1801 following the murder of his father. He encountered the Society of Friends in June 1814, while in London on his way home to St. Petersburg from the peace conference in France after his defeat of Napoleon. British Friends presented him with a statement expressing their gratitude for his efforts to circulate the Bible in the areas under his control, and to promote peace. They appealed to him to protect those of his subjects who, like Friends, declined to violate the spirit of the Gospel:

> On the 21st June ... three Friends were admitted to Alexander's presence. ... 'The Emperor stood to receive us: he was quite alone and dressed in a plain suit of clothes, and ... seemed to meet us as friends rather than as strangers.' The [Friends'] address [was] ... handed to him. ... He talked of his own experience of the guidance of the Holy Spirit, and of worship as an interior, spiritual exercise. [4]

The Quakers also sought the Tsar's support for popular education and eradicating slavery. After about an hour's conversation he shook hands with each of them and invited any Friends who might come to St. Petersburg "on a religious account" to call on him without formal introduction, saying, "I part from you as from friends and brethren."

Only three years later, this encounter with British Friends would lead to Daniel Wheeler's extraordinary "call" from God, and fifteen life-changing years in Russia for him and his family. Once again, the story is excerpted from the work of Richenda Scott, who relied on the *Memoirs of the Life and Gospel Labours of Daniel Wheeler*, published in London in 1842. Wheeler was an orphan who joined the navy and became an officer while still a teenager. During a stormy voyage he experienced "a life and power welling up within him which had nothing to do with his own desires or volition but was granted with the joyous surprise of a gift ... altogether the immediate work of the Holy Spirit in the heart." [5] A few months later he resigned his commission and returned to England to live with a married sister who was a member of the Society of Friends. In 1797 he became a member of Handsworth Woodhouse Meeting. He also married and started a business as a seed merchant.

But by 1809 Wheeler's health was declining, so he moved his family to the countryside and took up farming in addition to his seed trade. When he felt that the business was taking too much time from his spiritual life, he decided to support his family through farming, and he was very successful. During that period he began offering vocal ministry and traveling to Meetings throughout England to share his profound experiences of God. Richenda Scott describes the intensity of his struggle with his calling:

> In the early months of 1817 he was confronted with a difficult and momentous decision. Some years before the conviction had been borne in upon Daniel Wheeler that he would at some time be called to serve abroad, though where and in what capacity he had no idea. It was a bitter moment when the conviction came. For the first time since early

childhood he had known the securities of home, the joys and rubs of family life ... for which he was continually grateful. ... His first response was to shrink from the demands of his exacting faith, to feel that an almost insupportable burden was laid upon him. ... Then one day as he was pacing up and down his parlour, wrestling with his problem, his eye fell on a puzzle which his little son was piecing together on the table, "a dissected map". The name 'St. Petersburg" sprang into his vision with the flash of a revelation. Henceforth he had no doubt as to his destination, though for two and a half years he kept the matter to himself, mentioning it to no one. A little time after this first insight ... the thought came unbidden into his consciousness, "What if the Emperor of Russia should want a person for the superintendence of agriculture? – at which time a willingness was begotten in my mind to go. ... It was a prospect, I must acknowledge, at which I was ready to shudder." [6]

Meanwhile Tsar Alexander, like his grandmother Catherine, wanted an English Quaker to fulfill his plans, which in this case involved reclaiming the marshes around St. Petersburg. His letter to the Society of Friends eventually made its way to Daniel Wheeler who, without hesitation or surprise, made himself available for the Tsar's mission. Anxious about his wife's reaction to this proposal, he was relieved to find her sympathetic, and amenable to following what she perceived to be God's will. Daniel Wheeler sailed for St. Petersburg in June 1817. He examined the lands and marshes in the vicinity of the capital, and finding both the soil and the foliage similar to what he knew in England, wrote a detailed proposal for the Emperor. When they finally met, Tsar Alexander and Daniel Wheeler apparently enjoyed a fundamental accord, both on developing the St. Petersburg marshes, and on religious faith.

A year later, Daniel Wheeler returned to St. Petersburg with a supply of agricultural implements, seeds and cattle, his wife, six children, two other farm workers and their dependents, and a tutor for his younger children. Over the next fifteen years of very hard labor, they would clear and drain the bog, chop and haul trees and shrubs, and surprise their Russian workers with the integrity of Quaker business practices – paying each man a fair wage based on what he had accomplished. Regular Meetings for Worship and occasional visitors from England broke the pattern of the laborious days and the isolation of long Russian winters. "By the early summer of 1819 the first reclaimed plot ... was bearing healthy crops of vegetables, grain and grass. Sixty acres of turnips ... were snapped up in the markets of St. Petersburg as fast as they could be brought in." But the cold, damp, crude housing led to much illness, and for almost a year Jane Wheeler and five of the children returned to England to recover, leaving behind a very lonely (and also seriously ill) Daniel Wheeler along with his son, William. In 1825, Alexander I died suddenly. The turmoil of the Decembrist Revolt and the new leadership of Nicholas I upset the Quaker household. By 1828 Jane Wheeler and their two sons were reclaiming land in Volkova while Daniel Wheeler and their daughters were working in Shushari.

In 1830, Daniel Wheeler and his family spent several months in England for health reasons. Upon returning to Russia, he "felt the overpowering conviction that he must . . . go into fresh and as yet unknown fields ... into yet more distant lands. He obtained the regretful permission of the Tsar to leave, handing over the direction of all the work ... to his eldest son." During fifteen years in Russia, Daniel Wheeler oversaw the draining of 100,000 acres of waste and marsh, and brought some five thousand acres under cultivation. Then, with the full support of his family, he moved on to the South Pacific. Two of his sons carried on the Russian agricultural work for several years. Jane Wheeler died in December 1832. Both she and their daughter Janinka or "little Jane" are buried in Russia. [7]

The death of Alexander I, and the departure of Daniel Wheeler ended an era of Quaker connections with Russian leaders. In 1854 Friends called upon Nicholas I to avert war on Russia's Eastern borders and in 1858 they issued a "Plea for Liberty of Conscience" to leaders in Europe and the Tsar. In 1891 they learned that "a series of bad harvests, followed by an exceptionally hot summer with no rain, [had] produced famine conditions in the Volga valley." [8] The first Quaker delegation for relief of famine in Russia set out in November 1891. Anticipating his Soviet counterparts by twenty-five years, the Russian official with whom they met "stated, politely but emphatically, that the Russian government felt that the task of relief must be theirs, and had already constituted a committee ... to grapple with the problem. But what Friends intended to do as private individuals would not be hindered in any way." [9]

> After various delays, the ... Quaker emissaries ... got away to the Governments of Tambov and Saratov on the Volga. They found that famine conditions extended over fifteen Governments ... many of which were larger than England. ... A first hurried survey was made. ... How 200,000 people were to be fed with nearly all the horses dead or eaten, presented an almost insoluble problem. Many of the landowners were devoting themselves tirelessly to the relief of the peasants at considerable personal sacrifice, but they could meet only a fraction of the need. [10]

The Quakers proposed a comprehensive plan for preventing future catastrophes by irrigating the land between the Don and the Volga rivers. If it had been implemented, subsequent famines in the same area in 1906-7 and again in 1921-22 might not have occurred, and the 20th Century story of Quaker service in Russia would have been quite different. [11]

Events Leading up to the Russian Revolution

As Orlando Figes notes in his masterful account *A People's Tragedy, A History of the Russian Revolution*, the famine of the 1890s in rural Russia was only the first phase of an onrushing social, economic, political and cultural crisis that engulfed Russia well into the twentieth century. This period of great turmoil began with famine, in a country increasingly ill served by an autocratic government that was out of touch with the extremities of life for the huge majority of its people. It ended with a new agricultural crisis of massive proportions, which led to the consolidation of power in the hands of disciplined revolutionaries who were determined to completely rework centuries of life in both city and countryside.

The tsarist government was able to survive the famine of the 1890s only by virtue of a massive campaign including international assistance organized by the novelist and pacifist Leo Tolstoy and others. But by 1903, Russia was drifting toward a social and political crisis, as its leaders continued ignoring the common demands for political voice and social reform raised simultaneously by populists in the countryside, Marxists and workers in the cities, and middle class and professional western style democrats.

The crisis came to a head in 1904-05 as people from St. Petersburg and Moscow as well as the provincial countryside demanded that the autocracy yield some of its power. They called for political freedom, a bill of rights, a constitution and a legislature. Perhaps nothing would have come of these demands if two major events had not occurred. First, the tsarist government fatally blundered into an ill-conceived war with Japan. Then, on a cold January day in 1905 tsarist troops panicked at the sight of ten thousand unarmed workers demonstrating under the leadership of an Orthodox priest, while carrying petitions and icons. Women and children had been placed in the front of the demonstration to deter the soldiers from shooting, but the troops opened fire on them and the news of 'thousands of deaths' traveled quickly. Figes estimates that the true figures were closer to 200 killed and 800 wounded. [12]

The following spring and summer was a time of unbelievably unified action, leading to the general strike in October 1905, said to be the largest general strike in world history. The government appeared to capitulate, agreeing to the "October Manifesto" offering political freedoms and a constitutional monarchy – perhaps Russia's last chance to avoid a fatal class conflict and social upheaval. But the settlement of 1905 unraveled, done in by a government determined to retain absolute power, a populace tired of protest, and the deepening polarization of a desperate and increasingly radicalized mass of workers and peasants under the leadership of Marxist and socialist parties. Meanwhile, the middle and professional classes were torn between their desire for western political and economic freedom, their love of country, and their fear of revolution from those at the bottom.

Into this maelstrom of failed reform and unmet hopes came World War I, vicious and seemingly unending, a disaster for Russian society and government. By March of 1917, after nearly three years of bloodshed and defeat, mounting waves of strikes, bread lines, and desperately cold and hungry troops, the city of Petrograd (formerly St. Petersburg) was consumed in anarchy, revolution and mutiny. The Tsar abdicated, the moderate leaders formed a republican provisional government and a new Soviet of Workers', Soldiers' and Peasants' Deputies organized themselves to protect the revolution. During the spring and summer of 1917, as the war continued to go badly, the provisional government found itself shifting gears repeatedly. This served to radicalize the deputies and their grassroots supporters, and spurred the growth of Bolshevik influence. Finally, in the "Great October Socialist Revolution" Lenin, Trotsky, and the Military Revolutionary Committee of the Petrograd Soviet took power with remarkably little violence. The provisional government fled leaving Lenin and the Bolsheviks to form a government, which in turn was quickly engulfed in social strife, civil war and the radical re-organization of society.

This is the environment that the 20th century Quaker workers found when they entered Russia in 1917.

3. "WE ASSIST THE CHILDREN AND CIVILIANS IN ALL COUNTRIES, IRRESPECTIVE OF THEIR FORM OF GOVERNMENT"

THEODORE RIGG AND ESTHER WHITE, ARTHUR WATTS AND ANNA HAINES HELPING WAR REFUGEES AND CHILDREN; ENVISIONING OUTREACH 1916 - 21

The Great War, the Revolutions and the Civil War

The Great War (WWI) prompted Quaker relief efforts all over Europe. Similarly, across the entire spread of Russia – from the Volga region in the southwest, to Vladivostok on the Pacific coast, in the heartland of Moscow, and north to Petrograd and the Baltic – Friends established refugee programs, distributed food and built hospitals. But the center of Quaker Russian relief was the Buzuluk district of the Samara region, along the Volga River, near where previous Quakers had served in 1891. An area of some 1,000 square miles, it included at least 130,000 people, not counting the ever-increasing numbers of refugees from war-torn Poland and western Russia. For the next fifteen years, through revolutionary and civil wars and famine, the story of Quakers in Soviet Russia largely unfolded there. At their peak in the early 1920s, British and American Quakers operated more than one thousand separate feeding stations, along with tuberculosis sanitariums, agricultural schools, educational and construction programs, children's homes, and nurses' training centers. Through it all, a shared commitment to humanitarian service, opposition to war, and the belief in "that of God in every person" linked British and American Quakers whose perspectives often differed (and sometimes conflicted).[1]

With the United States' entry into the war in the spring of 1917, diverse Quakers from the Philadelphia area, including Rufus Jones and Henry Cadbury, formed the American Friends Service Committee (AFSC) to respond to the war and provide young Quakers with an alternative to serving in the military. American Quakers joined their British counterparts in the relief effort, sending six women to Buzuluk in 1917. Anna J. Haines of Philadelphia served as the official communications link between the relief project and the AFSC office in Philadelphia. Soon her independent perspective would be crucial as disagreements surfaced between British and American Friends.[2]

Robert Tatlock, writing for the AFSC's *Bulletin No. 16* ("The First Year of American Friends' War Relief Service" June 1, 1917 to May 31, 1918) described the extent of the team's work in an article entitled

The Bitter Cry of Russia

Twelve million refugees from a devastated area as large as the whole of France and Belgium are scattered for thousands of miles over European Russia and in Turkestan and Siberia. ...

The large number of refugees, the poverty of the lands on which they find themselves, the severity of the climate, the widespread lack of clothing, the local shortage of food, the prevalence of disease, the high refugee death rate, the insufficient nature of such few relief bodies as exist, and the long-standing nature of the trouble, all help to make the Russian problem, if not the most striking or the most vivid, still the largest and in many ways, the most dreadful civil phenomenon of this, or it may be, of any war. ...

The district of Buzuluk has an area the size of Belgium, and ... more than 20,000 ... refugees, 1,500 miles from their devastated homes. They had been passed on from district to district, finding no welcome and often hostility from the native population who had less than enough food and shelter and clothing for themselves. Many had been forced,

Quaker workers inspecting a village, surrounded by Russian peasants

through the carelessness of officials, across the Caspian Sea and far into the deserts of Oriental Turkestan, where the death rate arose [sic] to 55 per cent before their return journey into Samara. Friends have five centers, 20 to 50 miles apart, and have helped people in about 15 villages.

***Medical.** The tremendous need for medical assistance is disclosed by the fact that in the whole region of 100,000 persons, not a single doctor had been left, owing to the needs of the Army Medical Corps. Three hospitals in two years time treated over 70,000 out-patients.*

***Relief.** This is much similar to the social service work done in France, the distribution of clothing sent from England and the United States being the most important. This matter of clothing is often a case of life and death. Many families are forced, because of inadequate clothing, to remain in the fetid, disease-producing atmosphere of their crowded rooms during all the six months of winter.*

***Work-rooms.** A lack of sufficient women's occupations ... led to the establishment by our Mission of several work-rooms where women could find employment as a wholesome substitute for idle brooding upon their distress. The chief employment is the making of clothing; ...*

***Work for Children.** Scores of refugee children who have settled in this district have lost their parents and relatives through disease during the long journeys; they do not know the exact district from which they came, and are entirely unknown to any others of the party. An orphan home and trade school for 100 children has been maintained by the Friends' Mission.*

***Famine Relief.** The heavy hand of famine resulting from crop failures has recently increased the already almost unbearable distress of the people. The most important recent work of the Friends' Mission has been the ... purchase of food and seed grain from more favored districts.*

The demoralization of banking and transportation has made the problem a tremendous one and Friends have been co-operating with local governing bodies, both Zemstvos (old) and Soviets (new). In addition to loans arranged from Russian banks, Friends in England raised a special famine fund of $90,000 and we have sent $25,000.

***Looking Toward the Future.** In a country of such kaleidoscopic changes it is impossible to plan long in advance for changes of work to meet changing conditions. It is still the dream of many Friends to sometime engage in reconstruction work. ...* [3]

The momentous revolution of October 1917 at first had very little impact on Quaker relief efforts in Buzuluk. With the Bolshevik takeover in Petrograd and Moscow, local soviets assumed control in the Samara region, but the new officials were quick to assure the Quakers that their programs were urgently needed and should continue. Following a meeting to evaluate the food situation and relief needs for the winter, Theodore Rigg reported to the head of the British War Relief Committee "the conference was very satisfactory insomuch as it showed a willingness of the local authorities to cooperate with us." [4]

Both Rigg and Anna Haines sent long cables and letters to London and Philadelphia in late December, urging the expansion of Quaker relief efforts in Buzuluk and elsewhere. They also advocated sharing Friends' values along with material relief. In separate memos to Henry Cadbury (of the AFSC's Russia Committee) and Ruth Fry (head of the [British] Friends War Victims Relief Committee) they said, "I think also by reason of the fact that we are neutral in the various party conflicts that are raging in Russia ... we might be able to arrange some matters ... better than the local Russians here. ... I therefore have no hesitation in saying that now is the time to help. By helping now we will do something towards bridging the gap between the various parties in Russia." [5]

Meanwhile, across the Atlantic, AFSC Chairman Rufus Jones was also envisioning a Quaker role in US-Russian reconciliation. Early in November 1917, he sought U.S. government permission for the AFSC to expand its relief efforts in Russia with additional supplies, money and personnel. Jones' optimism was bolstered by an aide to Secretary of War Newton Baker who told him "the Russian frontiers are open again and [he] offers to assist us in securing admission for our mission." [6]

By the spring of 1918 the chaos in Russia deepened. The Russian people were fed up with the war and the army was demoralized. The March 3 Brest-Litovsk Treaty effectively acknowledged the Germans' defeat of Russia, and the Soviets relinquished control over Eastern Poland, Ukraine, Lithuania, Estonia and Latvia. American and British leaders' distress about Russia's withdrawal from WWI made them reluctant to deal with the new Bolshevik leadership, or even to allow Allied personnel to remain in Bolshevik or contested territory. The outbreak of the Civil War further disrupted communications and jeopardized existing international relief efforts, much less their expansion.

Conditions in Buzuluk had also worsened – Bolshevik commissars in Buzuluk were summarily executing political opponents – putting both the local authorities and the Quaker workers on edge. Meanwhile, Quaker team members John Rickman and Lydia Lewis had fallen in love and decided to be married. Having witnessed the executions, Rickman anguished over how to oppose the killings, without endangering the Quaker relief efforts. He wrote to his mother:

We therefore quite calmly resolved to go to the Tribunal and tell them that we had witnessed the scene of the afternoon and we knew how they would feel at having justice sacrificed to mob law. ... [We] came to the conclusion that the best way we could show them that we really did have confidence in them and that we did not go to them [only] to criticize their action was to go to them to be married.[7]

John and Lydia's strategy appears to have been effective. Summary executions ceased for the moment, the Quaker relief efforts continued without hindrance and the local official in Buzuluk certified their marriage.[8]

Staff in London and Philadelphia became concerned over the unrest and confusion and their inability to communicate with field workers. In April, AFSC Executive Secretary Vincent Nicholson told Anna Haines that, despite an initially positive response to her December 31, 1917 cable requesting increased assistance, the uncertainty and lack of information about the situation in Russia made the Committee reluctant to appropriate further funds. But they continued raising money and recruiting new workers, and by June Nicholson's perspective had changed. He wrote to Haines, "confidence in the future of our Mission in Russia has not been shaken at any time, and our interest in it has been steadily increasing." He added that although "a great body of sentiment ... is rather hostile to Russia ... our work as a center of English and American influence will claim an increasing interest, in a good many quarters." [9]

But it was nine months (March 1919) before Anna Haines received Nicholson's letter. On June 26, 1918, the Czechoslovaks and their anti-Bolshevik Russian allies captured Buzuluk, cutting off almost all contact with central Russia. Red Guards, Cossacks and Czech forces alternately arrested individual Quaker workers, and then eventually released them to return to their work. By September the Bolsheviks were back in control. Still, the principal problem was obtaining funds from London or Philadelphia. One Quaker doctor, G.H. Pearson, spent a week in Saratov trying to turn a letter of credit into cash.[10]

Theodore Rigg traveled to Moscow to seek funding and assistance from the British Consulate, repeatedly risking his life as he crossed both Bolshevik and Czech lines. On his return journey he carried both British and Bolshevik safe-conduct letters which he presented alternately as the need arose, making his way back to Buzuluk with 250,000 rubles hidden on his body.[11]

The Quakers in Buzuluk stayed on through the revolutionary period until the fall of 1918, but neither the support of the AFSC nor Theodore Rigg's heroics could sustain their program. Family concerns, political uncertainty, and the difficulty of bringing in new workers all took a toll. But perhaps the most decisive blow was the complete and decisive breakdown of relations between the Bolsheviks and allied government representatives in July and

Quaker Service headquarters in Buzuluk, 1921

August 1918. By October, American consular and diplomatic personnel, American Red Cross workers, and nearly all other British and American citizens had departed from Russia. Only the Danish Red Cross remained to protect Allied interests.[12]

Even then some of the Quakers refused to leave. Several, including Anna Haines, moved to Omsk on the western edge of Siberia, which was under Czech control, to work with the American Red Cross.[13] For Theodore Rigg and Esther White, the breakdown of relations, the Civil War and the beginning of Red and White Terror in Central Russia only marked the beginning of their work on behalf of Russian children.

From Relief to the Propaganda of Ideals

On his 1918 trip to Moscow to obtain funds for the Buzuluk program, Theodore Rigg first learned of the desperate plight of children in Moscow orphanages. He also glimpsed the need for Quaker engagement in the larger and rapidly changing post-war Russian situation. On June 9 he wrote to Ruth Fry that his perspectives were evolving:

> I have now been away from Buzuluk a little over a fortnight and find that the change has already ... broadened considerably my perspective on the Russian work. ... At Buzuluk, one is out of touch with the trend of events in Russia and ... frequently we miss splendid opportunities of development through not having sufficient contact with the heart of Russia. It seems to me more and more clear that a representative stationed at Moscow would be invaluable from the point of view of the development of work in Russia. ...

Rigg wrote, "the need for refugee relief seems to be on the increase with every passing day," and added that E.K. Balls was advocating a different approach. Instead of distributing relief directly, Quakers should work through Russian societies, and specifically with the Tolstoyans:*

> [Balls] is still desirous of assisting with relief work but he feels that our help ... should be rendered ...through ... the Tolstoyan party in Moscow, and our deputing to them a definite piece of relief work supported by our funds. ... The Tolstoyans can give to the Russian peasants and refugees even more than we can give ... and through our active support and alliance with the Tolstoyans we shall be doing more permanent good to Russia than by our own unaided efforts. ... At this stage we are passing from the sphere of actual relief to the propaganda of ideals which perhaps is not the primary concern of the Friends' War Victims' Relief Committee but which naturally Friends as a whole will be most desirous of helping.

Anticipating the creative tension that would continue for the duration of the work in Russia and throughout the life of the Friends Service organizations, Rigg continued:

> Now certainly is the greatest opportunity which has ever been offered to Friends in rebuilding a spirit of service among Russians who in idealistic outlook are closely akin to the Society of Friends. ... Thus our party stands at the cleavage of the ways—relief work both temporary such as at ... Buzuluk and a thousand other towns, ... and on the other side ... the greatest opportunities of influencing the Russian spirit in the rebuilding of a true democracy. [14]

Saving Children, 1918-19

Having envisioned the role of Quakers as reconcilers and re-builders of democracy, Rigg was quickly plunged back into the urgent demands for direct relief. He contacted the *Pirogovtsi* Society, one of the Tolstoyan groups in Moscow, which maintained four homes for Russian orphans. The young people had been dispersed to summer camps in Voronezh and Tambov. Representatives of the society were increasingly concerned about caring for the children on their return to Moscow in the winter, given their financial difficulties and the dire prospects for food and fuel in the cities of central Russia. Rigg's August 21, 1918 letter from Moscow to Ruth Fry portrays the broad sweep, the detail, and his perspectives on his work:

> It is now over five weeks since I wrote to you and ... I have been unable, since my arrival in Moscow, to find any means of forwarding [copies] to you. However, shortly there will be an opportunity, when

---

* As early as 1892, the novelist and pacifist Count Leo Tolstoy and his son opened some 270 free soup kitchens in Samara. After his death in 1905, his followers formed scattered groups of spiritual seekers, vegetarians and pacifists. Led by Vladimir Tchertkov, Tolstoy's secretary and promoter, these "Tolstoyan" groups flourished between 1916 and 1927 while Soviet policy encouraged religious and philosophical alternatives to the Russian Orthodox Church. But by the late 1920s even they were being persecuted, and a major crackdown occurred in 1928.

the British Consular staff leaves Moscow, of sending a letter through to England. ... Miss White and myself came to Moscow to see what could be done ... in regard to helping the *Pirogovtsi* Society to continue their colonies for starving children during the coming winter. ...

Rigg and White had to cross the Volga River twice, switching back and forth between territories controlled by Czechs and Bolsheviks. But Rigg's safe-conduct passes from his previous trip proved useful as he showed his British passport to Czech soldiers and his letter from Soviet Foreign Minister Chicherin to the Bolsheviks.

Owing to the great difficulties in traveling we were a fortnight on the journey from Buzuluk to Moscow. ... After two or three days in Moscow, we decided ... to make a short inspection of the four colonies in the Voronezh and Tambov Governments [approximately 200 miles away], so that we might have some idea of their possibilities before meeting the Committee of the *Pirogovtsi* Society. Traveling again was extremely difficult and this made our inspection at times even more interesting and novel than we expected. ... There were only two days [out of twelve] in which we were not traveling. Our experiences included a cross country journey by tarantass to cart from Anna to Voronsobka about 160 versts [around 1,400 kilometers], many weary waits at different railway stations, all kinds of railway travelling from 1st class to cattle truck and ended up by a night on the roof of a train under decidedly damp weather conditions.

On this last occasion, we had tried every carriage in the train ... for a place inside and finally after two trains had gone through the station ... we decided that there was no alternative but a seat on the roof.

We were much impressed by the good work which had been done at such short notice by the *Pirogovtsi* Society in removing their 570 [children] from Moscow to the country. ... Although they were in many cases poorly clad [the children] were nevertheless greatly improved in health by their sojourn in the country. ... It quickly became apparent to us that the colonies ... would have to be re-organized and fresh buildings found, if they were to continue ... during the winter months. In no colony was there anything like sufficient space for the winter needs of the children. ...

The workers ... had only offered their services for the summer. ... Practically speaking, new colonies smaller in size [and] staffed with new personnel would be required if the children were to remain in the country for the winter. On arrival back in Moscow ... we met with a fresh disappointment for we found that the Committee ... had now dwindled ... to a chairman and secretary who felt quite incapable, even with the financial help which we could afford them, of undertaking the organization of winter colonies for 570 children.

Our proposal had been that our Society should work as a branch of their Committee and should undertake the entire financial and organizing responsibility for two colonies of 80 children per colony. In addition [we] offered two subsidies each of 20,000 rubles for the organization and purchase of equipment for ... two colonies, which should ... be dependent directly upon the *Pirogovtsi* Society.

The two members of the *Pirogovtsi* Committee ... felt themselves incapable of assuming responsibility for the children in the present unstable political atmosphere. ... They ... invited me to . . . their interview with the Kommisar ... to state to him directly our willingness to assist in the formation of the winter colonies. We were kindly enough received by the Kommisar ... [who] recognized the importance of maintaining the children in the country if it was at all possible but doubted his ability to organize and find money for equipping so many winter colonies in the short ... time ...before the advancing autumn made a transfer of the children to warmer buildings a necessity. ... He agreed [to] our taking over the two colonies to provide clothing, boots and materials for the 160 children. ...

There is oceans of work to be done and tremendous need in every direction for the inhabitants of Moscow are all slowly but surely starving ... I trust however that we may yet be able to prevent the greater proportion of the children from returning to starving Moscow. [15]

On September 24, Rigg reported to Ruth Fry: The Soviet Department of Social Security and the *Pirogovtsi* Society had agreed to transfer the organization and administration of three children's colonies to the Society of Friends until March 31, 1919, when the Soviet government would resume responsibility for them. The Soviet Department also agreed to provide linen, blankets, towels and winter clothing and 100,000 rubles for repair and reconstruction. The Quaker representatives agreed to be responsible for organization and physical reconstruction of the colonies, purchasing food, and teaching academics and handicrafts. [16]

Thus began the first Moscow Quaker Centre, staffed initially by Esther White and Mikhail Khorosh, Tolstoyan and Secretary of the *Pirogovtsi* society. White recruited staff and provided general oversight while Khorosh served as liaison with the Soviet Department of Social Security, and Rigg traveled back

Building near Totskoye to be used as a children's colony

and forth to the colonies to make sure everything was in order. He also negotiated with local soviets and Commissars of Agriculture to obtain food and supplies.

This was a difficult time of turmoil, political uncertainty, economic hardship, and shortages of basic supplies. Bolshevik authorities had begun arresting their real and perceived opponents, but apparently White and Rigg experienced no difficulties. While in Moscow they stayed with Tolstoyans who were able to obtain food and fuel from the countryside, and were known for their anti-Bolshevik sympathies, but the Cheka (the *Extraordinary Commission to Combat Counterrevolution and Sabotage,* and precursor to the NKVS and the KGB) never bothered them either. Theodore Rigg marveled at the assistance they received from Foreign Minister Chicherin and the commissars in the Social Security administration, "at a time when all British and French officials in Moscow were imprisoned, we moved freely about the town and in the country districts." [17]

Esther White's letters provide additional insight and detail about the relief work and the political situation. On October 1 she wrote from Moscow:

> The last six weeks have been terrible for the children. It seemed to take an almost endless time to get our necessary agreements, guarantees and permissions drawn up. In the meantime, the colonies were left without sufficient funds for actual food. The weather was abominably cold and the children were dressed in the thinnest of worn out summer clothes – scarcely ... one garment apiece. ... They were housed in miserable quarters, some were sleeping on the floor without enough coverings and none of the houses were heated. I myself have been warm here in Moscow only when I'd been walking in the sun or else in bed, so I can hardly bear to think of what it must have been like down there in all the mud and rain we've been having for over a month. ...

> We have been extremely fortunate in our relations with the Soviet government. They are very glad for our help and are apparently perfectly willing to let us work quietly and as we please. Major Wardwell of the American Red Cross has been feeling uneasy at the thought of my spending the winter here but I'm sure if my position is in any way delicate, Mr. Rigg's is ten times more so. ... We have very fine papers from the foreign office and now besides that are actually working with the Soviet government. The situation at present for foreigners has eased up, so I'm sure it's the right thing for us to stay on as long as we're allowed to do good and they are allowing us to do it. [18]

In the midst of uncertainty and privation, Rigg and White managed to maintain a sense of humor. Rigg concluded his August 21, 1918 letter to Ruth Fry, with a request for "a Patisserie, a Confectioner's shop, an orchard and a loaf of bread." [19] Esther White's October 2 letter from Moscow gives her perspective:

> We've had many new and interesting experiences since the quiet and uneventful days ... [when] I nearly burst with excitement if a cart

arrived, but now I should nearly burst with excitement if I could find such a quiet, safe spot again. After ... May the ... orphanage improved little by little until you wouldn't have known it for the howling wilderness it was when we took it over. As soon as the children really found out that we meant to help them and could be trusted to do what we'd said we'd do, it became a new world. We got enough flour to give them good, white bread; we increased their food for breakfast and gave them some variety of diet. Then for the small children we got milk for in between lunches, and made them take naps in the afternoon, kept them clean and gave them decent clothes. It began to be a pleasure to see them and have them about. ... We sent away all the people we didn't want and found good ones to take their places, so really the orphanage could probably very much run itself now.

Then suddenly we were all involved in the taking of Buzuluk by the Czechoslovaks. It began on a Sunday night and was all over with by noon Wednesday, but it wasn't very pleasant while it lasted. Some of us got stuck at the country house, others at the Buzuluk house and [one] luckily at the orphanage. I was at the Buzuluk house. ... It got so hot early Wednesday morning we all got up about three AM, ate a hearty breakfast and then with mattresses and candles and samovars and money and food we all went down to the cellar with about fifty or sixty people from the neighborhood. ... I had often looked at refugees lying about on their belongings, but never had really supposed I'd be reduced to the same. [Five of us sat] all in a row in the darkest, blackest corner of the cellar you ever saw trying to make ourselves comfortable by the light of the feeble candle.

Kitchen of Quaker house in Russia 1920 – 1922

> We hoped ... to bring ... some three or five hundred children [out of Moscow] and establish them in the orphanage [in Samara]. The harvest there was unprecedentedly good this year. ... Bread was plentiful and cheap, and since we were so well known there, it seemed the sensible thing. ... However the political and military situation developed so rapidly ... it was quite out of the question to even dream of doing it.. [20]

Six weeks later Theodore Rigg elaborated on the uncertainties and his handling of a difficult situation in a letter to Ruth Fry:

> We have just received your telegram which you dispatched through the Dutch Ministry of Foreign Affairs. ... Isolated as we are, the receipt of such a telegram is exceedingly cheering. ... We very much wonder what news you have of the Buzuluk party, as we are unable so far to get in touch. ...
>
> We have done all that was possible ... to ensure the safety of the Buzuluk party in the event of... its recapture by the Soviet troops. We got the Russian Ministry of Foreign Affairs to send a special telegram to the Commandant of the Soviet troops ... asking that all consideration be given to the members of our party. A letter was also dispatched to the Ministry of War ... The telegram was dispatched in good time before the capture of the town afresh, but whether the Commandant ... actually received [it] ... I cannot say. We have now got the Ministry of Foreign Affairs to make inquiries ... as to whether our party continues to work in Buzuluk and if so to forward a list of the workers who have remained. ... I have received no answer but hope to do so in ... the next two or three days. In the event of no answer being obtained I would like to go and personally ascertain what has happened ... but for the present I am unable to leave Moscow and the work in connection with the Tambov colonies. However as soon as I can free myself I am thinking of ... undertaking a journey to Buzuluk, although [it] will be an exceedingly difficult one and in the event of our party having evacuated Buzuluk may place me in a suspicious position as far as the Buzuluk authorities are concerned.
>
> Miss White has continued to keep an oversight of our office during my absence in the colonies. ... Khorosh, our Russian representative, has done invaluable work in securing ... the material we require either free of charge or at the ... selling price of the Soviet. ... At the present time, such work as he has done could only have been accomplished by a Russian thoroughly acquainted with the Soviet Departments and endowed with much persistency. [21]

Frustrated by the difficulties of communications with the field, on December 10, 1918 the AFSC in Philadelphia asked the U.S. State Department to contact Esther White in Moscow. On December 21, the State Department replied:

> *Gentlemen:*
>
> *The Department has received your letter ... in which you inquire regarding the possibility of communicating with Miss White a relief*

worker under your care at Moscow by telegraph or by mail, and whether money by draft may be sent to her.

You are informed that the Department has been notified that the Swedish and Norwegian Ministers have been recalled from Russia by their respective governments. The Department regrets further to inform you that, in view of the abnormal conditions existing at present in Russia, it is impossible to communicate with Miss White at Moscow by mail, and also impossible to forward funds to her. With reference to communicating with her by cable, you are informed that the Department has endeavored to obtain information regarding Americans residing in Moscow but has been unsuccessful in its efforts. If, however, in view of this situation, you still feel that you desire to have an inquiry made regarding the welfare Miss White it is suggested that you deposit with the Department the sum of $25.00 in the form of a certified check or money order, payable to the "Disbursing Clerk, Department of State," for the purpose of defraying such cable expenses as may be incurred by the Department in making the desired investigation.

I am, Gentlemen,
    Your obedient servant,
        For the Acting Secretary of State
           (Signed) William Phillips
              Assistant Secretary [22]

Finally, the meager rations, the uncertainty, and the lack of communication overwhelmed the Quaker workers. With the children's colonies more or less set for the winter, Rigg was confident that Khorosh would be able to arrange the transfer of authority in March as scheduled. Both he and Esther White wanted to return home, to report on their work and recruit replacements. They left Moscow in February 1919 on a beleaguered train with Finnish and French nationals who had just been given permission to leave. Esther White was apparently the last American to leave Bolshevik Russia at that time. They arrived in London on March 1, 1919. [23]

Negotiating the Return

Even as Theodore Rigg and Esther White made their way back to London (and Anna Haines and others left through Vladivostok), the AFSC in Philadelphia and Friends War Victims Relief Committee in London were educating, recruiting and negotiating for the Quakers to return to central Russia. A report of the AFSC's Russian Committee was blunt: "no efforts should be spared to resume relief work in Russia." [24] Ruth Fry wrote to Anna Haines in March 1919 saying that British Quakers intended "to make an attempt once more to obtain facilities from the Foreign Office for a small unit to go to Russia" and continue cooperating with the AFSC. [25]

At the same time the Allies (US, Britain, France, Italy and Japan) were meeting in Paris to negotiate the peace treaty with Germany ending WWI. Significantly, they had excluded Russia from the Peace Conference due to the Bolshevik takeover. Lucy Biddle Lewis (the mother of Lydia (Lewis) Rickman from the original group in Buzuluk) was part of a small Quaker delegation at the Paris Peace Conference, urging the Allies to permit relief work to resume.[26] Quakers also tried to negotiate with the Bolshevik government in Berlin, Riga, New York and Moscow.[27] In January 1920 the allies lifted their blockade, and in July the U.S. State Department and the War Trade Board eased restrictions on relief and trade, thus making new approaches possible.[28] The AFSC promptly sought permission to send relief to Russia, accompanied by several representatives to oversee its distribution. Secretary of State Bainbridge Colby articulated the official position, "The Department will interpose no obstacle to the action contemplated by the American Friends Service Committee in sending supplies into Soviet Russia."[29] A State Department memo further elaborated, "Such representatives as you may send ... must go at their own risk and without the expectations of receiving the protection of this Government while in soviet territory."[30]

Meanwhile, British Quakers had already secured Bolshevik permission to return but only to bring in supplies. In March and April 1920, Hinman Baker accompanied fifty tons of goods, including dried milk, cod liver oil, soap, rice, oatmeal and medicines destined for babies, children's hospitals and sanitariums in Petrograd and Moscow. Gregory Welch, a member of the original team that went to Buzuluk in 1916 (and who would return several times), wrote about Baker's trip and the emerging controversies about politics, service, "Quaker Ambassadors" and Friends' goals:

> Conditions ... were indeed depressing. Lack of fuel had kept the temperature of most of the houses at round about freezing point all through the long Russian winter. [People were] living day and night in the same clothes, including overcoats harboring vermin so typhus is claiming many victims. The breakdown of transport has cut off Petrograd and Moscow from food supplies. Butter, meat, tea, etc. can be bought – but at prices that take a fortnight's salary per pound of each. The population is insufficiently rationed on black bread, cabbage soup and a cereal. Yet, half destitute, they carry on and as I read in a letter from Mr. Shappero, Head of a department in the Soviet government, "It is magnificent to see the poverty-stricken workmen of Russia striving after the ideal, and each bringing in their brick for the building up of the new social order."

> Hinman Baker met ... the heads of the children's institutions and the Commissars for Health, Education, etc. and arranged for the allocation of the supplies he had brought. ... He visited the orphanages, school feeding points ... hospitals and the child clinics and satisfied himself of their relative needs. The ragged and pinched appearance of the children was testimony enough. It is now satisfactory

to know that some thousands of these children will have eggs, milk, fats, etc. for a few months at least. He was satisfied with their method of distribution and felt more confidence in the present officials than those he would have met under the old regime. It is difficult to describe Russian appreciation. When Hinman Baker left Petrograd he was hugged and kissed by some of the officials. ...

His observations ... are valuable in that they bring us news of affairs as they appear to a visitor, as late as May. ... Briefly, he found the Communist party as enthusiastic as ever. (They compose about 1% of the population.) Fully confident that given transport and free trade they can demonstrate to Russia, and to the rest of the world, the ideal society. There are indications that Shop Committees are being abolished and industry, where there is any, controlled from the top. In Petrograd and Moscow there is almost no industry owing to the shortage of fuel and raw material. Under communal law all surplus stock, crops, and goods must be rendered to the state, which gives in exchange nominal sums of worthless paper money. The peasantry are opposed to this, and so long as the Government cannot exchange for their produce clothing, machinery and a thousand other things they need, the majority of Russia will be opposed to Bolshevism.

At the end of this month, we hope to be ... distributing another 1000 tons of child-relief. This is of course, temporary work. Our aim is to try and do something to help Russia as Quaker ambassadors. We hope that the way will open for a resumption of Friends Relief Work in Russia, and that we shall see the opportunity for the establishment of a more permanent nature than we have so far been able to accomplish. [31]

Following Baker's return to London in June, another British Friend, the engineer Arthur Watts, received permission to accompany another shipment of relief supplies. His letter of July 21, 1920 conveys the complexities of meeting and negotiating with Bolshevik authorities, along with some rare personal observations of Soviet life:

Peasants leaving home in search of food

Since I last wrote it has been possible to secure permission for Gregory Welch to pay a very limited visit to Russia ... on the principle that [he] has a special mission to perform ... regarding the repatriation of the children from Vladivostok. Permission for Hinman Baker is still withheld on the principle that he has no special and separate mission to perform. The authorities are very rigid in this matter ... So long as conditions of war continue I feel that there is little prospect of obtaining permission for more than one person ... unless of course the nature of the work makes it imperative. ...

I reported in my last [letter] on my visit to the Commissariats of "Labour and Insurance" and "Public Health." I have since visited the Commissariat for Public Instruction, and on Monday last a Conference took place between these three, a representative from the All Russian Council for child Welfare, and myself (with an interpreter). ...

I have had the good fortune to have the same interpreter at all my interviews and have had many talks with him besides, and as a result he thoroughly understands and takes a real interest in our work. He has thus been most valuable and greatly facilitated my work and I feel confident that he has made everything clear to the various individuals concerned.

On Saturday ... I went and did my bit at the "Voluntary Saturday Labour." I was greatly impressed by this practice and despite the fact that some of our Labour delegates had told me that it was semi-compulsory, felt that there was a real spirit of service amongst those who worked and I saw no indication of any sort of invidious compulsion. We marched several miles from the center of the city and were employed in removing and stacking a large number of contractors' tip trucks on the railway side. We then did the same with railway sleepers, whilst the women ... were engaged in removing sand for the construction of a new railway line. After it was all finished we went together to the railway station, where I learned that we were all entitled to an extra pound of bread, but it was unanimously decided to forego our claim in order that the bread might be given to those more in need.[32]

Gregory Welch arrived in July with another shipment of relief supplies, and a mission to assist the Petrograd Children's Colony. He worked alongside Arthur Watts in Moscow from July 24 to August 24, 1920, inspecting and distributing relief supplies and negotiating with Russian officials. But Welch brought another agenda as well. As he mentioned in his report on Hinman Baker's visit, he hoped to initiate a program of "Quaker ambassadors" – a more permanent presence in Russia providing educational and religious activities, particularly in support of Russian Tolstoyans.

Welch argued that a permanent relief operation was "impossible" because "the Soviet government considers the state must provide hospitals, food, [and] clothing and [it] has no place for philanthropic organizations. ... All we can do is supply materials ... they will do the rest." He advocated having Watts remain in Moscow only because his patience and energy would "gather prestige" which might ultimately open the way for a Quaker Embassy. Welch wanted the Quakers to support those who were "yearning for spiritual food" and in the process educate Russians interested in Quakerism. If this were not possible, the Friends should withdraw from Russia permanently. [33]

Watts argued the opposite: the endless meetings, detailed negotiations, painstaking inspections and distribution of relief supplies, and his work with the commissars of Education, Public Health, and Social Maintenance proved that long-term relief operations were both possible and effective. For him, the elaborate network of schools and children's dining rooms, military hospitals and soldiers' homes, material and infant welfare centers, civilian hospitals and maternity care centers, along with distribution points for pensioners, refugees and soldiers' families all demonstrated the desperate need for major Quaker relief. In Watts' view, if Quakers remained completely aloof from political or religious or philosophical influence they would be allowed to stay in Bolshevik Russia, and thus demonstrate their faith through their work.[34]

Their differences came to a head at an October 1920 meeting in London. Gregory Welch, newly returned from Moscow, attended, as did Lucy Biddle Lewis representing American Friends. According to Lewis, Welch told the committee that Arthur Watts took a "rosy view" of the Soviet government and was even "a communist himself" and that "under his auspices our efforts would be construed as an expression of sympathy with Soviet methods." Lewis suggested that Welch's critique arose in part because the Soviets had not allowed him to remain in Russia, because his anti-Bolshevik sentiments and his ties to the Tolstoyans were both too strong. Supporting Watts' role, Lewis concluded, "what we had been waiting for ... seemed within our grasp and the work could be underway raising money for relief."[35]

Following a long discussion, the London committee agreed to instruct Arthur Watts to send a statement of the Quaker mission's philosophy and objectives to the Russian government before proceeding with any further agreements on relief. But when they received a copy of the statement, the AFSC Executive Board immediately convened and cabled London with its strong disapproval, "Do not approve any written message. Believe representatives able to state message and arrange conditions at proper time."[36]

Arthur Watts responded in two ways. On October 18, he wrote an eloquent letter to his principle political liaison, Santeri Nuorteva, the "Director of the Entente and Scandinavian Section of the Commissariat of Foreign Affairs," conveying the delicate balance between spirit and politics in Friends' service:

Dear Friend:

My Committee in London has written to the effect that before they are able to decide on establishing relief work in Russia on a more permanent basis, they wish you to clearly understand their motive in sending such supplies.

I am convinced that you already fully realize that in giving what little help we have been able to give for the children of Russia, we have merely given an outward expression of a spirit of love and sympathy towards a stricken people without any political significance. Such help does not of course signify any sympathy with or acceptance of the political aims for which you stand or the means by which you attain them. This is of course clear from the fact that we assist the children and civilians in all countries irrespective of their form of government ... in Germany, Austria, Poland, Serbia and Switzerland ...

I believe that my Committee is always anxious to give material help wherever it is needed without attaching any condition as to their being allowed to spread the religious views held by the Society of Friends. They feel however, that honesty demands that you should know of our desire to come into religious fellowship with people in Russia who share views similar to our own.

Quakers ever since our rise, over 250 years ago, have held very strongly that no social reconstruction which is merely material, or which relies on physical coercion, can achieve all that is needed. Unless it is accompanied by a corresponding change of spirit we feel that it is bound to fail. This together with our views on the sacredness of human personality has led many of us to suffer imprisonment rather than participate in the taking of human life in war whether waged for imperialistic aims or for human or religious freedom ...

There are in Russia many groups of people who share views similar to our own and it is only natural that we should desire to cooperate with them in religious fellowship.

I do not think that my Committee has any desire to make the continuance of our relief work in Russia conditional on receiving permission to form some sort of liaison between our Society and these groups, but they feel that you ought to know of our desire and [they] ask whether you would view favourably their sending representatives for this purpose. [37]

The next day he wrote a detailed rejoinder to the London committee, voicing his dismay and his belief that their proposed statement was not only inappropriate, but might jeopardize any possibility of ongoing Quaker relief. He told the committee:

There is no danger of your being suspected of sympathy with or acceptance of the aims of the Russian Government or of the means by which they attain their ends. You are much more likely to be regarded as bourgeois philanthropists attempting to persuade the people against their government. ... Did you demand a statement from the Tsarist government that our help was not to be taken as indicating approval of their aims and methods?   ... I wonder if Christ thought of issuing a statement of aims before raising the Centurion's daughter. If the Good Samaritan had drawn up a careful minute we might have admired his "Quaker caution" but it would have spoilt the point of the parable. ... I believe that the best message that we can give to the Russian people at the present time is that there are Christians who are large-hearted enough to give disinterested relief. ... There are thousands of children who will suffer hunger and cold in Russia this winter. You can only help a few. Are you going to let those few shiver whilst you satisfy yourselves that you are not misunderstood? [38]

In early November, Anna Haines, (formerly of the Buzuluk team), stopped in London on her way to join Watts as the American co-anchor of the team in Moscow. After meeting with Ruth Fry, Gregory Welch and others she wrote her assessment of the controversy to AFSC Executive Secretary Wilbur Thomas:

> The Committee has given a great deal of weight to Mr. Welch's recommendations. ... Perhaps much of his attention has been focussed on the miserable physical and mental condition of a small group of Tolstoyans with whom spiritually Friends have much in common, but who cannot be helped individually. ... Welch does have a good knowledge of Russian conditions, and a real love for Russian people; his mind just doesn't work along political lines. [39]

Subsequent conferences enabled Welch and Watts to proceed amicably. The London Quaker commissioners, William Albright and Frederick Libby, recorded their enthusiasm for the new team of Haines and Watts, as "just the right Friends to undertake this work and if the hopes outlined can be realized, we feel their work may pave the way for the sending of further reinforcements ere long." [40] Anna Haines received permission to re-enter Russia on November 24.

Haines and Watts plunged immediately into a demanding life full of tedious negotiations and hard physical work, which resulted in numerous breakthroughs for the Quaker relief mission in Russia. They negotiated an agreement with *Narkomprod*, the People's Commissariat for Food Production, for Friends to store, control and distribute food and medical supplies from the United States and Britain. They obtained use of an office and warehouse from *Tsentrosoyus*, the Central Association of Russian Cooperatives. Haines wrote to Wilbur Thomas, "People who have not lived in Russia can scarcely appreciate the length of time needed to carry through any matter of business. What we have accomplished has meant in almost every instance a grim settling down to a four or five hours wait in some office." [41]

The English and American residents of Moscow invited some of the Soviet foreign staff, including Santeri Nuorteva, to a Christmas dinner. Haines reported to Thomas that at dinner Nuorteva said that the Friends "were the only social service organization [in Bolshevik Russia] against which Soviet Russia had no score for misuse of their mission." And she added "such an inheritance of confidence makes us very desirous not to do and not even to be asked to do anything" that might jeopardize the work.[42] Shortly thereafter,

Quaker Star

Nuorteva demonstrated his confidence by authorizing AFSC to distribute relief supplies from the American Red Cross, the American Relief Administration, and Britain's Save the Children Fund, "on behalf of and in the name of the above mentioned organizations" so long as Friends continued to perform in the same manner as before. [43]

Within weeks "Friends International Service, Society of Friends (Quakers), Department of Help to Children" was printed on letterhead stationery. The Quaker Star was prominently displayed alongside signs in Russian. By May they were distributing relief supplies to all the city homes for children. A detailed exploration of Anna Haines' work appears in chapter 7.

4. A FIRST-HAND ACCOUNT OF THE FAMINE
THE STORY OF A QUAKER WOMAN IN RUSSIA, BY ANNA HAINES

When one has seen garbage carts full of dead babies, and older children and grown-up people dying from starvation on the streets, and the farm machinery which is almost more important in Russia than human life, scrapped and rusting on the wayside, one loses all desire to follow the fashion of beginning a talk with an epigram or a funny story.

I have been to the heart of the famine country.

I went back there to the Samara province, to villages in which I had lived ...and I could ... compare the life of the peasants under present famine conditions with the way they had lived in other years, when despite the war there had been no actual famine. In these villages I have eaten more beautiful bread than I have ever seen in this country, bread which really was as light and white as our Angel food, and when one compares what they are eating now, one realizes what the famine means.

When it was understood that one of us wanted to make an investigation, Dr. Semashko, the commissar for public health, made me a member of the Russian Commission ... to investigate the conditions of children and see how Moscow could help.

I speak a little Russian, enough to go about among the peasants, and I could check up these official figures with the accounts given by the Orthodox priests, who are the most conservative members of the community, and by the agents of the old cooperative stores, and by the individual talks with the peasants I had known in other years.

We went from Moscow two days to Samara, the largest city in the famine area. ... A boxcar was assigned us to ride in. There were about sixty other freight cars on that train because it was going to Tashkent and everybody in Samara applies for a place on that train. There were more people on the roofs than inside and the inside was as full as it could be. Unfortunately there was a slip-up; we were pushed up and down and could not get room. Finally we found a car in which *forty-six children were being evacuated from the city of Samara to better orphanages in Tashkent. There were three teachers in that car, all shivering with malaria, the kind that gives you a temperature of 106. The children were in complete control. They were fighting with their fists and tongues, to keep other people, grain speculators and travelers, out of the car. We put our case before them, and said that we were there to help children, and not fleeing or escaping from the city. Then we waited to see what would happen.*

Those children had to retire into the car and hold their little council or soviet to decide whether we should be taken aboard or not. Finally the door was opened. The spokesman, who was about 12 years of age, said that as we were not there on a selfish motive they would give us the privilege of riding there. It was really a sacrifice on their part. For 15 hours no one could lie down in the car. Many of the children had dysentery and most of them had malaria, yet they were most cheerful, none of them cried—they also had bugs, and that was one of the reasons why we kept awake all night.

The next morning we arrived at Buzuluk and left for the three days' journey on down to Tashkent. For the entire four days the children had one pound of bread for their food ration. ...

We spent one night lying on the floor of the home of a man whom I had known before as the richest man in his village. One of his daughters-in-law lay beside me, and she said that every morning twelve of them went out on the prairie as far as they could go with one horse to collect the grass and little leaves from bushes ... along the streams. There are no trees. They bring the grass and leaves in and dry it and mix it with ground-up horses' hoofs, and ... they make the little black pancakes they have been eating for the last two months or more. They have to put the hoofs in because it has no gluten at all. It would not stick together unless it has some mucilage substance to hold it together. If they worked as hard as they could, she said, there would not be enough food for the family. Some would not be there when Spring came—very stoically and very quietly they face that fact. The great majority will not be there when Spring comes. ...

In place of their normal crop of a thousand pounds of wheat per acre, this year there was a harvest of about fourteen pounds. In many places it was far less than that. ... In March they had 4,100 horses; in September 2,100. In March there had been 3,800 cows; in September 1,600. ... The sheep had decreased from 9,200 in March to 3,200 in September, but the pigs had decreased most of all. In March there had been 342 pigs in this township; in September, 2. Those particular figures were interesting because in Moscow, when we used

AFSC workers hauling clothing

to go out to the children's institutions and ask them what kind of food they wanted, they used to ask for butter and fat instead of sugar or candy. They realized that was what they needed.

They planted 40,000 acres of wheat and rye in that township last autumn... more than enough to carry them over winter. It was on those 40,000 acres that they harvested 14 instead of 1,000 pounds per acre. This year only about 15,000 acres had been made ready; ... [but] they had seed wheat for only about 3,000 acres. If more seed wheat is not brought into that neighborhood there will be almost as bad famine conditions there next year as there are now.

Under the Tsar the whole township had about eight teachers. About one-quarter of the children of school age had had seats in the schools. Last year and the year before that teaching capacity had been increased to twenty-one teachers and almost all of the children could have gone to school. This fall when I went down, there were only six teachers left. There had been no food and no salary for them, and not being residents of that neighborhood they had gone away. Four of the six were expecting to leave as soon as they could get horse transportation to get them away. It was more than a day's trip up to the nearest railroad. ...

I went over to call on the agent of one of the co-operative stores, one of the most intelligent men of the village. He had been agent for them under the Tsar's regime, then under Kerensky's and then under

Clothing distribution in Novo Semokino

the Bolsheviks. I asked him how business was, and he smiled and said there was not any business. "My shop has been vacant for months. My salary for the past several months would be only large enough to buy me a medium sized watermelon." He said the richer people in the town had been living recently by taking the long trip of fifty or sixty miles to the railroad station and exchanging their clothing with the bread speculators. Only the rich people, he said, could do that, because only the rich had the horses strong enough to make this hundred-mile trip, and only the rich people had surplus clothing enough to exchange. As I was leaving the house, his wife followed me out. She noticed that I had a tiny camera and asked me if I would take the baby's picture. She and her husband would try to walk away, but she knew the baby could not possibly survive the rigors of the winter and she would like to have something to remember it by. ...

    The next day we took an automobile trip to the county seat to visit the homes established for children ... either orphans entirely or children deserted by parents who thought that perhaps the state could do more for them. We went first to a home established in July, when this migration of peasants began to be noticeable. The place had been planned to hold about 60 children from 3 to 14 years old. In September it had already 450, and another house was being opened in the village. For these 450 children there were exactly 31 cups and bowls to eat out of, and there was no place in that village where you could buy more. Their ration was about three or four ounces of grass bread a day with a little bit of rye flour in it still, and horse-meat soup a couple of times a day. The rooms were almost bare; a few children had beds to sleep in. No chairs and nothing at all in the way of amusement. A small room held eighty-seven children; they sat around and picked lice off each other; that kept them busy all day. Some of the children went out into the streets and picked up rotten potatoes and old watermelons that were thrown away by the peasants coming in. The manager said that at first he prevented them from doing that, but finally decided that perhaps they could get a little bit of nourishment ... and he decided to let them. ...

The home for babies from a few weeks old to three years was very much more dreadful, because while older children could eat the black bread and the horse-meat soup, babies could not live on it. When asked where the home was the people in the street said, "Wait and you will be able to hear it." I do not know how many of you can stand long the mewing of a very hungry kitten. We could hear the babies two blocks away. ...

We went over to a children's hospital which had been started about two years ago by the health authorities. The young doctor said that in 1920 he had lost only 12 of the 40 children at the hospital, whereas in the month of August 57 had died. ...

As far as I know the Friends are the only foreign organization which is trying to do anything for adults as well as for children. Most of us feel that it is a very serious thing in a neighborhood where there are actually famine conditions to feed only the children. We are already beginning to get reports that where the children are being fed in certain cities the families from contiguous neighborhoods emigrate into those cities and desert their children, having given up any hope of keeping the family together as a unit for the Winter.

And I think the economic situation in all Russia will be seriously affected if we allow the farming population of that neighborhood either to die or to run away entirely. It will mean that there will be no farmers there next spring to plant seed wheat when the snow melts for the spring planting, or to harvest the crop for other years.

The head of the Famine Bureau in Chicago ... [told me] there were five billion bushels of corn in this country which was entirely surplus. ... The farmers ... would be glad to see [this corn] removed because it will glut the market for three years to come and keep prices

Food distribution from "health train" 1921

far below what they should be. All of us on the Atlantic seaboard know that there are ships lying idle here. Is it quite enough, with the surplus of corn rotting in this country and with ten million starving to death on the other side? Is it quite enough for the American nation to feed only 1,500,000 children?

Excerpted from a publication issued by the Russian Famine Fund, New York (1922).

5. "Why Don't You Work Like The Quakers Do?"
Friend Hoover, Friend Jones; The AFSC and The ARA 1921-22

Rufus Jones and the early American Friends Service Committee

The story of American Quakers in revolutionary Russia cannot be separated from the story of the American Friends Service Committee. And the story of the AFSC in its first ten years, although it included hundreds of volunteers and staff in many locations, owes much to its first Chairman, Rufus Jones: Quaker activist, educator, historian, and professor of religion at Haverford College. Rufus Jones was 54 years old in 1917 at the time of the founding of the AFSC and the launching of American Quaker work in Russia. He brought diverse Quakers in the United States together with Christians from the broader ecumenical movement. His deep friendship with John Wilhelm Rowntree (the pivotal figure in the rise of modern British Quakerism) was crucial to British-American cooperation in the post WWI era.[1] These relationships, coupled with his respect for and friendship with Herbert Hoover, established the direction not only of the work in Russia but of the AFSC as a whole.[2]

Rufus M. Jones

Born into a strong Quaker family in South China, Maine in 1863, Rufus Jones's faith was shaped by years of teaching, journalism, travel, and engagement in the struggles of American Quakerism. He also endured many personal trials. His first wife, Sallie, died of tuberculosis in 1899, and their precious son Lowell of diphtheria at age 11 in 1903. In 1905, his friend and collaborator, John Wilhelm Rowntree, died of pneumonia. Out of this crucible of pain and loss Rufus Jones's faith and mission was tested, and deepened.

Once, as he was walking in Birmingham, England, Rufus Jones saw a child beating on an iron gate that had swung shut, locking her out. She was sobbing for her mother and as Jones watched, the mother came and opened the gate. Gathering the frightened crying child in her arms, she said "Didn't you know mother would come?" Instantly, Jones recognized a parallel with his own situation, which he expressed as, "Didn't you know God would come?" He knew that God was on the other side of the gate, of the closed door. Like the mother, God would understand the suffering and open the door, even more, like the mother, God suffered too. [3]

This ever-present reality of religious experience became Jones' touchstone. He was utterly opposed to creeds or statements of belief – or anything that would tend to rigidify or reduce to formulae the nature of God's relationship with human beings, which he believed was a constantly changing, active encounter. He asserted that Friends beliefs could not be captured in words but as with George Fox or John Woolman, they had to be experienced.[4]

Rufus Jones always linked his belief in a vibrant spiritual life with his conviction about the importance of political action in the world. He was convinced that awareness of 'the God within' also mandated individual action in the world, and that whatever external changes Friends advocated had to be accompanied by inner spiritual change. As he wrote in one of his rare diary entries "We must work in two directions: (1) for better political relations and ideals, for making war outlawed, and (2) for deeper spiritual interpretation and comprehension." [5] Political, economic or social change devoid of the personal and spiritual could never last. In 1927 he wrote,

> Our real mission as a Society of Friends ... is to help form the right spirit and the right atmosphere for the bringing of a better civilization for which we long. ... We must form the habit of sharing and cooperating. We must be as ready to sacrifice as we now are to compete. There is no substitute for this new spirit and this new way of life. ... We shall need experts ... but ... we shall never get our happy, peaceful, joyous world until we learn to love and understand and share and become brothers to one another because we are children of a common Father.[6]

The outbreak of the Great War in Europe challenged Friends in the United States. For Jones it was a spiritual crisis that tested his convictions about Christian faith and the particular activist responsibilities of Friends. As he wrote in the fall of 1914, the war was "one of those appalling events which test to the bottom our central faith in God, in human goodness, in cosmic rationality and in onward progress."[7]

The United States' entry into the war in the spring of 1917 prompted Rufus Jones to challenge American Quakers to connect their positive spiritual vision with a path of service. He was not able to attend the first meeting of the little group that formed the American Friends Service Committee on April 30, 1917, but it is a mark of their high regard for him that they asked him to be their Chairman. He hesitated because he feared that the work would demand too much time from his teaching and writing, and his other responsibilities to American Quakerism. The Committee assured him that he would only have to chair meetings and consult occasionally. No one could have anticipated the enormous commitment of time and energy that the AFSC would consume over the next three decades of his life.[8]

AFSC's initial organization reflected the different relationships, among Friends and in the wider community, that Rufus Jones and others had developed in the early years of the century. In the beginning, the Committee was an ad-hoc group, under the auspices of Young Friends, with representation from diverse Friends' bodies (Five Years Meeting, Friends General Conference, and Philadelphia Yearly Meeting). Soon this structure became an independent board, with representatives of the three Friends groups. Rufus Jones was an ideal choice as Chairman in part because he came from a Meeting that had never suffered the devastating split - between the Orthodox and the more radical Hicksites [see glossary] - plagued Philadelphia Friends. He came from New England Yearly Meeting where, despite different styles of worship, Friends worked together harmoniously. He had strong ties to mid-western and Evangelical Friends even as he lived in Philadelphia and enjoyed good relations with members of the "unprogrammed" Friends General Conference and Philadelphia Yearly Meeting. He worked closely with British Friends, teaching at the Woodbrooke Summer School and writing (with Charles Braithwaite) the multi-volume History of Quakerism. Jones also maintained a deep relationship with Ruth Fry, Secretary of the British Friends War Victims Relief Committee.[9]

As tensions arose between the Americans and the British because of different working styles, problems of communication, fundraising, and governmental relations, Rufus Jones consistently advocated close cooperation. The British trusted him even when relations with impetuous Americans in the field were strained, and the Americans trusted him even when they (often) were exasperated with their more deliberate British counterparts. The correspondence between Jones and Ruth Fry was particularly noteworthy. She wrote him many personal letters, and sent him copies of her draft reports and all her correspondence with Executive Secretary Wilbur Thomas in the AFSC office.[10]

Rufus Jones faithfully upheld AFSC's mission to relieve suffering, and the religious and spiritual basis out of which the work grew. He was always willing to meet and work with any government or agency when there was relief to give and God's work to do. In a 1939 lecture at Oberlin College, Jones reflected upon the AFSC and its central meaning in his life:

> Things that matter in this world are done by God through people. If we are going to have the Kingdom of God it is not going to come in by some sudden bolt out of the sky, but it is going to come by the process of building it in the lives of men. If we are going to take care of the wreckage of the world, and if we are going to try to head off things that lead to wreckage, and if we are going to have any part in the work of the world, we have got somehow to cooperate with God.

> One of my great mystic friends of the fourteenth century said, "I want to be to the eternal God what a man's hand is to man." That is what we have been trying to do. I think that it is what the world has

got to come to in the future. We shan't be satisfied with mere abstract schemes and we shan't be satisfied with mere philanthropic methods. We have somehow to get into the life and heart of humanity, and have there got to be purveyors of that higher, richer life, which is a stage of the kingdom which is God's kingdom.[11]

The Role of Wilbur Thomas

Wilbur Thomas was born in 1882 into a Quaker family in Indiana, and he earned his BA degree from Friends University in Wichita in 1904. He later earned Bachelor of Divinity at Yale (1907) and a Ph.D. in Philosophy from Boston University (1914) where he wrote a dissertation on "The Social Service of Quakerism." As pastor of the Boston Monthly Meeting of Friends in Roxbury from 1908 until 1918, he worked to bring that congregation together with Cambridge Friends Meeting. Then, in 1918, at the peak of relief efforts in France, he left to work in the AFSC office. Although Thomas was nineteen years younger, like Rufus Jones he was an alumnus of Moses Brown School. The two men had become acquainted through New England Yearly Meeting and Thomas shared Jones' conviction that cooperating with God was essential if they were going to repair the wreckage of the world. Both were also sure that the way to unify Quakers was through service, rather than theology or doctrine. But it was Rufus Jones's brother-in-law, Henry Cadbury, with whom Thomas was particularly close. When Vincent Nicholson, AFSC's first Executive Secretary, was drafted in July 1918, Cadbury, a professor at Haverford College, was invited to step in. But Haverford would not give him a leave and he recommended Thomas. Wilbur Thomas served as AFSC's Executive Secretary from August 1918 through 1929. He was AFSC's principle champion of Russian relief, while Henry Cadbury chaired the Russia committee and was Thomas' staunch ally throughout the early period.[12]

Beginning in 1920, with Anna Haines' second Russian mission (see chapter 3), Wilbur Thomas worked tirelessly to raise funds and interpret AFSC's Russia work. By 1921, he had established close relationships with pro-Soviet labor, radical, and relief groups in the United States. He helped organize a fundraising coalition for famine relief, made up largely of labor organizations and left-leaning groups in the New York City area. He garnered respect and financial support from the Women's Peace Society, the Russian Famine Fund, Raymond Robins (former Red Cross official in Russia and advocate for American recognition of the Bolsheviks), Lillian Wald, and others. In August, 1921 he wrote to Rufus Jones, "We are working on the plan now of letting the labor organizations and all other organizations that care to do so form a national committee ... simply announcing that they distribute through the American Friends Service Committee." [13]

Wilbur Thomas' commitment to Russian relief is evident in his correspondence and in the huge number of speeches he gave all over the country to raise money. Thomas clearly stated that the famine and the suffering of the Russian people resulted not just from Bolshevik terror and an illogical economic system (essentially the analysis of Herbert Hoover and many others), but also from "decades of slavery or serfdom ... the terrorism of the Tsar's police, and the horrors of Siberian exile." He gave the Soviet government some credit, "working under tremendous handicaps, the government made great efforts to meet the situation." [14] This analysis of the famine's causes was supported by reports from the Quaker workers. Field director Homer Morris wrote in

Wilbur Thomas (left) and a delegation visiting Russia

March 1922, "the conditions in Russia, which we are attempting to cope with, are the direct result of seven years of war, revolution, raids, banditry, and two years of crop failure. ... The government is doing everything that is possible to attempt to meet the situation, and we have the most hearty cooperation from all government officials." [15]

Thomas' priority was to complete the work that had begun during the famine – to work closely with the government, both in the Volga valley and elsewhere, to transform relief into reconstruction. "Steps must be taken" Thomas argued repeatedly, "to provide the peasant with the means of earning his own living. ... Animals, seeds and tools must be made available for the use of village groups. ... It will take at least five years for these peasants to get back on a self-supporting basis." And Friends had to show that they would stick with the Russian people through this transition. Thomas concluded:

> The Russian people must be made to feel that they belong to the brotherhood of man and that the people in other countries are directly interested in their welfare. ... These Russian people need *both* food and friendship. [16]

Thomas' vision clearly laid the conceptual framework for Nancy Babb's later reconstruction work (See chapter 6). He was quick to correct any

Quaker field staff who assumed that the end of direct famine relief meant the end of Quaker work in Russia. Late in 1922 he wrote

> There is going to be need for service in Russia for many years to come. ... There is no end to agricultural and reconstruction work, development of nurses training homes, schools, and various things in which the people, who desire to cultivate friendship and good will between nations, can be interested. .... There is to be more or less continuity of work, though the character of it may change year by year.[17]

Herbert Hoover and the American Relief Administration

In November 1918, President Woodrow Wilson appointed Wartime Food Administrator Herbert Hoover (later Commerce Secretary under Harding and Coolidge), to direct the agency that would later become the American Relief Administration (ARA) charged with providing food relief and reconstruction for Europe following World War I. Born in 1874, in the Quaker community of West Branch, Iowa, Hoover studied geology in the first class of students at Stanford University, later becoming an engineer, businessman and U.S. President. Like Rufus Jones, Hoover's roots in the Society of Friends extended back many generations on both sides of his family. Yet scholars disagree on the extent of Quaker influence on his life and work. George Nash, one of Hoover's principle biographers, asserts that Hoover was not at all influenced by his Quaker roots, nor did he make any effort to maintain ties or live his life according to Quaker precepts.[18] Another biographer, David Burner, emphasizes Hoover's frequent associations with the Quakers up through 1931 when, as President, he provided funding from the ARA and the Rockefeller Foundation for the AFSC to feed hungry coal miners' children in Appalachian West Virginia. Burner argues:

> We cannot be sure that he consistently thought of himself as a Friend, yet all kinds of similarities between the Quaker mentality and Hoover's suggest themselves: a blunt plainness; a belief that people will work well together and that in rational discussion minds can be persuaded to meet; a dedication to peace; and in these things a shrewd involvement in worldly matters and a conviction that good common reason and strategy accord well with the conscience and its affairs. The universe as the engineer perceives it has the orderliness of number and physical law; the universe of the Quaker has the order and harmonies of spirit. Quakers practice cooperativeness; Hoover, who wanted a cooperative social system, spent much of his private career amidst technical and financial institutions that required the intricate combining of separate labors and inventions.[19]

Hoover's relationships with the AFSC over relief in Russia can best be characterized as *ambivalent*. The first encounter dates back at least to 1919 when the Quaker delegation met with him in Paris to negotiate for permission to assist central Russia. Hoover made no promises, but hinted that Quaker relief might be permitted if and when the blockade was lifted.[20] A year later,

Wilbur Thomas supported Hoover's decision to extend ARA feeding in Austria and Poland, rather than subcontracting it to AFSC, because he believed that would make it easier for AFSC to obtain Hoover's support for expanding work in Russia. [21] For a brief time Hoover was Vice Chairman of the AFSC, and Rufus Jones served on the Executive Council of the ARA.[22]

The story of American governmental relief efforts during the Russian famine of 1921-1923 is well documented in the official history, Herbert Hoover's memoirs and Bertrand Patenaude's comprehensive new history.[23] But these accounts, and most of those that rely on them, date the origin of western famine relief to Maxim Gorky's famous appeal of July 13, 1921 and Herbert Hoover's response of July 23, which resulted in the Hoover-Gorky agreement of August 20, 1921. [24]

Moscow, July 13, 1921

To All Honest People:

The corn-growing steppes are smitten by crop failure, caused by the drought. The calamity threatens starvation to millions of Russian people. Think of the Russian people's exhaustion by the war and revolution, which considerably reduced its resistance to disease and its physical endurance. Gloomy days have come for the country of Tolstoy, Dostoyevsky, Mendeleyev, Pavlov, Mussorgsky, Glinka, and other world-prized men, and I venture to trust that the cultured European and American people, understanding the tragedy of the Russian people, will immediately succor with bread and medicines.

If humanitarian ideas and feelings-faith whose social import was so shaken by the damnable war and its victors' unmercifulness towards the vanquished – if faith in the creative force of these ideas and feelings, I say, must and can be restored, Russia's misfortune offers humanitarians a splendid opportunity to demonstrate the vitality of humanitarianism. I think particularly warm sympathy in succoring the Russian people must be shown by those who, during the ignominious war so passionately preached fratricidal hatred, thereby withering the educational efficacy of ideas evolved by mankind in the most arduous labors and so lightly killed by stupidity and cupidity. People who understand the words of agonizing pain will forgive the involuntary bitterness of my words.

I ask all honest European and American people for prompt aid to the Russian people. Give bread and medicine.

Maxim Gorky

The only antecedent that is (rarely) mentioned is the work of Norway's Foreign Minister Fridtjof Nansen, who appealed to the Allies in Paris in 1919 for food relief to Bolshevik Russia. The "Hoover-Nansen Proposal" got caught up in the politics of the Russia question at the Paris Peace Conference. It was finally offered to the Bolsheviks in the context of a cease-fire and the unilateral end to Bolshevik hostilities against the White* forces in the Civil War, which they ultimately rejected on the grounds that the West was "interfering" and using food as a political weapon.[25]   Thus, almost all discussions of the origins of western Famine relief to Soviet Russia in the 1920s fail to mention the crucial influence of British and American Quaker relief efforts after 1917.   They ignore the precedent-setting agreements that Quakers negotiated with the Bolshevik government in 1920 and 1921, and the extraordinary personal relationship between Herbert Hoover and the AFSC Chairman, Rufus Jones.

The Quakers' Unique Relationship

Although all Quakers were gone from Bolshevik Russia from March of 1919 until the summer of 1920, both British and American Friends were vigorous in pursuing both the Allies and the Bolsheviks for opportunities to return.   With the lifting of the Allied blockade, in the spring of 1920 both sides granted permission to resume sending supplies and for relief workers to return.   Arthur Watts and Anna Haines became the nucleus of the British-American team in Moscow in the summer and fall of 1920.   Early in 1921 they successfully negotiated to expand Quaker relief work from Moscow to the provinces.   Watts cabled Wilbur Thomas, advocating expansion to Buzuluk and Tambov provinces where Quakers had previous experience:

> So many and such strong pleas have come to us to take up relief work in the country districts that we have taken the matter up with the Foreign Office and have received permission for other Friends Service workers to come to Russia to work in the provinces, providing supplies are sent in sufficient quantities to warrant their coming. [26]

Georgi Chicherin, Foreign Affairs Commissar, opened the door to expansion with an invitation to Friends Service in April 1921 that clearly expresses both the Soviets' appreciation and their specific limitations on Friends' activities.

> The activities of your organization in Moscow from the time you were enabled to renew them have deserved nothing but appreciation and support from us. ... Insofar as the proposed assistance will be rendered and go through you, i.e. through people who have really proven their absolute abstinence from politics, and insofar as it will be in the future conducted and rendered in the same spirit in which it was conducted by you for the last year it will not be hindered in any way by us. ... As regards permission for the entrance into Russia of any additional

---

* "White" forces in this context refers to all those monarchists, social revolutionaries, Mensheviks and moderate democrats who opposed the "Red" (communist or Bolshevik) forces.   Part of the reason that the Red Army won the Civil War was that the Whites never coalesced into a unified opposition.

Russian children wearing clothing donated by Americans

personnel of your organization, we wish to state that we do not intend to limit their number.[27]

By May 1921, local Moscow officials permitted the Quakers to distribute food and medical supplies to all city homes for children. With Chicherin's letter in hand, Anna Haines embarked on a trip to the Volga in May and June.[28] There she worked out an agreement with a large Russian committee formed to secure relief from the emerging famine. Arthur Watts informed Wilbur Thomas, "We are assured that our workers will be permitted to work in the famine area if supplies are sent in sufficiently large quantities from England or America."[29] On this basis, the AFSC embarked upon a major fundraising effort for flour and other supplies, and began recruiting relief workers. In August, Wilbur Thomas reported to Anna Haines:

> We will be able to organize a big committee in New York City that will be representative of labor organizations and those who are sympathetic with the idea of Russian relief. ... If we can have a few selected American personnel as workers, we probably can get about $5,000,000 worth of supplies during the next year. [30]

The breakthrough agreements to revive and expand relief efforts in Buzuluk deserve special attention because they served as precedents for Hoover's negotiations with the Bolshevik government in the fall of 1921, which resulted in the compromise known as the Riga Agreement. It would allow the ARA to bring in its own personnel to distribute supplies, while the Bolsheviks maintained control over the railroads, the ports, and ultimately the ARA relief workers themselves. In contrast, the Quakers obtained unique agreements allowing them to manage their own warehouse, distribute supplies and coordinate relief. Arthur Watts explained to Wilbur Thomas, "our office and storeroom will be entered through a separate door the key of which will be in our keeping."[31] In a subsequent letter, he outlined how Quakers would track supplies to their destinations:

In Moscow the supplies are stored in a warehouse which is managed by us and is used exclusively for supplies donated by or though the Friends International Service. ... We have to sign all receipts for supplies entering the warehouse and all orders for goods to leave [it]. ... In making the actual distributions we undertake to do so in conformity with a plan agreed upon by the Department for Protection of Children's Health or such other department as may seem necessary, and ourselves.[32]

Once the Haines-Watts program was well underway, Friends hoped to use some of the ARA monies that the European Relief Council had earmarked for Vienna and Warsaw to extend their efforts to feed children in Moscow. Hoover's reaction to this proposal was conditional, arguing in a January 26, 1921 letter to Wilbur Thomas, "We are not justified in using money subscribed by the American public for the feeding of Bolshevik children so long as the Bolshevik Government holds [around six] innocent American citizens prisoners in Moscow." He offered "to advance food supplies to the value of approximately $100,000 ... on the condition that the Bolshevik authorities are informed that the continuance of such assistance depends upon the immediate release of American prisoners."[33] Unwilling to be identified too closely with the American government, the Quakers refused to make their food relief conditional on the prisoner release.

Negotiations with Herbert Hoover

But before the work in Buzuluk was fully underway, the extent of the famine prompted Gorky's July 13 appeal to the American people. Hoover asked Wilbur Thomas and AFSC Chairman Rufus Jones to come to Washington to consult. Jones could not go (he was in Maine), but Thomas took a train down and had breakfast with Hoover. According to Thomas' account, the visit was "very satisfactory." They talked about how the German relief was proceeding but Hoover's "main concern" was his proposed response to Gorky's appeal. He outlined an ambitious plan for feeding children in all the cities of Russia, while demanding the release of American prisoners and he asked Thomas "if this would interfere with any of the work which we were doing." Thomas assured Hoover that it would not, and encouraged him to reply to Gorky. Hoover then asked about Friends' plans for expanding work in Russia, and in particular, how much money they would need. Thomas estimated $2 million. Hoover "did not commit himself to any amount but stated frankly that he would give us a considerable amount of supplies." Thomas concluded that Hoover "was very kind and entered very sympathetically into our problems."[34]

By August, Hoover's attitude had changed considerably. The negotiations which began in Riga in August had bogged down in disagreements.[35] The Bolsheviks, using the Haines-Watts agreement as a model, stipulated that relief workers must absolutely stay out of Russian politics and not interfere with local Russian relief committees. During one impasse, Hoover again called

Wilbur Thomas to Washington. Thomas described that meeting to Rufus Jones: according to Hoover, the Russians "agreed to all the points excepting the search and seizure policy and the state control of food, which means that the Soviets want to have the supreme authority to organize committees in any local community ... [while] Mr. Hoover insists that his men shall be free to go and come and to have their own property inviolate."[36]

Hoover's motivations were complex. He really believed in relief, but he was hostile to the Bolsheviks and all left-leaning liberals, socialists and other sympathizers. In his examination of the official American (ARA) response to the Russian famine, Bertrand Patenaude asserts that Hoover shared the conviction that relief workers should make no attempt to influence Russian politics. But he saw a very pragmatic use for food as a weapon of western foreign policy. "Hoover believed that if he could only relieve the Russians' hunger they would return to their senses and recover the physical strength to throw off their Bolshevik oppressors. The ARA example of energy and efficiency would itself serve to bring further discredit upon the 'foolish' Soviet system." [37] Thus, Hoover felt that the very existence of a separate Quaker program in Russia was problematic. Wilbur Thomas outlined the controversy in a letter to Rufus Jones:

> He especially wanted us to have our committee take the position that we would not work in Russia unless the Soviets could agree to the same plans that he (Hoover) had laid down for his work. In other words he asked us to take his demands and insist upon the Soviet authorities accepting them for our work before we went any further. We told him that this was absolutely impossible; that we had been working in Russia for a year in a very satisfactory way; that we were non-political, and that any such action at this time would give political color to our work. He insisted that Litvinoff and the Soviet authorities were constantly saying ... "Why don't you work like the Quakers do? Why don't you accept their plans?" It was evident that this was a very irritating factor; and he got so angry about it that he literally pounded the table, and swore like a trooper.[38]

Hoover went on to threaten, "In case the Soviet authorities refused to accept his demands ... the State Department would not issue passports for any relief to go into Russia, and ... he and President Harding ... would make a statement advising against any contributions for Russian relief." Thomas held firm, however, and told him, "We couldn't see it that way at all. ... We had been there for years ... our work was going ahead satisfactorily to us, and ... we saw no occasion to change our program at the present time, particularly as everyone would misunderstand and think we were playing politics." [39]

Also in August, Thomas had written an encouraging letter to Anna Haines and Arthur Watts about AFSC's ability to continue financially supporting the work. "The All America Fund for Russian Famine Relief is functioning [and] other committees are being formed all over the United States and we will have things under way within a short time." At the same time, he cautioned that

> The Hoover negotiations are making a great deal of stir in this country. We are very anxious about the outcome, for if they fall through they will turn the tide of public opinion against Russian relief in a very large way. It will be extremely difficult for us to get support from the wealthier givers in case this happens, but of course the working people will go ahead supporting us just the same.

He closed with AFSC's commitment to continue its support regardless of the outcome of the Hoover negotiations, "In case any difficulty arises ... we may be going against the wishes of our government. ... We are going ahead, for we believe that the best way to help bring about better world conditions is to show a spirit of good will and kindness to everyone and everywhere, irrespective of nationality, race, or creed." [40]

The Riga Agreement signed on August 20, 1921 was a compromise between the ARA and the Bolshevik government, giving the ARA personnel limited authority to bring in and distribute supplies under watchful Bolshevik control. The ARA specifically agreed "that its personnel in Russia will confine themselves strictly to the ministration of relief and will engage in no political or commercial activity whatsoever." Anyone who violated this agreement would be subject to dismissal by Bolshevik authorities. And contrary to Hoover's desires to establish some ARA presence in the cities of central Russia, the agreement focused on food, clothing and medical relief to the sick and children only in "the famine stricken areas of the Volga." [41]

Although the Riga Agreement contained no mention of AFSC work, Hoover strongly insisted that the AFSC should continue its work in Russia only *as a part of and under the same restrictions as* the ARA. AFSC launched a series of intense meetings. Cables and letters flew between Philadelphia, Moscow, London and Buzuluk as American and British Friends and Quaker Service in Russia struggled to balance the Quaker organizations' desire for cooperation and autonomy with the material benefits that Hoover and the ARA could provide. At a long meeting of AFSC Executive Board and its Russia Committee in August 1921, two key issues were raised. Would cooperation with Hoover compromise Quaker integrity and control over "disinterested" famine relief? And to what extent would this affect the relationship with liberals and radicals, particularly the labor organizations that were providing the bulk of the funding for the relief efforts? Helen Todd, representing the coalition of labor organizations known as the "All American Commission for Russian Famine Relief," noted that these groups had expressly not wanted to contribute through the ARA because of Herbert Hoover's anti-Bolshevik policies. Several others pointed out that Hoover wanted "the moral support of Friends" and Friends to accept his conditions, in order to continue their relief work. [42]

But problems of fundraising lingered. Rufus Jones asked the fundamental question: how much money could be raised from other sources? Could the All American Commission come up with the ARA's anticipated contribution of over $1 million? Helen Todd responded, "If Friends have to make a stand and Friends have to turn to labor for support, it is impossible to believe that labor would not help them." Jones noted that AFSC had three options, "(a) To cooperate with Hoover and accept his terms; (b) to reject his terms and turn to labor for support; (c) to withdraw from Russia during the period of Hoover's activity there." He personally felt that any separation from Hoover would be very difficult, putting AFSC "in a hole with our constituency, the Society of Friends, which believes in Mr. Hoover and would not favor an alliance with radical labor." [43]

Both former Executive Secretary Vincent Nicholson and current Executive Secretary Wilbur Thomas argued that Friends could be persuaded to break with Hoover and join labor in a special fundraising effort. Then Thomas proposed a different solution: AFSC should agree to limited cooperation with Hoover, maintaining independent control over a specific geographic area, while keeping their own identity and authority for publicity and fundraising separate from the ARA. Some members agreed with "the idea of asking for a definite area with permission to raise funds" while emphasizing the need to avoid a break with Hoover or with labor. Others felt it "would be better to withdraw than be sunk" – competing with ARA for funds would be impossible. One member noted that "the essential thing is that food should be distributed" and that a way be found to continue. Another could not believe that "Mr. Hoover would put himself in the wrong so far as to make us withdraw." Emma Cadbury wondered why it was not possible to co-operate "both with Mr. Hoover and with the Soviets." Finally, Rufus Jones brought the group together and a minute was written.

> Friends should ask [for] an arrangement whereby they should continue their work in Russia, maintaining their identity and controlling the work according to their own plans and ideals, but possibly being assigned a definite area of territory or class of population ... and also controlling publicity in America. Emphasis was laid on the importance of Friends maintaining the standards of true relief and avoiding even the semblance of political interest ... and on the Friends fitting into the great problem of relief in Russia without interfering with Mr. Hoover's work."

The split with either labor or Hoover had at least temporarily been avoided. The Committee asked Rufus Jones, Wilbur Thomas and James A. Norton to represent AFSC at a discussion of all relief organizations with Hoover in Washington on the following day.[44]

Representatives of the American Red Cross, the American Jewish Joint Distribution Committee,[45] the YMCA, the YWCA, the Federal Council of Churches, the Knights of Columbus, the Catholic Welfare Council, and the

AFSC met with Hoover. Wilbur Thomas' assistant, James Norton, took notes for a confidential memorandum, particularly covering AFSC's concerns about independent authority and control. Hoover opened the meeting by laying out the enormous job facing both the Russian government and any foreign relief organizations, including ten provinces facing severe drought, and 44 suffering from famine at some level. Following some general discussion, Rufus Jones again raised the question of AFSC's present work in Russia and its relation to the new agreement. AFSC wanted to be assigned a specific district for relief where it could maintain its own identity and control as it had since entering Russia in 1917.

Hoover responded that he did "not desire to destroy the identity of any organization" but asked if AFSC would be willing to distribute American relief supplies strictly through American staff, thus disrupting its work with British Friends. Jones responded that AFSC had "always cooperated and are now cooperating with English Friends. It would be difficult to break from them, but we could probably arrange something."

Finally, Herbert Hoover and Rufus Jones agreed, subject to some grumbling from Wilbur Thomas, that AFSC would work in a specific district under the ARA. AFSC would maintain its own identity, but American aid would be subject to ARA control, and American Quakers would at least nominally be under the jurisdiction of the ARA in Russia. At least on paper, AFSC would have to break with British Friends. Both the Jewish Joint Distribution Committee and the American Red Cross also agreed to work under the ARA conditions.[46] The ARA assigned jurisdiction over the Buzuluk district to Friends and from 1921 through 1922, relations between the field staffs proceeded harmoniously with ARA providing approximately $415,000 in direct funding as well as significant staff and facilities support to AFSC.[47]

Negotiations with Staff in the Field

Jones and Thomas immediately informed both the AFSC staff in the field and the British Friends' War Victims Relief Committee about the new agreement. Their cable to London of August 24 noted the "temporary" affiliation of AFSC with ARA, and asked London Friends to "either cooperate in our assigned area or work in area assigned you." In his draft report to English and American Friends in Russia, Jones noted, "it would be impossible for our organization to continue its work in Russia during this period of emergency relief without making some form of affiliation with the ARA, whose work is to be on such a large scale and with such facilities or operation that no other relief body could satisfactorily work in isolation or maintain an independent status." He went on to note that the ARA agreed "to give us a definite district or area of distribution in Russia, and that our organization shall maintain its own identify and work according to its own ideals." He added that Col. William Haskell, the Director of the ARA in Russia, had assured AFSC that this arrangement did not need to jeopardize the relationship with English Friends. Either the English would be included with the American personnel in the AFSC-assigned area, or the ARA would assign English Friends their own area.[48]

Quaker Service and Russian staff, Buzuluk 1922

Jones and Thomas had to respond to the concerns from abroad. Walter Wildman, Director of Friends' relief work in Moscow, sent a telegram asking, "Are American Friends still bound under Riga Agreement? English Friends desire separate agreement with Russian Government."[49] And from London, Ruth Fry cabled, "Advise freedom from Hoover and acting internationally ... English Friends strong desire cooperate with you in new work [in] famine area which Hoover suggestion precludes ... consider Friends direct dealings with Soviet of greatest value." [50] In a long letter to Ruth Fry dated September 16, Wilbur Thomas tried to soften the apparent break with British Friends, and said that AFSC was "unable to see our way to any other course." He argued:

> Our message is bigger than any one group or groups of Friends and ... these limitations ... are some of the clothes which we have to wear for the time being in order to give our message. Certainly such things cannot stand between Friends themselves for underneath it all we know that we are one at heart and purpose in all our work. It is not alone an American message of goodwill nor an English message of goodwill, not an English-American message of goodwill but a Christian message of goodwill that we wish to give.[51]

The next day, in a letter to Anna Haines and Arthur Watts, Thomas acknowledged:

> This will cause you a considerable amount of anxiety and perhaps you will feel like criticizing us very severely. ... [But] this does not mean that we will have to break with English Friends. As far as we are concerned we will keep in the very closest cooperation and sympathy with the English Friends' work, and I hope that they will either assume responsibility for a district with us or accept a district adjoining ours so that there can be no misunderstanding about the cooperation of the Friends among themselves.[52]

Thomas rightly anticipated the anxiety from the field. Watts, Haines, and the Quaker Service staff isolated in Russia had forged strong Anglo-American bonds during several difficult years. Their first-hand experience of successes amidst hardships and the evolution of their unique Quaker style, compounded by the difficulties of communication with Philadelphia, London and even Moscow, gave them confidence in their work and made it difficult to accept direction from a remote central office. In a cable and follow-up letter, (which crossed Thomas' in the mail) Anna Haines articulated six reasons to oppose the ARA agreement. Primary among them was the ARA's status as a "semi-official organization" which aroused great skepticism among the people. She noted, "the ARA will probably have a very fleeting contact with Russia. Friends have had and should have a more permanent relationship." She argued that no "step involving such changes in our official relations in any country should be taken without consulting with the unit in the field." [53]

Arthur Watts was vehement in his opposition to having any restrictions placed on their work, but he was also clear that the program would proceed. His letter of September 24 also indicates the complexity of on-the-ground arrangements:

> It is difficult for us to make any alternation in our plan of work with the exception that for the time being we are developing our famine work almost entirely with funds secured in London. ... We are strongly of the opinion here that it is desirable for us to work free from Hoover's control but with friendly cooperation in the field and we have in fact recently negotiated the loan of forty five tons of flour from the ARA.[54]

A few days later, Watts focused directly on the main points of contention:

> We feel ... that it is most important that we should retain our individuality and that the test as to how far we are likely to do this will be in whether negotiations with the Russian government are made by us as a Friends Unit or whether they will have to be made through the ARA. If the latter is the case we feel that probably the English and American Units will have to work under a separate agreement. ... We sincerely hope that we shall be able to continue as a joint unit as we are certain that cooperation of this kind adds considerably to our testimony as many Russians seem to think it strange that English and American organizations should be able to work as one.[55]

In October 1921, Anna Haines left for consultations with London and Philadelphia, and to pursue nurse's training in order to return to Russia yet again. Her departure heightened the anxiety of the English and American field staff who wanted to work together unhampered by the ARA bureaucracy in the midst of the expanding famine. As Arthur Watts reported from Buzuluk at the end of October:

> We have undertaken a work which we find cannot be limited. ... We have therefore got to rise to this occasion. ... The difference in the attitude of the people and officials towards the ARA and ourselves is quite marked. We have a unique position here in Russia and the very

fact that we are unconnected with any government or semi-government organization has meant a tremendous lot in the development of our work on friendly lines of mutual cooperation. ... To have two sets of Quakers negotiating with the same local authorities would require a considerable amount of explanation. ... We are all anxious to continue the cooperation as far as ever we possibly can.[56]

Adding a personal note of frustration, Watts wrote of his fear that the ARA agreement would endanger the whole endeavor to bring about joint British-American relief work in Russia:

> I was particularly asked ... to try and open the door for you. This was finally accomplished ... since then everything has been done to open the way for fuller cooperation. ... Now you have gone and thrown this all away and a lot more of the good relationships which Anna Haines helped to build up. ... Now we may expect November 1921 to bring to Russia the picture of Friends International Service becoming two separate organizations one of which at least will be nationalistic. ... The period of Hoover feeding will pass but we hope that Friends will still continue. ... If we are not completely buried under Stars and Stripes or Union Jacks or have not been swallowed by Lions and Eagles we may try again to reestablish by November 1922 what we have lost in 1921.[57]

Nancy Babb, the first American relief worker in Buzuluk after the famine (See chapter 6) had a very different perspective. Wanting to be free of ideology or politics, she focused on maximizing material assistance. On November 10, she complained to Wilbur Thomas about Arthur Watts and British Friends, and asked to develop an American sector, under the ARA:

> I find the work very much handicapped through the pending arrangements for Friends to work in two separate units ... In spite of all the political snares which the English seem to think will befall us, ... I am inclined to think we shall be able to work with more freedom from politics under the ARA than we are now able to do under the English unit. Moreover I do not believe we as Friends should be continually knocking any relief organization now in Russia or in any way refer to any other organization as being political when we at present are so justly accused of being here to help the government more than the people as a whole.[58]

Ultimately, Quaker relief work in Buzuluk and Moscow proceeded as a harmonious British-American effort in close consultation with the ARA, which simply assigned the Buzuluk district to Friends. Emma Cadbury's prescient hope that it would be possible "to co-operate both with Mr. Hoover and with the Soviets" prevailed. Ruth Fry reported to Wilbur Thomas on December 1, "after all, the two units in the field will be able to work together very much as if they were one, and this practical cooperation is what we have been hoping for and rejoicing in." [59]   Watts and Haines negotiated a new agreement with *Narkomprod* (the People's Commissariat for Food Production) on September 16, and the Buzuluk relief effort received a major infusion of international

Quaker Service headquarters in Buzuluk, 1921

supplies from the Soviet Foreign Ministry. Both agreements showed the vitality of Friends personal connections with Soviet officials, despite the Riga Agreement. [60]

Political and Fundraising Controversies

Starting as early as 1890 and through the onset of WWI, American liberals followed events in Russia closely. They noted that an increasingly desperate, sick, hungry and heavily taxed peasant class had more than doubled from around 55 million in 1861 to 115 million in 1913, while the land available to them had grown by only about 50 percent. Meanwhile the Tsarist government suffered a costly defeat in the Russo-Japanese war. A complete breakdown of the social order seemed frighteningly likely unless the monarchy could be replaced with a democratic form of government. But WWI and the beginnings of the revolution split the liberal community. In 1919 the Bolsheviks unsuccessfully attempted to take over Hungary and undermine Germany while spreading shrill rhetoric about the benefits of international communism, and a "red scare" gripped America. Some liberals became disillusioned with Woodrow Wilson's ill-fated League of Nations, and the Russian Revolution's early violence. This was compounded by unprecedented labor unrest in the United States. The police in Boston and railroad workers in Chicago and Pittsburgh went on strike, and there was a general strike in Seattle.

AFSC staff and committees reacted to these events in a variety of ways. Some, like Wilbur Thomas, Arthur Watts and Anna Haines held out hope for the Revolution's potential, while others were more skeptical and disinclined to get involved. As a result another controversy persisted until the end of the ARA involvement with Quaker relief: the relationship between AFSC and left-leaning Americans – labor organizations and others – who were willing to financially support AFSC while they accused Hoover of being anti-Bolshevik. "We might as well be frank about this," Hoover had said. "There are various groups of Reds raising money for Russia. They are using the Quakers as a cloak. I think the Quakers should take the money. I don't care what color it is, but the question of fathering such propaganda the Friends must determine for themselves." [61]

In August 1921, the liberal and radical supporters of AFSC were condemning the Riga Agreement as a sellout to Hoover and a compromise of AFSC's vaunted integrity, and Wilbur Thomas began having second thoughts. He cabled Rufus Jones,

> Convinced get practically no support later ... and as no Hoover money available cannot make respectable showing any given section. Rather than break with English Friends suggest discuss turn unsolicited funds [over to] English Friends withdraw Americans or undertake only Jewish [Joint Distribution Committee] and solicit only for Ukraine. [62]

In a subsequent cable he suggested that the Executive Committee and Russia Committee meet to reconsider the agreement with Hoover, and urged Jones' attendance. He later explained his reasoning, "It is an impossible situation to campaign for funds and say, 'Give to us and not to Hoover.'" [63]

Jones was not convinced. In a cable to James Norton at the AFSC, he laid out his thinking, "I stand solidly by settlement made with Hoover yesterday. If it stops labor contribution, we must face it and tell Hoover frankly what has happened. Confident he will use us in district and support with his funds." Jones followed up his cable with a long letter of explanation:

> There is no other course open to us. ... The opportunity to go in and carry forward our work of relief in Russia under our own name and with our own ideal is all we can expect at this crisis. To stand out and line up with the radical wing is to end our career of service and to defeat the end we have in view. If our funds fail, as they very likely will, we must either ask Hoover to use us as his distributing agents or work quietly with English Friends who are evidently securing funds through a nationwide appeal. [64]

Still, AFSC would have a hard time competing for funds with a quasi-government program like ARA. Some people feared that contributions from the All America Fund for Russian Famine Relief, Federations of Labor and individual unions were being hampered by the ambiguity of the relationship with ARA. They wanted to break with the ARA and publish a clear public statement of AFSC's aims. Lewis S. Gannett, radical publisher and member of the Fund for Russian Famine Relief, articulated the issues:

> Take that agreement. I have had some difficulty defending any interpretation of it to friends here. If labor people learned anything during the war it was not to trust that laws, speeches, or agreements would be sympathetically interpreted. ... We cannot start work until we know where we stand. The fundamental fact which is not subject to argument or rationalization, is that labor groups profoundly distrust Hoover and will not give money to be expended under his direction. ... I should like, both from the point of view of money and of principle, to see you issue a statement, which, while perhaps also including a direct appeal for funds ... would somehow include pretty explicitly ...

independence and friendly cooperation with the Soviets and with English Friends.[65]

Rufus Jones still wanted a public statement from Hoover and the ARA clarifying AFSC's independence. Another meeting resulted in a letter from Hoover to Jones, which AFSC immediately made public, "The efforts being made by the Friends Service Committee to secure charitable subscriptions for their work of famine relief in Russia have my fullest support." Hoover went on to clarify that "none of the organizations cooperating under the Riga and European Relief Council agreements which you have accepted, are in any way losing their identity or supervision of their own distribution." [66]

Almost immediately Hoover had second thoughts about how his statement might be used by the left-liberal press and all his detractors. He wrote a follow-up letter:

> Since you left my office it has occurred to me that I should confirm formally the fact that the letter which I handed to you this morning was an entire settlement of the relationship of the Friends Service Committee and the American Relief Administration. I do not want this thing to be constantly turning up because a militant group of red minded people are trying to undermine the American Relief Administration through the Friends Service Committee." [67]

Rufus Jones reacted promptly. He had been defending Hoover and the ARA agreement, but now it was time to defend the AFSC, Wilbur Thomas, and those on the left who supported Quaker relief. In a clear, blunt and heartfelt response to Hoover, he upheld AFSC's integrity:

> I should ... not feel it right to pass over in silence your reference to the attempt of certain 'red minded people' to 'undermine the American Relief Administration through the Friends Service Committee.' I have always been a sincere and genuine friend to you and loyal to your great work. I would not tolerate for an instant any action on the part of the Service Committee while I was an officer of it, which would array it against you or tend to undermine your reputation or your efforts. I have no affiliation with or leaning toward reds or pinks, and I do not intend to have them or anyone else use me or our Committee to injure you. I am concerned solely with human service and with getting as much of it done as possible. I am conscious that something has annoyed or offended you and altered your attitude toward us, but I am convinced that we have been perfectly fair and square and honorable in our relations with you.[68]

Hoover responded with an equally straightforward affirmation of AFSC and of Jones, although he still felt compelled to attack their leftist supporters:

> I have no reserves about the American Friends Service Committee. If there is anything in which I have implicit confidence, it is the rightmindedness of the people with whom I have been born and raised. ... I think you will agree with me that the propaganda in the New Republic and in the red press is enough to cause some anxiety lest through such intrigues conflict would be created between American

organizations and do infinite harm to the whole cause of saving life in Russia. Now that I know this does not originate with or has no sympathetic support from the Friends themselves the whole matter is at rest in my mind. No one has a higher appreciation of the singlemindedness of your own efforts than I have." [69]

Still, problems with Herbert Hoover persisted. Hoover wanted the AFSC to commit not only to aid a particular district, but to feed a specific number of people until the harvest of 1922. In a November 1, 1921 letter to Rufus Jones he reasoned, "if the Friends secure $15 why cannot they undertake to care for one specific child or adult until next September, and extend the number of persons in ratio to the money? Otherwise it is a question of giving a man his breakfast and letting him die before dinner." [70]

For Jones, this approach at first seemed to compromise AFSC's integrity and the diverse relief work being carried out in Buzuluk. On January 2, after another conference, Jones wrote to Hoover, thanking him for his "friendly cooperative spirit" and his "recognition of the principle that our present basis of work in the field shall be preserved and that our unit as at present organized and planned shall be maintained." Then, with the promise of ARA food supplies, Jones agreed that AFSC would feed 50,000 people and more if additional money or food became available. He asked Hoover for another statement of support for AFSC to be used publicly in a nationwide fundraising appeal. [71]

Within less than two days, a very different public statement threw the AFSC into a crisis. Hoover and the ARA asserted that there was little need for additional food or flour for Russia, and that Russian port and rail facilities were completely tied up handling ARA shipments. It appeared that the left's charges had been accurate, and Hoover wanted to undercut the Quakers' straightforward, principled collection of funds and supplies for relief. Wilbur Thomas was furious. In a January 1922 meeting, he bluntly accused Hoover of sabotaging the AFSC effort. Other members of the Quaker delegation were shocked at his vehemence. [72]

Once again Rufus Jones appealed to his old friend. "Having undertaken the collection of money and food supplied under the Riga Agreement and with your approval, and having a large collection of flour under way ... [Friends] find it practically impossible to make a satisfactory readjustment. We would ask if there is not some way whereby we can preserve the interest and goodwill in this campaign of the American people." Jones offered to give the flour to the ARA to go with their shipments, if only Hoover would retract his statement about the need being over. He urged Hoover to "recommend . . . that all individuals or organizations who wish to contribute toward further relief in Russia send their contributions to some one of the strictly American organizations ... including AFSC." Hoover declined to make a new public statement, although he did promise "to temper his remarks" and to continue

Donation of flour from the people of Pasadena, California

supporting the work of the AFSC if asked. Then he expressed frustration "at the hysteria that is being injected into many of the begging programs, as witnessed by the telegram which I have received from one of your committees ... [that] displays a lack of truth that ought to shock every Quaker." [73]

The AFSC Executive Board met to formulate a reply and, at the suggestion of Rufus Jones, decided to ignore the last statement. In a letter drafted by committee, Wilbur Thomas thanked Hoover for being "willing to phrase your statement to individual inquiries so that we can proceed with our appeal for funds for Russian relief. ... We are going ahead with our appeal in an effort to provide for the needs of the famine sufferers in the area already determined upon by Mr. Haskell." [74]

The controversy continued. Wilbur Thomas and his colleagues at other famine relief organizations remained convinced that Hoover was determined to control all the relief efforts, and strangle the independent organizations. In early February they resolved to try once again to persuade Hoover to support continued fundraising for famine relief. Requesting a statement similar to the one they had proposed in January, Thomas appealed to Hoover:

> One thing our Service Committee desires in the matter is an arrangement which will enable us to carry through honorably and efficiently the piece of work which in the progress of circumstances has been committed to our care. We should have no difficulty in securing sufficient funds for the feeding of our district were it not for the impression on the public mind which I have referred to above. [75]

Although Hoover declined to issue the statement, he wrote to Jones, "If what the Friends want is an endorsement from me ... I am perfectly willing to give it. ... So far as your work in Russia is concerned I am and have been only too willing to cooperate." Hoover pledged to provide AFSC with food *pro rata* to make up any shortfall from the fundraising effort. But he also urged Jones to keep "the Committee … free from association with radical groups for I cannot conceive a greater negation of all that the Quakers stand for than a regime that carries on its banners, 'Religion is the opiate of the people.'" [76]

Jones, directed by the Executive Board to respond to Hoover, ignored the concerns about radicals. Instead he chose to "express to you my hearty appreciation for the way you have dealt with our committee and its work. … I have always intended to have our work on lines which would meet with your approval and that of the sound, sober judgment of the country at large."[77] Ten days later, Jones drafted a more detailed response to "Friend Hoover," thanking him for the statement and the commitment of supplies, and pledging that AFSC would "be very careful not to become entangled with radical organizations, although we shall feel free to accept unsolicited contributions which they may desire to turn over to us." But he apparently thought better of sending it, because there is no record of a final copy being written, or received by Hoover. [78]

Divisions Within the AFSC Leadership

Rufus Jones repeatedly cautioned Thomas to be more circumspect in criticizing Hoover, whose cooperation was essential to the Quakers' work in Russia. Thomas responded coolly, "I have been just as careful to send out the things which were favorable to Mr. Hoover as the ones which were unfavorable. Unless there is further objection I propose to continue to follow the same course." [79]

Jones was not the only AFSC Executive Board member to be critical of Wilbur Thomas and his difficulties with Herbert Hoover. Charles Evans had attended the January 1922 meeting where Thomas lost his temper. He was so upset that he wrote an agonized letter, offering to resign from the committee if Thomas could not hear his criticism, and reach an accord. "I do not wish to be an obstructionist," said Evans, asking the committee to find a quiet time for heart searching and guidance instead of accusation and calumny.[80] William C. Biddle, who had also been at the meeting, wrote to Jones on February 10, expressing his "strong feelings and convictions" that Thomas had gone too far. He called on Jones to stop the accusations against Hoover:

> We talk about our testimony against war and in favor of peace, and we should not talk and act to or about individuals in the same kind of antagonistic spirit that brings on war between nations. … I question whether we are not losing instead of gaining in this big work the committee is trying to do.
>
> I have arrived at the firm conviction that if members of our committee cannot … cease from talking about Mr. Hoover and his men they way they have done, but even cease thinking in those lines, … they are not the ones to send to interview Hoover. … Unless this criticizing

spirit can be absolutely eliminated, we had better withdraw from our attempted cooperation with the Hoover organization.[81]

Radical and liberal criticism of the ARA and Hoover continued unabated, with occasional implicit comparison to Quaker Service. Wilbur Thomas maintained his connections with leftist supporters of Quaker relief, many of whom continued sending funds to AFSC while criticizing Hoover. On February 26, 1922 *The New York Call*, a socialist periodical, published an article by A. C. Freeman, titled "Hoover Sabotages Russian Relief." The author criticized Hoover for insensitivity to the continuing famine, and creating bottlenecks in shipping. He concluded:

> No information has reached us which would lead us to believe that the need for help is past or that continuing relief will not be needed for many months. Mr. Nansen says otherwise ... the Russian Red Cross says otherwise; and the English and American Quakers say otherwise. In view of Mr. Hoover's extraordinary misinformation in the past we cannot take his latest announcement as authoritative, and we urge men and women of good heart to give and to keep on giving for the relief of the people of the Volga basin.[82]

Although they are not named in the article, the detailed contradiction of the ARA's assessment of the famine could only have come from the Quaker workers in the field. The article caused a sensation and Hoover was furious. In a stinging letter of March 6, he called on AFSC to specifically repudiate its information, its accusatory tone, and its criticism of the ARA. Some members of the AFSC board were so upset that a special board meeting was called on March 11 to consider a response. Two letters were drafted: one to Hoover and one to the *New York Call*. Rufus Jones was absent due to illness but the drafts by Charles Rhoads and Charles Evans reflected his sentiment and approach. In the letter to Hoover, the AFSC apologized and disclaimed any role whatsoever in its writing or in supplying any information to the *Call*.

> It is a matter of sincere regret to us if ... in the inability to relieve distress in Russia there has been a confusion of the facts expressed by you with an implication that you were personally hostile to our relief work in Russia. We know that this is not the case. ... We deplore as you do this tendency to lose sight of the fundamental necessity to relieve starvation in Russia. ... We disavow in advance any attacks upon you personally or on your conduct of Russian relief which may appear in the press and in which the name of Friends organizations may be introduced.[83]

In its letter to the *Call*, the AFSC was even firmer.

> As [the article] contains statements which we regard as untrue we find it our duty to ask you to give full publicity to the following statement: Your article states "Far more serious is Mr. Hoover's obstruction of the Friends in their efforts to raise money." ... This statement is both unfair and untrue. ... You should know that within the limit of means at hand, Mr. Hoover has assured us that he will support the work of the Friends in the event of our supplies failing

support. Over the experience of several months our Committee has found that Mr. Hoover has done far more to support our work in the Russian field than any original plan contemplated.[84]

The animosity between Herbert Hoover and Wilbur Thomas – two strong-willed and highly opinionated opponents – was never resolved. Despite the mediating and consensus-building efforts of Rufus Jones, Charles Evans and others, the tension between the AFSC and the ARA persisted. All parties seemed relieved when the ARA announced on July 5 that its relief efforts in Russia would terminate as of September 1, 1922. This reunited English and American Friends and facilitated a new agreement between Quakers and Soviet authorities, but for the first time since early 1921 Friends could no longer rely on the ARA to ship its supplies.

In October 1922 the Quakers and the Bolsheviks negotiated a new agreement. The Quakers agreed to continue relief in Buzuluk and Moscow for one year, and to extend their efforts into a reconstruction phase. New programs were proposed, including loaning up to 1000 horses "free of cost" to the peasants, developing weaving, spinning and clothing manufacture, and constructing hospitals, clinics and other public health facilities particularly in the Volga valley. In exchange, the Soviet government pledged to ease the entry of Quaker personnel and their "free and uninhibited travel." They agreed to provide housing, storage facilities, transit and transportation from border points for all supplies, along with motor transport and communications. All relief was to be distributed "without regard to race, religion, or social or political status." Friends would have "power to enter into negotiation and make contracts with local authorities," so long as those contracts "are in general harmony with this agreement." [85]

The next several years would be both innovative and tumultuous, both from the standpoint of relations with various Bolshevik authorities, and discussions among English and American Friends. The controversies over the spirit and politics of Quaker relief – that began with the dispute between Gregory Welch and Arthur Watts – were by no means ended. And despite the vigorous efforts of Rufus Jones and other members of the AFSC board, the controversy with Herbert Hoover continued to have a damaging effect on Wilbur Thomas. Over the next several years increasing numbers of Friends – among them Julia Branson, Clement Biddle, Agnes Tierney, Caroline Norment, Carolena Wood and Alfred Scattergood – expressed their concerns about Thomas' sometimes "imperious" leadership of the AFSC, his single-minded focus on Russia and his associations with radicals. In 1926 Rufus Jones appointed a committee whose members spent a year meeting with and advising Wilbur Thomas, and for a time a sense of unity and purpose prevailed, but by December 1928 Thomas had been persuaded to resign, effective the following February.

6. "Who wished for food had to work!"

Nancy Babb and the Totskoye Projects, 1921-1927

What Nancy Babb saw of the famine:
She lived in the worst famine district where people died in such numbers
that it was necessary to employ gravediggers to bury them
Where all cats and dogs were eaten and some people
Where even the thatched roof of the houses were used as food
Where people were afraid to be out in the evening
for fear of being murdered and having their coats stolen off their backs
And bandits were frequent.

What has she seen since?
Nancy Babb has witnessed the passing away of all the above conditions
and the organization of a regime of law and order.
She has seen the schools gradually restored, also hospitals,
bridges, cultivation of land, replenishing of work

From Nancy Babb's diary (undated) [1]

The American Quaker Nancy Babb was one of the most remarkable people in the story of 20th Century relief efforts in Russia. From 1921 to 1927 she worked in the Totskoye district, east of Buzuluk, but the heart of her unique reconstruction program began in 1922. In 1928 she summarized the range of her activities for a reference letter:

> This is to certify that Nancy J. Babb has worked as a representative of the American Friends Service Committee in and for Russia as follows:
>
> 1917-18, Mogotovo Hospital and Outpatients - Nursing and Doctors assistant - 8 months
>
> 1918, Buzuluk Center - Bookkeeper, manager of summer Friends Settlement and organizer of book binding trade school for refugees - 7 months.

1918, Survey of Siberian Russian refugee conditions and the organization of relief, schools, hospitals and delousing stations for the refugees in ... Omsk "Quaker Department of Red Cross" - 9 months

1921, Organizing the Russian Industries in the army barracks throughout Germany - 4 months.

1921-22, Organized famine relief work in Buzuluk (receiving, storing and distributing shipments, organizing working quarters) - 4 months

1922-27, Totskoye District

(a) Famine Relief - supervisor of feeding program - 6 months.

(b) After Famine relief - reconstruction organization - 18 months.

(c) Medical relief - malaria epidemics, children's clinics and feeding of undernourished children, orphans, etc. - 2 years.

(d) Establishing, building, organizing and equipping a new hospital center and reconstructing a demolished summer sanitarium with farm attached and supporting both ... through salvage of supplies - 3 years (Note, that overlaps (c).)

Note: During the last five years Nancy Babb worked quite independently of all other Americans and English under the Friends International Service, organizing and directing ... [only] Russians ... in a district of 63,000 population composed of 43 villages. Her work was carried out in cooperation with the local Russian officials but entirely under the control of Friends. [2]

Nancy Babb, Buzuluk, 1921

Nancy Babb was undoubtedly the most energetic of all Quaker staff in the field, and she was the last Quaker representative to leave the Buzuluk area. She also had a reputation for being difficult to work with. None of the other British or American Quaker volunteers stayed with her for very long in Totskoye, preferring to join other units, and there were times when Russian officials complained to her Quaker supervisors in Buzuluk and Moscow. But her no-nonsense, practical and fiercely independent approach to work won her respect, support, and eventually overwhelming gratitude among local officials, soviets and district committees, and the peasant communities with which she worked.

Born June 8, 1884 near Franklin, in Southampton County, Virginia, Nancy Babb was a lifelong Quaker. She graduated from Corinth Academy in Ivor, Virginia, and Westtown Boarding School, obtained a State teaching credential from the University of Virginia, and studied biology, bacteriology and chemistry at Temple University. She worked as a teacher in Virginia and as a tenement house inspector in Philadelphia before volunteering to go to Russia with the first group of American Quakers in 1917. There she worked with Anna Haines and others on behalf of WWI refugees in Buzuluk and Mogotovo. When the Russian Civil War forced the Quaker operations in Buzuluk to close in the fall of 1918, she joined the American Red Cross in Omsk, Siberia, for several months, and then she returned to the United States. Upon hearing the news of the famine in 1921, Babb was so determined to return to Russia that she offered to work with the American Relief Administration if Quaker Service could not place her in a responsible position. In 1925 she described her motivation:

> I have worked conscientiously and continuously ... to give constructive relief as far as possible ... that my work might be to these innocent people a living testimony of justice, Christianity, and the spirit of Friends Service. [3]

Babb arrived in the village of Totskoye, fifty miles east of Buzuluk toward the central Asian steppes (about 1000 miles southeast of Moscow), in December 1921, with the first trainload of clothing and relief supplies. The food included flour, sugar, lard, salt fish, grains, corn, canned foods, cod-liver oil and frozen carcasses of Australian meat (which she said "might have been carcasses of rhinoceroses, wild buffalo or anything of the sort, judging from the size"). Totskoye was the political headquarters of one of the districts where the famine had been the most acute (see Anna Haines' description, chapter 4). It was also three miles from the nearest railway station. She quickly set up warehouses for the supplies. Many years later she recalled those first days in Totskoye:

> Over each door of our warehouses and offices we had posted the Quaker stars well known by their four black points, alternating with their four red smaller points. ...

> The next morning my one American companion, with her interpreter, went away, leaving me alone and with no passport, in this village of eleven hundred, to organize the Quaker relief work for forty-three villages covering an area of three thousand square miles with sixty-three thousand population. Many were already dying of starvation and freezing for the want of the clothes which they had sold to buy food to keep them alive up to this time.

This village of Totskoye ... had no warehouse suitable to accommodate our supplies. These we were compelled to store, during the first year, at the station in care of the government, the Quakers holding the keys while the government had to be present each morning when the seals were broken. Rather dreading the daily cold drive through blizzards to this station and fearing having my face frozen frequently, I wanted to live at the station, but the good-natured official assured me that the Quakers really should not settle at the lonely station. After looking around all one day, finally they found me a four-room tiny, one-story peasant cottage which had been nationalized by the government and had been recently occupied by seven families, including one typhus case. ...

I was told that my house was on the famous Bandit Row, but the kind-hearted Russo-Japanese army cook, now a Russian government official, begged me not to fear the bandits, as the twenty Communists already killed and buried on my street would prove to have been the last to perish. In a few days the government was going to send a whole battalion of soldiers to defend the town, and some of these were going to be quartered in my little cottage for my protection. A week after we had organized the feeding, five hundred people arrived in front of our house. The warehouse man's wife became hysterical. ... A rap on the door, quickly followed by a second rap, announced that someone had arrived with demands. I opened and sure enough, there stood a large group of men. "Who are you, and on what authority have you come here?" I asked kindly. They replied calmly, pointing to their rifles:

"We are Soviet soldiers from the Red Army sent to defend the town against bandits. Please give us quarters here, so we can look out for your personal protection."

I told them that we were Quakers and did not need the protection of arms nor did we fear the bandits. They looked amazed. They were a lot of men, mostly very dirty and evidently hungry. Giving them each a loaf of bread, I asked them to leave me alone. I was very busy with the food committees. Moreover, they would find all our houses marked with the Quaker stars, and at such places their services would not be needed.

The next day the head of the village soviet, the governing committee, was astonished on hearing the story. He was surprised to find us without armed protection. ... [The local helpers] all informed me that unless I conformed to the rules and allowed the soldiers to remain for protection they would have to leave me. To this I replied, "Go where you feel comfortable, but I shall remain here." They then began to become more calm.

In a few days bandits came to the village where our food supplies were housed, but the committees, not wishing to disturb me, met the bandits themselves, explained the stars and that the Quakers were feeding little children ... all regardless of race, creed, or party affiliations. The bandits looked at the food and forbade their men to take any, but took all the soviet horses. [4]

Nancy Babb built a prodigious array of projects in the post-famine era. She raised flax, hay, potatoes, grain, and vegetables to supply children's homes and sanitariums. She established a machine shop, an agricultural school, an adult literacy school, a tractor pool, horse

Nancy Babb's house in Totskoye

and land banks, and several children's homes. By 1924 she oversaw clinics to serve mothers and babies and to treat malaria and tuberculosis. She managed an enormous number of cottage industries where peasant women made window curtains, clothing and embroideries while the men were organized into WPA-like work brigades digging wells, exterminating rats, repairing structures and constructing an entirely new district hospital. Babb also persuaded numerous village committees and government officials to cooperate with her in supporting these projects.

The Home Industries and Food in Exchange for Work

Babb was uniquely able to link her plans with local governments' reconstruction goals. She had the insight – earlier than any of the other Quaker workers – to require work in exchange for food or material goods, thus helping whole villages recover their self-sufficiency. She sought to make all projects self-supporting, or to enable the local people to take them over, thus enabling Quaker support to shift to other work – a later hallmark of almost all AFSC international relief efforts. As she summarized the story later,

> As soon as the winter was over a reconstruction program was organized in cooperation with the local government. Who wished for food had to work! This led to the rapid organization of inspectors of labour of many kinds, who co-operated with my central committees in seeing that the roads were staked out or repaired, orphanages provided, adult schools organized, furniture made, schools repaired, medical stations repaired, club houses, public halls and libraries repaired, home industries established - such as embroidery and weaving - farm buildings repaired, land ploughed for those who had lost their horses in the famine, hay cut, bridges built, plague exterminations undertaken, typhus

barracks arranged or built ... and countless other activities too numerous to mention. [5]

Early in 1922, Babb recognized that the need to move from famine relief to a cooperative reconstruction program neatly coincided with other objectives. The Soviet government wanted to declare the famine over, the ARA wanted to end large-scale relief, and both British and American Quakers were reassessing their financial support. But her reasons for moving into reconstruction were more basic, reflecting her perception that long-term relief sapped the initiative and even the dignity of those who received it. In her 1922 report to Quaker Service, she outlined her approach:

> There are still many things which we should be doing to help the unfortunate famine victims but ... the time has come to decrease the number of rations issued free and to require of every family some definite return for his ration. ... The spirit with which we do this and our willingness to help them in worthwhile reconstruction work will be cherished quite as much as the loaves and fishes. There will be difficulties and many problems but in this work it is more than possible that we shall be able to demonstrate our real desire to help them, and at the same time demonstrate international unselfish service! [6]

The projects depended on three-way cooperation: the peasants provided labor; the local government provided construction materials and support; and the Quakers provided organization, food, materials, and money. On capital projects, such as buildings, Babb offered Quaker support on a 50-50 basis with the local government committee.[7] By the winter of 1923, Babb's efforts were virtually autonomous from the rest of Quaker relief in the Buzuluk area. She had an independent warehouse along with bookkeeping, distribution, and agricultural and medical work, all moving towards self-sufficiency. In February 1923, she described how her approach was working:

> Knowing ... the local conditions, I have required some *volosts* to feed their orphans for the past four months, or at least to give them bread. Now the homes are being fed entirely by us on the condition that the local government provide more beds, and warmer and more sanitary quarters with their own funds. In this way, we have not only saved food but have encouraged a local pride in the homes and mutual aid and friendship between the government and the Quakers. ... Through the industrial scheme and the exchange of rations for work, since last May we have gathered many supplies for industry and food for horses ... cut hay, etc., all of which was done without a single additional ration. ... We also secured seed without any additional cost. ... I am confident that in all my plans for relief ... I have the full sympathy of the Russian government. I am on the other hand not understood or appreciated by those of our group who do not understand what Friends should do or how our work should be conducted. [8]

The key strategy was to provide any capable adult with food in exchange for productive work, while children and those who were sick or elderly would continue to be fed. Thus the greatest need was not for food, but for materials:

Sample of peasant embroidery

clothing, books, pencils, paper, wood, window glass, and raw materials. She formulated a plan:

> To allow all the very poorest to work for food rations even though the work is not half-time and to give him a child's ration where the work is limited ... To lend the local government a limited number of rations for all the others who ... have working animals or such trades as will make it possible for them to plough for children's homes, hospitals and the poor, or to assist in the construction of children's homes, hospitals, bridges, roads, etc. The government to return the food, *pood* for *pood* the first of September ... to be invested in constructive relief, such as school supplies and books, window glass, animals for Children's homes, clothing material, and raw supplies for trade schools. All constructive relief to be arranged for by the Quakers and the Government mutually but under the supervision of the Quakers until complete. [9]

By June of 1923, she reported that the village of Gamaleyevka had successfully implemented this policy, "all able bodies, men and women on the July feeding list are required to do four days work." [10] The "home industries" were perhaps the most innovative of all Nancy Babb's initiatives. Starting in 1922, she collected raw wool, food relief bags and scraps of old clothing so that hungry people could rework them into items to be distributed in their own communities. "Through this plan the wool collected does not go out of the famine area but comes to the most needy while the less needy are happy to exchange raw wool for old clothes. [11] In October 1923 she wrote:

> From our bags the poor women are making window curtains for the children's homes and embroidering rich designs with bits of gay wool obtained from the bales, also curtains for the community house in each *volost*. Many of the bags being in such wretched condition, they have been requested to mend all the bags in need of same and to make shirts and breeches of the better ones. For each 12 bags so repaired and for each two pairs of breeches and shirts a woman receives a food ration. The mended bags should sell at an increased price after being washed. ... [12]

Nancy Babb's October 1924 report summed up the significance of these industries for the entire operation of post-famine relief and reconstruction:

> The home industries originated as an attempt at employment during the famine when it was necessary to feed so many people who knew so little about skilled work. In this time every sort of employment which appeared to be useful and possible, was given to prevent pauperizing the peasant. This included hay cutting, ... brick making, wood cutting,

road marking, dam making, canal digging, and all kinds of home industries such as sewing, knitting, weaving, spinning, and embroidery ... on bags with scraps of wool, from the bales of raveled stockings, sweaters and anything possible. Finally we succeeded in getting a limited amount of flax and embroidery thread from Moscow. ... As the number of famine sufferers decreased and the conditions became more normal, the amount of public work decreased and the home industries became more thoroughly developed. ...

Owing to the great number of people being employed, and the great variety of work done, no one work was emphasized; but the particular articles of clothing were made which were most needed for the orphans in the homes and institutions. Such things as complete supplies of *valenki* (felt boots), socks, linen blouses, sweaters, hats, gloves, coats, dresses, shoes, baskets, furniture and the like were produced to supplement what we had received from the border. In this manner we have been able to entirely clothe over 600 children in 14 orphanages ... during the past three years, also to make clothes distributions to every family and widow in our district without work animals, and also to the various committees and Government employees who were working for only food rations.

The industries have filled a double service in the past, making it possible to employ the destitute who must have relief. ... At the same time it has provided us with the supplementary clothing and equipment absolutely necessary for support of our relief program and orphans. It was never commercialized, nor intended to be. But in the meantime such interesting work has been produced that quite a demand has been made for it locally, which we have only tried to fill insofar as the production of these articles will afford employment to the party for whom relief must be provided. Work could in many cases be ... far more skilled and attractive but ... not ... by the one entitled to employment. Linen could be bought already woven but it would rob the widow ... who needs work and cannot do embroidery or fine work. Capital could be invested in more expensive material; but the peasant who cannot do anything but knit or spin, would be without work ... until they can be taught to do other handwork. [13]

As the home industries developed, and Babb persuaded government officials to make material grants to her, other Quaker workers adopted her approach and the need for materials grew. Harry Timbres, in the neighboring village of Sorochinskoye, affirmed the value of home industries among all the women peasants:

I cannot ... emphasize too strongly the need for large quantifies of wool and flax for the organization of women' industries. ... Given sufficient raw material I see no reason why every woman who receives our *pyok* [food ration] this winter could not be required to work for it in spinning or weaving. A standard on piecework could be fixed, and the materials distributed monthly in the villages and then the women as they brought in their work could receive their payment for it and take more wool or flax for more work. Every place I have gone the women have greeted with enthusiasm the idea of working for their *pyok*: they would all much rather work than remain idle. [14]

Children's Homes

Nancy Babb's agricultural work and home industries grew out of the need to provide jobs for adult peasants along with food and clothing for homeless children. When she came to Totskoye in 1921 she found some 800 homeless orphans under the age of fifteen living in fourteen badly neglected "colonies" whose ranks had swollen as a result of the revolution, civil war, and now famine. Recalling that work with children was an original component of Quaker assistance to refugees (See chapter 3), she felt compelled to step in. Jessica Smith, another Quaker worker observed:

> It was that ghastly Children's Home with its wretched, half-stared ... inmates that concerned us most. [The peasants told us:] "Yes, yes, we know. It is bad there, very bad. But there is little we can do. There is not enough food, and how can we ask the peasants to give more when their own children are near starvation?" ...
>
> [We] told them of the transformation that had come about in other children's homes the Quakers had helped — how the children had grown healthy and happy. But that if they expected to receive Quaker food they must first show what they could do themselves to bring the home up to the standard we required. And before we went the peasants had pledged a fund from their own fast-vanishing stores to "clean up the children's home" and had forgotten their own need in their eagerness to help the children. ... They would find a new director, they would have beds built for the children, the place would be so clean when we came again that we would not recognize it.

The visit to the orphanage also provided an unanticipated opportunity to explain Quaker values:

> As we started to go there was a stir among the peasants in the back of the room, and at the door they called us back. A big blond *moujik* spoke up. "Please answer one question before you go. We do not understand why the Quakers have come to help us. We have heard that we must pay them back for everything they give us within a year. Is it true?"
>
> [We] reassured them quickly. "The Quakers are sending the food freely. They believe that the people of different nations should help each other when they are in trouble, and when there is plenty in one country and little in another, the richer must share what he has. The Quakers do not believe in war, and they feel that when the people of the world understand and love each other they will not want to fight any more. That is why some of them have come over themselves."
>
> The peasants nodded. The big *moujik* was satisfied. "Good, good, that is what we believe. That is what our communist government believes. We shall be able to work well together." [15]

In the fall of 1922, Edwin Vail reported from Gamaleyevka, describing the difficult work and numerous problems that were requiring more constant attention, time and energy from Quaker staff than at first anticipated:

The sanitary conditions in the homes are none too good, but we have been making a little progress in getting yards cleaned up and toilets built. We visited #16 ... and found it incredibly dirty. We have given orders for a thorough cleaning up, and if our orders have not been carried out when we visit there in the next few days, we shall have to refuse them further products. ... In the meantime the children ... in the already established children's home have suffered from a complete change of personnel, and the fact that we granted them an inadequate number of *pyoks* to help them with their harvest, so that they have worked too hard in the fields. As a result half of them have been sick. ... [16]

Children's home, Totskoye, 1922

Cooperating with the government and the peasant committees to clean, repair, furnish and provide food for the children's homes enhanced the human connections so critical to this part of Quaker work. At Christmas in 1922, Quaker workers personally visited every home to give presents to the children. Babb reported:

The picture of the happy faces of the little orphans receiving their first Christmas presents is far more beautiful and interesting than a pen or brush can paint. ... We were more than pleased with the splendid effort on the part of the government to cooperate with the homes in preparing the Christmas trees and their most primitive hand made decorations. ... Each little child proudly carried its little bag, containing a toy, nuts, candy, tooth brush and tooth paste in its hand and at night fastened the little bag with its first worldly possessions to the bed post. If the little children in America could understand the joy which they have spread among the famine stricken orphans they would feel amply repaid for every penny spent. [17]

The Quakers' feeling of personal connection and caring for the children was fully reciprocated. Archives at both AFSC and at the Hoover Institution on War, Revolution and Peace have many letters like the following:

Dear Miss Babb:

In the beginning of my letter I want to tell you a few words about my life. I am a girl of sixteen. I am studying in town in the Pedagogical School, and being an orphan and very poor, I am living in very hard conditions, not possessing even clothing and shoes, and other things necessary for existence.

I had to go to school half clad and almost barefoot until my last every shabby shoes were worn out. . . . . I began to despair thinking I would not have the possibility to continue my studies when suddenly I have received a good pair of shoes and a dress that you have sent me. You cannot imagine, dear Miss Babb how glad and happy I have been this day.

Will you permit me now in this letter to express my gratitude to you and in your name to all the Society of Friends. ...

With deepest esteem, yours,
Elisabeth Vassina [18]

By early 1923, through the combination of Quaker supplies, government and village support (especially construction materials), and peasant labor (in exchange for food rations), Babb had transformed all of the children's homes in her district. She wrote:

Children's homes have been given additional bedding and clothing to allow each child a separate bed and three changes of underclothes, shirts, and dresses. This applies to all except three of the fourteen homes, two of which will be ready next month also to accommodate single beds. ... The last visit to the homes showed marked improvement in sanitation though far from what American standards would endorse. Our ideas are so difficult for them to adopt owing to the great difference in their own training and the existing conditions, but with constant encouragement we still hope for improvements.[19]

Education and "Message Work"

Upon seeing the large number of homeless children in Totskoye, Nancy Babb became concerned about their education. In October 1922 she wrote to the AFSC advocating basic literacy training as well as trade and agricultural schools for both children and adults.

Owing to the great number of orphans from the famine, and the lack of any trade schools ... it seems a most urgent duty to assist in organizing a large trade school at the Agricultural Farm. ... However no house is available to accommodate the ... 100 boys who should be placed. We have ... over 700 full orphans and 14 homes. One school well equipped would be far cheaper than to work at 14 schools. At the farm the machines and shops are already organized and only the buildings are needed. ... Also there are capable and educated instructors ...

Recommendation: Donation of $500 and assignment of a capable energetic man to devote his entire time to this work. This man should be prepared to live at the school most of the time while [we] would provide him with all the necessary ... supplies ... and secure as much cooperation from each *volost* as possible. This would be a useful way of using up many workers who must have food anyway. Without some funds it is hopeless to think of doing the work, as local funds will not be available other than labor and transport. Bricks and lumber also nails are absolutely necessary.[20]

Due to opposition from Soviet authorities, Babb's ambitious plan was never realized, but she did not give up. Instead of a single central school, which would have required resources, permissions, funds, and personnel, she simply started smaller trade schools in conjunction with the various village operations. With the full support of local officials, for many years several of these schools provided on-the-job training in carpentry, making bricks, shoemaking and other work with leather, blacksmithing, and machine repair. [21]

Night schools for adult literacy were relatively easy to implement, extremely popular and consistent with Bolshevik priorities for peasant literacy and political education. Having estimated that only 10 percent of the population could even write their own names in 1922, Babb garnered support from local Boards of Education and urged every Quaker worker to teach reading and writing.[22] Even without books, pencils or paper, progress was rapid. The minutes from a Quaker staff meeting reveal:

The Adult Schools are to be opened for three hours each school day for twenty nights a month, and only illiterates allowed to attend. Teachers are responsible for the enrollment. At the end of the first month the pupils must have learned to write their own names. Teachers are responsible for the pupils coming up to this standard. Examinations will be held. [23]

One Quaker reported to Babb from Gracheyevka in January, 1923,

There is a greater interest in the Adult schools than in anything I have seen started in the district with the exception of the public work. The people are ready and eager for the schools, and we shall be run off our feet with them next month. It is ... imperative to have a large stock of school supplies, for there is nothing in the schools for adults. ... I also think it one of the most valuable points of contact that we have with the government for it is also eager to have schools started, and the representative here ... seems much interested in our activities. [24]

The popularity of adult schools raised a fundamental issue: could Quakers teach adults while remaining silent about their personal convictions and religious practice? And to what extent would committees in Philadelphia and London encourage Quaker workers to actively speak and teach about Quakerism? During their relief and reconstruction efforts, this question was never far from the surface, but for the most part Babb and her fellow workers agreed that no special efforts were needed. Without feeling any inclination to proselytize, they saw no conflict between the services they were providing and unapologetic clarity about their religious beliefs. Thus, they wanted to have Russian and English materials about Quakerism available for anyone who asked, but they did not want to conduct any specific program or effort to advance or publicize their faith.

Nancy Babb was convinced that if Quaker service in Russia was properly done – and if the perennial question, "Why are you doing this?" was answered honestly – Russian peasants, intellectuals, and Soviet officials would naturally be led to inquire about Quaker beliefs. When this happened, Quakers should be prepared to respond both verbally and with printed materials. Thus, she was confident that, over the long run, Quaker influence would rise and the Religious Society of Friends would find a foothold among the Russian people. She articulated this in a meeting with the "Message Committee" of AFSC while on leave in Philadelphia in the winter of 1925. Their minutes record:

> Nancy J. Babb was asked to speak of the work in Russia, from the point of view of the Quaker message. She is strongly of the opinion that we ought to have some Quaker literature available for the workers to use in response to inquiries about the principles of Friends. She finds that the Russian people have a strong philosophic tendency and that they frequently ask questions about our beliefs: even Soviet officials are privately interested. Propaganda methods of introducing religious material are very offensive to the Soviet regime; but individuals in private life are free to follow their own inclinations in the matter of reading or of worship.
>
> Quakers have more influence in Russia than most other foreigners, because of the disinterested relief work for the people. Nancy Babb is very much impressed with Russia's need of Friends. [25]

Public Works

While the peasant women were primarily employed in the home industries, the men were enlisted in a range of public works projects desperately needed by all the villages. They repaired roads and bridges, built and refurbished schools, and insulated the doors of public buildings. For the children's homes, clinics and sanitariums, they made boxes, trunks, and beds, repaired shoes, dug wells, cut firewood, planted bushes, and cleared fields to grow gardens and grain.[26] In Sorochinskoye they built dams and small reservoirs both to conserve water in times of drought and to protect against perennial flash floods. Harry Timbres wrote:

> The kind of work which presented itself as likely to keep the greatest number of men busy was the building of … reservoirs. These are simply large dams built at the end of a ravine to keep the water in so that the cattle will have a convenient watering place in the summer instead of having to be brought in from the grazing fields every night.

This is of course only fall work. For the men in the winter I could find no work that would keep large numbers of them busy. [27]

Still, the big problem was materials, and those for public works were much harder to acquire than the wool, flax, old clothing, and discarded feedbags needed by the women. One worker in Sorochinskoye bluntly stated the case to a Soviet official:

Our district needs materials for reconstruction and relief work as follows: bridge timbers, bridge steel, bridge steel rods, bolts, building lumber, carpenter tools, saws, axes, hammers, glass, nails, wool, flax ... for repair of bridges, schools, hospitals. We supply food for workers but must be assured government supply materials. ... Number of people we aid depends on amount of materials you can supply. [28]

All of the Quaker district supervisors were constantly searching for materials to keep the public works projects going. Edwin Vail wrote from Gamaleyevka in August 1922:

We have been doing everything possible to get our reconstruction program started, and to get the people to work on jobs for the community but most of the plans that come in to us call for lumber, glass, nails, tools, and building materials of all kinds which it is impossible to get within the *volost*, and which the authorities feel that it is hopeless to expect from the government. ...

In Shestakovskaya *Volost* we have given fifty monthly *pyok*s for the building of new wells in every town. The old ones were in a dreadful condition – the new ones will be provided with covers and made more sanitary. In Matveevskaya *Volost* we have granted forty monthly *pyok*s for the repairing of all the school buildings. ... In Bogolubovskaya *Volost* we have granted special *pyok*s to a sanitary commission whose job is to go through all the villages and see that streets and yards are kept clean, and also to carpenters for repairs on the children's homes and the hospitals. ... At present the greatest need is for materials. ... [29]

Besides constantly scavenging and cutting timber in the woods, the Quakers obtained materials from local and regional Soviet officials to rebuild the public infrastructure of their districts, thus providing jobs, saving on relief supplies, and removing peasants from the welfare rolls. But Nancy Babb increasingly understood that the only long-term solution was to view all of the Quaker relief and reconstruction work in each district as a seamless, interconnected and interactive web. She recognized that the work depended on a complex mix: materials from government; labor from peasants; food relief from the ARA and Quakers in Britain and the United States; financial support from AFSC and British Friends' budgets; and agricultural products from the land under Quaker cultivation. The linchpin of her entire program during the 1920s was the growing prosperity and success of the agricultural operation and its related industries. Hay, potatoes, vegetables, grain, farm animals and wool could be sold or exchanged for metal, glass, bricks and other materials that could not be grown. [30]

By the winter of 1923, Babb and the other Quaker workers understood themselves more and more as facilitators and coordinators of an intricate network of projects. As Edwin Vail wrote only half in jest from Gamaleyevka in January1923,

> My official title is now District Supervisor. ... But I think the term ... is entirely too limited when it really includes Food Controller, Clothing Commissar, Commissioner of Public Works, Highway Commissioner, Patron of Education and Dramatics, Political Boss, Philanthropist, medical advisor, etc. [I am] Food Controller because all food for the general population and Children's Homes is only issued after my O.K. of the lists [and] Clothing Commissar because I am omnipotent in the clothing warehouse. [I am] Commissioner of Public Works because all those who are able to work must spend two weeks on public work before receiving their *pyok* [and] Highway Commissioner because I have to see that proper bridges are built for motor transport this summer. [I am] Patron of Education and Dramatics because I make it possible for working adults to count school hours as work, and subsidize infant theatrical organizations by the donations of old dress suits, silk waists, flowered hats, and other choice articles sent over to keep Russians warm. [I am] Political Boss because I remove incapable directors of Children's Homes who have been put in by political pull by simply writing a note refusing to issue more products until he is replaced [and I am] Philanthropist because I generously give to certain worthy unfortunates and those gifted in the art of asking playing cards, trench mirrors (out of soldiers kits) etc. [I am] Medical Advisor because the pseudo-doctors supported by us know next to nothing, and many peasants don't trust them. [31]

Agriculture and Agricultural Industries

The agricultural work in the Totskoye and Sorochinskoye districts centered on the 1,800 acres of land that the Quakers initially cultivated on behalf of the children's tuberculosis sanitarium. The horse bank, land bank, tractor bank and machine shop allowed the peasants to share animals and tools that would have been too expensive for them to own individually. Babb and Quaker Service believed it was much more productive to encourage the peasants to work their own land, rather than expand beyond their 1,800 acres and hire peasants to work it.

In 1923, Nancy Babb explained that they could not grow hay on land that had been badly neglected during the Revolution. Instead, Quaker Service exchanged the cheese from peasant and Quaker cows for animal fodder. Then, by planting grains, they made the land productive. By 1925, she could boast of producing her own "bread, cereals, fats, butter, milk, cheese, hay, clothing ... but not fruit, eggs, tea ... which cannot be secured from the farm." [32] And in 1926 she wrote, "the farming department has been placed practically on a self-supporting basis, with over 150 head of cattle ... stables, barns, poultry, grazing facilities, reconstruction of all previous buildings, addition of several new ones, cheese industry, bees and lastly the planting of 50 *dessiatines* [around 110 acres] of trees to preserve the sandy soil and protect the institution from dust and sand storms." [33]

To complement the work of the farm, and provide additional jobs for peasants, Babb and her associates began an ambitious array of agricultural industries. These included hauling hay, collecting and distributing seeds, and digging canals in the snow-covered ploughed land during the early spring, to hold in the moisture at the time of the thaw. [34] One of the biggest projects involved repairing and reopening an abandoned machine shop to maintain tractors and other agricultural equipment. Karl Borders, the AFSC field director in Sorochinskoye described the strategic importance of the machine shop in 1922:

> We had taken on our tractor drivers and garage men with the understanding that they would be continued in our service during the winter. ... Now that our agricultural season is over, we began to look around for something for them to do, when Narosky discovered this machine shop. In view of the increased tractor program for which we hope and the great amount of general repairs on farm machinery which needs to be done in this district, the Transport Department thought it would be an excellent thing to repair this shop, use our idle men, and thus kill a whole flock of birds with one stone. ... This will mean repairing our own machinery and that of the farmers, teaching the boys a trade, and leaving the town in the possession of a rehabilitated shop. [35]

But the key to revitalizing the agricultural area was acquiring horses. As Edwin Vail noted in August 1922, the entire problem of moving the peasants from reliance on Quaker feeding to self-sufficiency could be summarized very simply, "Their houses are stripped of everything, they have no clothes, and most important of all, their animals are all gone. The one greatest need of all everywhere is horses." [36]

Bringing Horses to the Peasants

The idea of purchasing and distributing horses was first broached in 1921, at the height of the famine. Friends both in Russia and Philadelphia saw that horses were dying almost as fast as people and to rebuild a self-sufficient agricultural economy, they would obviously have to be replaced. Friends in the Midwest first proposed sending American horses to Russia, in a gesture of goodwill like the flour campaign of 1921-22. The idea was intriguing but the logistics were formidable. The animals "would probably come to a port on the east coast of the Black Sea, go overland in cars to the Volga and ... in barges to Samara, then in cars again to Buzuluk or Sorochinskoye, a terrible test of horse flesh. Only good horses can stand the trip and many will certain die on the way." [37]

Soon the team focused on finding horses somewhere in Russia. In the fall of 1922, Quaker Service in Sorochinskoye purchased 160 horses from areas where better rainfall offset the worst ravages of the famine. 155 horses survived the two-day overland journey. They had been numbered and branded with the Quaker star, appraised by a joint committee of local government representatives and Quaker Service volunteers, and made available for purchase to needy peasant families. 500 additional horses were purchased for the Buzuluk area. Plans were made to expand this program for the coming year. [38] As Nancy Babb noted in a letter to Anna Haines, it was impossible to make progress with a token number:

A peasant woman and the horse she got from the Quakers

I have just returned from a 40-mile trip ... requiring three days through rain and mud whereas one usually makes it in one day by motorcycle. The purpose was to distribute the 29 horses which we had sold at 1/2 price to the poor peasants who were formerly owners of horses and cows but now were without. ... It was pitiful to find so many families in this sad plight and our horses were not sufficient supply. 1/10th of the families [were] without either horses or cows. Today I received again 12 horses for my district ... where there is only one horse for 30 people. If we only had 1000 horses it would make a sign but nothing more. [39]

At their conference in November 1922, the Quaker staff discussed whether tractors or horses were better for re-establishing agricultural self-sufficiency. The peasants preferred horses, however, "The Committee on Horses ... agreed that from the educational standpoint [and] introducing improved methods, [it would be] best ... to bring in tractors. [We] recommend ... the purchase of 1000 horses ... [and asking] Philadelphia ... for $9,000 for tractors and $41,000 for horses." [40] Their report to Philadelphia provided a realistic assessment of the situation:

Whereas, it is not a moneymaking possibility to plough and farm in this part of Russia, it is possible in the course of three years to make the farming department more than self-supporting. [It is] cheaper to plough with tractors in heavy land than to pay the peasant to plough. The plowing done [with tractors] is also deeper, and can be done at the right season. While waiting for the peasant to plough his own land your possibilities are spoiled for a good harvest; as he will always – and rightfully so – plough for himself first. There being so few horses after the famine it will be a long time before the peasant can afford to plough for others. In the meantime the grain is needed to support the above institutions; and if we count on buying all these things from the peasant, we shall have to pay a fabulous sum for them. The same tractors are

Petrov, the head horse buyer and Ilya Tolstoy on a Khirgiz pony that will go to a peasant family

going to be used for harvesting, sowing, threshing and milling; for that reason it would be most necessary to consider the purchase of the additional parts of the tractors and continue the work already undertaken as outlined in the above report.[41]

In the winter of 1922-23, Quaker Service developed a much more ambitious plan for purchase and distribution of horses, which Director Walter Wildman believed was "the key to a gradual economic restitution." [42] In February 1923, they negotiated agreements for Alfred Smaltz and Ilya Tolstoy (Leo Tolstoy's grandson, a friend of Quaker Service and an expert on horses), to travel to Siberia, purchase between 500 and 1000 horses, have them examined and inspected, and bring them overland to Buzuluk and Sorochinskoye. According to this agreement, all the horses would be exempt from local or federal taxes or duties of any kind, thus keeping prices affordable for peasant families. [43]

Tolstoy and Smaltz left for Siberia March 1. They soon discovered that "everyone in Russia who could gather funds was there buying horses," requiring them to offer a higher price than they had anticipated. Fortunately the Friends were carrying gold bank notes whose value had increased enough to cover the difference. For several days the group purchased horses at the large market, always "subject to the approval of Tolstoy." As Wildman wrote later, "our agents all knew and loved horses and one of the satisfactory features of the entire expedition was the uniformity of type of horses purchased, a sturdy young horse well adapted to the needs of the peasants."

Smaltz recounted one crisis that called for Tolstoy's negotiating skills. "In moving one party of horses out ... two government horses grazing on the roadside mingled with our herd of semi-wild horses and were driven away. The authorities soon missed their horses and before night two employees of the Quaker mission were in jail for horse stealing. A situation over horse passports developed out of this trivial incident which threatened to upset the whole expedition, but considerable eloquence on Tolstoy's part and a prolonged tea party settled everything pleasantly." [44]

Fifty-five days later, having survived spring thaw and floods, the horses finally arrived in Orenberg on June 25. By this time, Friends had proposed a plan for replacing more than 70% of the working horses lost to the famine. They would invest $10,000 in a revolving fund to purchase horses for resale to the peasants on a nonprofit basis. All proceeds would be used to keep prices at or below cost, in order to distribute the horses to the greatest number of peasant families rather than those most able to afford them. In exchange, Quaker Service asked the Agricultural Department for a representative "with full authority to act as a liaison officer between the Society of Friends and the local governments," and for transportation, inspection, and taxation issues to be facilitated on their behalf. Since they would remain under Quaker supervision for projects in Buzuluk and Sorochinskoye, the Quakers also asked that the horses be exempt from military service or government mobilization." [45]

Within a week the Agriculture Department accepted the Quaker offer, and asked that the program be expanded but said they could make no guarantees with respect to "exemption of the horses from the mobilization." Still, the Department promised to facilitate the transportation, inspection and taxation issues, and during the subsequent two years, the government did not mobilize any of the horses. [46] This agreement should have cleared the way to bring in the horses, but once again Ilya Tolstoy's patient intervention was required. When the horses arrived in Orenberg, "the whole matter was up again for discussion and only [his] proper presentation ... settled [it] satisfactorily." The horses arrived in Sorochinskoye on July 5, where there was a grand celebration, highlighted by Mitoslav Rostropovich who played a serenade on his cello. [47] Alfred Smaltz described the expedition to Wilbur Thomas:

> The success or failure of the expedition was chiefly in [Ilya Tolstoy's] hands. This imposed upon him a responsibility well beyond his years but he has fulfilled it to a gratifying degree. His responsibilities not only called for the endurance of physical hardship but also the careful handling of difficult and delicate situations which have been a severe test of his energies and abilities. Besides his knowledge and love of horses which made that phase of the work agreeable to him, he has a genuine appreciation of the spirit that inspires Quaker efforts and he has been able in a simple and dignified way to convey that message to all whom we have met. [48]

Babb described how much the peasant families appreciated receiving the horses. She also highlighted the process by which the horses were distributed, and the relationships that were built between the peasant families, the local government, and Quaker Service:

> Last week was an unusually busy one owing to the sale of horses and a long time consumed in travelling over the muddy roads to ... distribute horses. The Cossack drove the horses down a day ahead. The prospective purchasers were summoned and acquainted with the contract before our arrival so that the signing of contracts and sales took place immediately upon arrival of O.D.K. [Quaker] representative.
>
> The pleasure in distributing these horses was as great as the joy of the peasants who received them. It was most gratifying to see how fairly the committee distributed the horses when once they understood

Peasants are drawing numbers from hats to select horses brought by the Quakers

the basis of distribution. Of course here were more applicants than horses and the largest family with the greatest number of workers ... received the horses. ...

One man had lost his last cow in hauling O.D.K. product. Another had lost all from the winter bandits. Some had ... sold their horse to buy bread from Tashkent which ... never came, while most of them had eaten not only their horses but every dog and cat and were glad to have survived "thanks to the Quaker food." Others most disappointed in not receiving begged us to go again to buy, and some asked if the Quakers would not be willing to buy for them in case the Government would lend its long promised sum ...

The horses were in such a weakened condition that we also gave them ... oats ... to feed them up before beginning work. ...

Recommendations: Buy as many more horses as possible in the early Spring and distribute them in the same plan. Continue to sell them cheap and allow the peasant easy payments. [49]

Parry Paul's Tractor School

In May, 1923 the Quakers had imported about a dozen Fordson tractors to complement the agricultural work with the horses. Parry Paul, who was in charge of the "Transport Division" in Sorochinskoye (where four of the tractors were located), perceived the long-term value of the tractors to help Russia improve and modernize her "greatest industry," agriculture. In the following unpublished vignette, written in 1924, he provides another glimpse into the Quakers' visionary response to the famine.

On the edge of the busy market-place at Sorochinskoye, Russia, stands a low brick building painted yellow. At both ends it has big iron doors that clamp shut and are fastened with a huge iron lock. The dusty windows too have iron shutters. I am told that this was formerly a sclad (warehouse) where some prosperous wheat merchant of pre-war days stored his products, profitably purchased from the peasants of the district.

For a year this building has been used as a garage by the Friends Relief Mission operating in the famine district of East Buzuluk – the only garage between Buzuluk town and Novo-Sergeevka, a distance of 150 miles on the Tashkent railroad. ...

I stop in the garage on a dull gray snowy day in December. In one room, cold and unheated, stand the Ford motors and trucks that serve the Quaker Mission even up until Christmas, that scout over the snow long after the peasants have begun to drive about in their *saniis* (sleds). The other room is heated by a stove that resembles a large rusty can. ... The floor is black and oily – machines have been repaired here for over a year; the sides of the room are lined with work benches and shelves containing a few spare parts. In one corner there is a pail of oil and an empty barrel.

On one side of the room stands a partly torn down Fordson tractor covered with chalk marks and arrows. On the other side is a blackboard, and in front of it two planks have been thrown over some soap boxes; on the planks sit the members of Parry Paul's Tractor School.

Last May when the Fordson tractors arrived in Sorochinskoye, and the steppe land west of the village was ready to be plowed for millet, I ... sent out a call for drivers. The very countryside responded. Experienced chauffeurs there were none in the district, or if there had been, they had died of hunger or moved away. But blacksmiths and carpenters and tinsmiths and eager young fellows who had worked in

Fordson Tractor in Buzuluk, 1923

machine shops – plenty of these volunteered. Not one of them had ever seen a tractor. Not one of them but was dying to drive one. To them tractors represented the genius and culture of the fabled and overdrawn America. And to those of them who were communists, these tractors symbolized the hopes and ideals of the Soviet to improve the methods of agriculture on the vast plains of Russia. ...an earthly reward almost too joyous and generous to be true.

From the group of applicants I picked ten or so, who looked as though they could steer a machine. I put them on the tractors, and in no time they were running them day and night, to be sure with some errors and smashes and bad handling, but they were learning day by day to solve the mysteries of the powerful little motor tugs that had been put into their hands.

The story of their achievements is too long to recite at this point: the 165 acres of land plowed for millet, the 700 acres turned for fall rye and next spring's wheat, the 52 tons of potatoes harvested from the land plowed for the Children's homes are but a few results of the machines at work, pulling plows or harrows or seeders or wagons full of hay or millet in the sack.

By the end of the summer the ten chauffeurs knew something about tractors. The practical experience in making the little iron insects work in the fields had given them a knowledge of gas engines and cylinders and crank shafts and valves that could not have been gained in any other way. But I was not yet satisfied with the training … [so I] established the tractor school to systematize and make coherent the knowledge these men had gained in the fields. So this dim day in December I find sitting on the planks in the garage ten chauffeurs – listening eagerly to an explanation of the cause and effect of over- and under-lubrication, the action of the float and the needle valve, the throttle and the choke, and other things that an expert should know about a Fordson tractor.

I use the question method of teaching. Clad in a black leather suit and a warm cap, I stand before the class, and fire question after question. A part of the Fordson engine is clamped in a vise on the table beside me. I use the engine and the blackboard and a pointer stick, and last but most important, mechanic-interpreter Sergei Mucha in explaining my points to the class of ten, all of whom are quick to respond with answers when questions are put to them. The practical experience of the men comes out in almost every answer. They check each other up and explain and correct. And on a box beside them sits Gregory Yeremin, the transport messenger boy who has been with this department so long that he knows almost as much about motors as the *chauffeurs – he laughs and his round cheeks glow with merriment when the others make a mistake and he happens to know the answer. The men sit in their shubas or in their overcoats that came in the Quaker bales, for the tin-can stove gives little heat. Some are smoking hard; all are thinking hard. They have to keep up with me and Mucha and the errand boy.*

"Now if the electrical system is okay, and the carburetor works, and the kerosene is in the tank, what may be wrong?" I ask, turning to Mitya Lukim, aged 21, the smartest chauffeur in the class.

Mitya scratches his red head, puffs at his mahorka, and delivers the answer to Mucha, who passes it on to me, and I in turn emit a satisfied "Pravda!" (Right!)

"And what else may be wrong?" I ask Leon Lukim, Mitya's older brother.

Leon has an answer just as right as his brother's. "Pravda!" ...

"Now if the tractor is smoking and the smoke is blue what's wrong?" I fire at Bill Nasdukim, the oldest chauffeur, and like every other eligible rabotnik (worker) in these parts a former sailor in the Black Sea Navy, in the good old days of Nicolai.

"Too much oil" answers Bill. "Pravda ... and if it is blackish?"

"Kerosene – too much" answers George Stolnikoff before Bill can think again. "Pravda." ...

This is the Tractor School: everyone on his toes to learn, some with notebooks and pencils recording the new facts that are thrown up by the lesson. And all of them are lads who might have been dead had the Quakers not arrived with food in December 1921.

The background of these boys reveals a wide range of struggle and experience. Take the Lukims. Their father ran a machine shop in Sorochinskoye before the war. Leon was drafted in the Czar's navy, and worked in a submarine chaser in the Black Sea. After the revolution when

Parry Paul (center) and his tractor school students

the Whites began to cut their capers in Samara, he was drafted again, to work in a military machine shop running between Orenburg and Buzuluk. When the counter-revolutionaries were finally dispersed, he returned to Soronchinskoye. The father died in the fall of 1921. The two boys were left to support their mother and three sisters. Then the famine came. Leon was sent to Tashkent for food, but he came down with typhus and brought back practically nothing. The family was desperately poor and without food, and the famine was at its height. Then the Friends' Mission came and I sent out my call for tractor drivers. And both boys qualified. That saved the family. The boys learned so fast – their father's machine shop had trained them well – that they were soon supervisors of the busy tractors, Leon by day and his brother by night. ...

As he was writing his story in 1924, Parry Paul anticipated that another shipment of tractors would arrive from America the following spring. Quaker Service would then distribute them to agricultural communes which in turn would re-pay the Quakers in wheat or rye, thus becoming full owners of the machines. Paul further assumed that the young men of his tractor school would go with the tractors to the communes. There they would demonstrate and supervise their use, thus creating an ever-widening circle of benefits and assuring "the success of the agricultural reconstruction plan of the Friends Mission this year. Moreover it will help Russia in the way that she most needs help, as the darker shadows of the famine recede a little. It will help Russia technically in the upbuilding and improvement and modernization of her greatest industry, the cultivation of the soil." [50] But unfortunately, Paul's vision was not realized. With the changing political situation in Russia, and the evolution of Quaker priorities both in the US and England, neither additional tractors nor horses were delivered.

The Hospital and Medical Work

Nancy Babb's most enduring contribution to relief and reconstruction was undoubtedly her medical work. Most of the clinics and sanitariums that she started and nurtured outlasted their agricultural and cottage industry counterparts. [50] The hospital that she built in Totskoye shows her skill at facilitating cooperation among peasants and government officials, and it remained the area's only hospital until the late 1970s, after which it became a children's community center for more than thirty years.

There were significant reasons to focus on medical work after 1923. As the acute famine was over, fewer adults and children were dying from malnutrition, but disease remained a great problem. Medical work also meshed with the priorities of local governments, without provoking the ideological difficulties of education. During the 1920s, Quakers in the Buzuluk area created clinics for mothers and babies, and to treat typhus, typhoid, and malaria. They established sanitariums for tuberculosis and rheumatism, and finally built the hospital. Edwin Vail in Gamaleyevka underscored the value of the medical work:

[The peasants] have worked too hard in the fields. As a result half of them have been sick. At present we have a nurse caring for them, and have granted special *pyoks* [food rations] for a month to workers to clean up the place thoroughly ... There is a great deal of malaria, dysentery, and typhus throughout the district. Eight people died of cholera in one little hut, but we established an isolation barracks at once, where we moved all the sick people, and ... with personnel and medicines [we] were ... able to check the further spread of the disease. [51]

Babb's statistics on her clinics, particularly for mothers and babies and for malaria, show the rapid escalation of the caseload between 1923 and 1925:

During the last six months there were organized seven clinics in the most destitute villages, where all children were invited. ... On the basis of need and medical examination those too poor to provide adequate food for their children received food from the Quakers in exchange for work at home industries or gardening. ... In addition, ...a series of lectures is prepared and delivered weekly, in each clinic, to educate the parents along the lines of elementary hygiene, sanitation, child-feeding, home nursing, prenatal work and infectious diseases.

In Totskoye Village with a population of over 12,000 there was only one midwife trained to help the mothers. Such complicated cases as could not be handled by the untrained midwives, had to be sent 25 miles to Buzuluk. The Quakers have appointed a physician, one trained midwife and some nurses to hold, not only consultations for mothers and babies but to answer calls in the village and to try to work with the untrained midwives, giving them as much information and assistance as is possible. A milk kitchen is being opened for the undernourished babies; and regular lectures are given to which all mothers are invited. The attendance is very good and recently one woman remarked, "At last somebody has come to help the women." We hope they will also learn to take better care of the babies whose death toll is 50%.

Most of the drugs, and the salaries of the workers here have been given by the Quakers. ...There being no hospital within 25 miles of the villages and no doctor except the Quaker ones it is not difficult to realize the great help which the Quakers are giving, and the great need of a real hospital here. ... When the Government can advance more funds for medical relief or when the Quakers are able to allocate more funds and some of its equipment to this hospital, we shall be able to conduct a regular hospital, which is much needed. [52]

An excerpt from Nancy Babb's Annual Report for 1924-25 reads:

Number of children received from the opening of the Health Center, April 1924: 2,924. Number of personnel, number of children fully examined, number of visits to children at home: 487. Total number of visits to clinic and consultation: 3100 age 0-3 years; 5398 age 3-14; total 8498. Number of lectures and talks given 33; number of clinics held by doctor 250... [53]

By the end of 1924, 44 malaria clinics were operating in a territory of 2,000 square miles. They treated more than 20,000 patients, having purchased large quantities of quinine sulphate and quinine tablets. [54] The Buzuluk clinic was so highly regarded that local authorities wanted to restrict its services to certain groups of people as a way of rewarding political behavior, but the Quakers insisted on keeping it open to the whole area despite long lines and waiting lists. [55]

As Quaker doctors and nurses began seeing large numbers of patients and as their medicines began saving lives, the demand rose exponentially. What began as a "Health Station," where people got some medicines, some consultation and advice, food for children, and outpatient treatment [56] soon grew to serve 3,000 patients a month, and ultimately led to the construction of the Totskoye hospital. [57]

In another significant innovation, Nancy Babb organized a very popular "Consultation for Mothers and Babies" along with a series of educational programs at the clinics. Over the course of 1925-26, Dr. V. K. Boyanus spoke on diet and hygiene during pregnancy, scarlet fever, women's and children's diseases, malaria, infection, abortion, contraception, nutrition, breast-feeding, the mothers' role in child rearing, syphilis, gonorrhea, and child welfare, to audiences that averaged 30-40 persons per lecture. [58] Babb and Dr. Boyanus expanded the lecture program into a comprehensive public health campaign. They mapped every house in the village of Totskoye, and developed a committee with an advisory nurse or a representative from each sub-district, who was responsible for visiting every single home in her district, and personally inviting the mothers to attend the clinics and lectures. In 1925, Babb and Boyanus planned to expand this program to the surrounding rural area of 63,000 people. [59] Babb wrote to Wilbur Thomas in July 1925,

> Our daily dispensary is caring for about 1000 adult patients. ...
> Also the drug store [is] issuing over 5000 prescriptions monthly, and the
> consultation for mothers babies and children to 14 years of age, ... [has]
> ... over 1800 children and an average monthly attendance of 800
> children. The midwife is busy in her educational work trying to save
> the mothers from the ignorant illegally practicing midwives. The
> children's ward in the hospital has been closed this summer for want of
> funds and the personnel transferred to the sanitarium. ... Instead of
> closing up the work here the government wants to help to enlarge it,
> providing a maternity ward and some beds for adults in another
> building adjoining the hospital. Minor repairs are now being made
> preparatory to winter work. ... [60]

When Ruth Fry arrived from London in January 1925, both home industries and agricultural work had become secondary to the expansion and development of medical projects. In her journal, Fry wrote of paying a visit to the "imposing Hospital Compound" with clinic, children's wards and a TB ward that Nancy Babb had organized. [61]

Ruth Fry on a visit to Samara

By the middle of 1925, as the famine emergency appeared to be over, funds were declining, and Quaker Service in London and Philadelphia began cutting expenses and consolidating the Russia work. In the fall, AFSC Executive Secretary Wilbur Thomas informed Babb that Quaker Service wanted her to begin closing down her projects, and prepare to return to the United States permanently. Outraged, she quickly became creative. She wrote to Thomas:

> With the uncertainty of funds to properly finance a tractor program, late arrivals of shipping and the uncertainty of being able to keep the land I did not foresee a single bit of profit and before I should waste Quaker money, I decided to transfer it all to [the] medical program. ... The *Oozdocom* was good enough to give me 10,000 rubles for my old tractors and ploughed land on condition that I would use the money to build an additional ward to our little hospital at Totskoye. Of course they would not have objected to having the money anywhere but ... I agreed to the proposition as something had to be done quickly and there seemed no better way out. If the local help is forthcoming on which I am counting, I hope to manage to squeeze through with our building and repairs to completion of both the hospital and Sanitarium by next Autumn, though we are certainly making the ruble squeeze to do it. That is, if you don't fail to send us the budget.

Thus in a few strokes she seized the initiative and consolidated all of the Totskoye district work into the medical program. In exchange for materials, equipment, and land that she turned over to them, the local government promised to help her complete a new hospital. Without authorization from either London or Philadelphia, Babb committed Quaker Service to the hospital and sanitarium with contracts extending to October 1927.[62]

When Thomas protested her *fait accompli*, she simply informed him that it was "not possible" for her to come home or for the work to be closed up any sooner. If he ordered her to do so she said she would "officially" close up the work on October 1, 1926, but she would remain until the contracts were honored and completed. She argued, "in a country where it is said that so many contracts are violated, I am glad that the Quakers have stood by their word till the last. ... Friends have ... helped to restore to health hundreds of little children since the famine. What hate and revenge and war had demolished Friends have restored for the use of innocent little children." And, as for the fledgling hospital,

> Totskoye Health Center, another child of the Friends (now in a state of adolescence) should have reached the age of discretion in another year if Friends do not forsake it at this critical hour. ... Personally I shall be glad to be free from this by September 1, but fortunately or unfortunately I am not temperamentally fitted to accept the statement, "when joy and duty clash let duty go to smash" so I should like of my own accord without involving the committee, to stay over until I see the job finished properly and know that the funds entrusted to me have not been misused. . . . We have given so much of our means, time and selves to the work I hate to see it neglected just at this most critical moment. The *gubernia* medical chief has said that our children's clinic and health center was the best in Russia probably and certainly the best system in the *gubernia*. [63]

In October 1926, the sanitarium had been turned over to the government, but the hospital was not finished, and Babb was determined to see it open. Despite the delay, she was upbeat in a letter to Thomas, expressing both the excitement and the cooperative achievement that the hospital represented:

> Here in Totskoye, we had already well under foot the plans for construction of needed brick building to [add] to our hospital campus when you wrote about the plan to cut off funds from America in September so it was too late to change. Good luck came our way and in more than one way the local people, government, and Samara *gubernia* officials have assisted to such an extent that it looks quite like we should have our hospital ready next summer for occupancy even though floods, illness, liquidations, and a dozen other things have tended to delay us. ... I am sending you a plan of the location and the new building which is a beauty and left here for ages to express the good will of Quakers for even peasants.
>
> Now ... the Foreign Department assures us that the *Narkomzdrav* [The People's Commissariat for Public Health] will take all possible steps to get the 50% promised by the Government to furnish and equip same. You will probably be interested to know that it is the first large building of its kind since the war and our little village is quite proud of the fact that they have it here built from their own bricks made in the village. One dear old peasant remarked last week, "Every holiday I go to see that Hospital, which is a wonder. Now we are going to get our peasants to build some good bridges to match it! [64]

Several years later, Babb described how the hospital was built:

> *How I built the hospital:*
>
> *I. By request of the Government in order to enlarge the first group of buildings given for a temporary hospital in 1923;*
>
> *II. Financed entirely by the salvage fund from equipment supplies and machinery left over from the time of the famine*
>
> *III. Deficit of 8000 rubles according to original contract part by the local government*
>
> *III a. Plans of Nancy Babb accepted with few changes and endorsed by the Gubernia building department also by the Gubernia Board of Health*
>
> *IV. Work supervised by agent of Friends paid monthly to see that work was done according to several contracts. All work was done piecework; first year the Quakers supplied the material. 2nd year all work was given out to a contractor by the Quakers. ...*
>
> *Materials were supplied (a) locally from newly organized brick factory; (b) lumber from the forest 100 miles away via RR; (c) plumbing from Moscow, 1000 miles away; (d) glass from Ufa, 400 miles away; (e) paints, alabaster, hinges, screws, cement etc from Samara City 200 miles distant; (f) nails, tin roofs, stone filling and minor supplies from Buzuluk 50 miles away.*
>
> *Labor supplied as follows: Architect released from Government service to make pencil plans and supervise the work; engineers and contractor invited from Samara; Bricklayers from Orenburg, Carpenters from Buzuluk, painters from Buzuluk; transport of bricks and sand done as ... contribution by peasants and partly by Buzuluk transport company.* [65]

Nancy Babb's Legacy

On her departure in 1927, the medical staff of the Totskoye clinic and hospital gave Nancy Babb a letter expressing their appreciation:

> You have been able to lay the foundation of a great work at Totskoye which from the first demands an independent existence. The medical personnel has realized with you step by step the establishment and growth of the Center which has developed fully along the broad educational lines of sanitary and preventive medicine. The protection of the health of babies; the preschool age and the mothers, the maternity home, the hospital ward; drug stores, children's sanitarium, day camp for tuberculosis; and the plan of lectures, each of these departments you have placed on a firm basis. In addition to all the above, you have been able to erect of newly made red bricks a splendid hospital – the best of the district. ...

The medical personnel which you have assembled from beginning of work has watched its continual growth and believes that your work will never die, and that the best memorial of your services in far Russia and the recognition of the highest service is the further extension and support of the center. [66]

Upon her return to the United States, Nancy Babb was frequently called upon as a public speaker. She was active in many civic organizations in the Philadelphia area until her death in June 1948. But the memory of her contribution remained alive in the village of Totskoye seventy years after her departure. Ivan Leontivich, a retired 86-year-old schoolteacher, lived across the street from the former hospital. It had served as the village's primary medical facility until the 1970s before becoming a children's community center. In an interview with David McFadden and Sergei Nikitin, in 1998 he described running around the newly poured basement as a child, and he recalled the day the hospital opened. It had been raining for days, and all the roads had turned to mud. On the morning of the opening the sun came out and all the beds, tile floors, and equipment gleamed. He said, "I will never forget the muddy boots on the new clean floors, but also the wonderful happiness on the faces of the people as they saw their new hospital." [67]

7. "The Days of Our Life" Anna Haines and the Politics of Medical Relief, 1919 - 1927

Anna Haines' first two tours, 1917 - 1921

Anna J. Haines was a member of the first Quaker team that went to Buzuluk to help with the WWI refugees in 1917. When civil war conditions forced the team to leave Buzuluk in 1918, she went to Omsk, Siberia, (as did Nancy Babb) and then home to the United States. She returned to Russia again in the fall of 1920 as the first American representative alongside British Quaker Arthur Watts in Moscow (see chapter 3). These experiences convinced her that Russia's greatest need was for medical support so she went back to the United States in October 1921 to study nursing, in order to resume her service to the Russian people. Her third tour in Russia began in 1925 and lasted almost two years.

Anna Haines' background is remarkably similar to that of Nancy Babb, but in temperament and vision they were very different. While Nancy was an independent activist whose lasting monument was a hospital in Buzuluk, Anna was a more patient team player, and a conscientious report writer who sought to establish a western-style nurses' training school in Moscow. Born into a Quaker Family in Moorestown, New Jersey in 1886, Anna Haines was educated at Friends Academy, Moorestown School, Westtown Boarding School, Bryn Mawr College and later, the Nurses Training School of the Philadelphia General Hospital and the Pennsylvania School for Social and Health Work. While living in Philadelphia, she taught in the public schools, did settlement work and served as a housing inspector for the Department of Health.[1] Her careful writing skills and contributions to the strength of the Moscow team are evident in her November 25 letter to Wilbur Thomas exploring the subtle nuances of the Gregory Welch/Arthur Watts controversy of 1920:

> The series of committee meetings ... brought out considerable discussion particularly on the part of Gregory Welch and Arthur Watts. ... Their point of view continued unchanging, Gregory Welch feeling that Russia's greatest need was for personal work along spiritual lines with the emphasis on a Quaker form of religion, and that the material relief which we might bring in should be used not exactly as a lever but as a point of contact for the more important other side of our mission. Arthur Watts felt that material relief was what could best be understood

by the great majority of suffering Russian people, and that it should be administered at present as an expression of disinterested Christian love. Later when the country is not in such an abnormal political and economic state he felt that the Quaker Embassy type of work would be possible without being misunderstood, as it is almost certain to be at present.[2]

Once settled in Moscow, Anna Haines arranged for the office, and the "*Friends International Service*" letterhead stationery printed in English and Russian, with its eight-pointed Quaker star. Then she settled into providing "ballast" as she put it, for Arthur Watts, joining him at endless negotiations with Bolshevik authorities, and overseeing the distribution of relief supplies. More than any other member of the various Quaker teams, she has provided a detailed glimpse of the life of a relief worker in her chronicle of 48 hours in the winter of 1920, which she titled:

The Days of Our Life

One of Andreev's plays with the above title, recording a succession of trivial and apparently meaningless details in the life of very ordinary people, has become so popular in Russia that we have wondered if you might not like to have some such commonplace diary of the days of the Quaker Unit here. It will not be a formal report— reports are supposed to employ the good old rhetoric virtues of "unity, mass and coherence" and our days show none of these! It will merely be a chronicle of 48 hours, almost any 48 hours in the last three weeks.

7:30 AM: Alarm clocks go off. No one else in either of our hotels thinks of rising for two hours yet. A.W. [Arthur Watts] gets up and prepares breakfast for himself and two Russian staff, after which they all cycle to the warehouse. A.J.H. [Anna Haines] decided to sleep ? hour more and eat breakfast as she walks to work, there being no means of preparing food in her room, and black bread being easily munched en route. Fifty minutes' brisk promenade (cabs are awfully expensive, and as A.W. says every time he passes her on his wheel, "walking is very good for the health") carries one past three railroad stations. ... At that time of day [they] are giving forth hundreds of country peasants who have come to town with a few pounds of bread or cans of milk to sell to whoever is rich enough to meet their exorbitant demands. The streets are crowded with other pedestrians also on their way to work and with the long queues of people waiting outside ... to receive their rations. ... Almost every one is dragging a little handmade sled to which are fastened ... little sacks of food or little babies or little boxes of tools. Faces are a bit thinner and grayer than they were three months ago, as the food shortage combined with lack of fuel for transportation has really brought famine conditions to many citizens of Moscow. Near the warehouse the streets grow narrower and dirtier, and in one of them a real village well supplies the neighborhood with drinking water. Our quarters are in the basement of a large concrete building, fitted with electric lights which work, and steam heat which doesn't.

9:15 AM: Every one gets busy measuring or weighing or counting out the supplies which are ... apportioned to the various institutions sharing in our first consignment. There are 82 of these orders and

The Kremlin Gate, 1919

at the time of writing sixty-odd have been made up, so that our store-rooms, which only last week looked so neat and well arranged, are now frowsy with piles of soap and stockings and oatmeal and lard and petticoats, all mixed up together waiting for the Children's Sanitarium ... to come and claim them.

Two workers have been given to us by the manager of the warehouse: one lazy middle-aged man and one energetic middle-aged woman. While they discuss religion and politics, we cut up the soap (with an axe, other tools being scarce), and pack odd quantities of lard in vacated soap boxes, thankful that all labels are printed in English. Our clothes get shiny both from friction and from the fat, but manual labor has the advantage of keeping one warm. We are interrupted by ... a bustling little housekeeper from some children's institution ... [inquiring] to make sure that so much stuff is really coming into her possession, and on having her pile pointed out [she] hastens away to secure a horse and sled before the goods vanish. Soon she is back with ... sacks for clothing, which ... she zealously counts over to ensure receiving the whole list. Alas a pair of stockings is missing! Business of the whole Unit and all employees [stops to] hunt for these stockings! Unfortunately that particular pile of clothing was near the door and many people have passed in and out in the last two days. Another pair is at last substituted and the little housekeeper sent on her way rejoicing, after about ten papers have been signed to bear witness to the fact that she has received the goods; that she has a perfect right to drive through the big gate of the warehouse yard with these goods; ... that she has a right to travel on the railroad with them, etc. etc. The Unit settles down to splitting soap again with gloomy comments on the depravity of a hungry people (the loss of that pair of stockings rankles). Time passes and another housekeeper comes to claim her goods; the resultant shifting of several boxes of lard reveals the errant pair of stockings, which had fallen behind a counter.

The Unit goes to dinner, its faith in hungry human nature revived.

12:30 PM: When we are working at the warehouse we have permission to receive a dinner apiece at the working man's restaurant in the neighborhood, run by the Tsentrosoyuz. It is a low-ceilinged, steamy room filled with oil-cloth covered tables and long benches, where on the presentation of a proper ticket one receives a tin bowl of soup containing a bit of fish or meat, and a plate of boiled buckwheat or millet greased with a bit of sunflower oil. One must bring one's own fork and spoon or eat with one's fingers – which procedure is quite 'comme il faut'. We enjoy going, as we meet all sorts of people there and the food is really very good. We are considered somewhat of a curiosity and somewhat of a nuisance because of our invasion of the kitchen in the (to us) laudable desire of washing our hands.

1:15 PM: Although feeling ourselves competent to attend to the partition of things like soap and lard, we became a bit shy on being confronted with a carload of medicines, not being just sure what proportions of strychnine and cod liver oil agrees best with infants and adolescents. On applying to the City Health Department we received the services ... of the Chief of the city Pharmacy Department, a very pleasant gentleman of the former 'intelligentsia' but not averse to hard labor and dirty work. ...We hope to become better acquainted with this man and his family ... [and to visit] two of the children's hospitals.

4:00 PM: Closing time. The ceremony of sealing the door of the warehouse is performed each night. It takes several people to hold the candle, melt the wax, dampen the seal, etc., but finally the reconstruction star shines out in uncracked purity of line, which is supposed to guarantee the intactness of our supplies throughout the night. We shake hands with the manager and six or eight workmen and depart for A.W.'s room at the Savoy.

5:30 PM: The Unit and staff ... starts to collect its supper. Some of this comes from the hotel dining room, some from the cauldron of boiling water which can usually be relied upon in the service room of the Savoy and some from the fast dwindling stores brought in for private consumption by Welch and Baker. A.W. affects to scorn these toothsome extras, but the rest of us put up no pretense. Our only anxiety is that the next installment may not arrive by the time these are gone.

While the dishes are being washed (A.W.'s room comprises office, bedroom, dining room, kitchen and bicycle garage, also ... carpentry shop and photographic studio) the [Russian] Assistant Secretary for Foreign Affairs strolls in, apologizing for his lack of a collar and pleased with a cup of real coffee which we hasten to boil up again. We learn a little foreign news and some internal gossip before he has to depart to his office. The whole Foreign Department does most of its work at night, as they say fewer cranks bother it then.

7:00 PM: The Unit starts in on accounts and the warehouse stock book as it seems a shame to waste the active part of the day on this work. When papers get spread over every available flat surface the maid comes in to clean the room – it being locked during her other waking hours. On her departing heels treads a Tolstoyan bright of eye and eager to talk on every spiritual and mental subject. Others come and go, Red soldier comrades, translator-stenographers, neighbors stalking cigarettes, transient American businessmen, but the Tolstoyan stays on forever ... [At] 10:30 ... A.J.H. tramps off to her quarters a mile or more through the dark, snowy streets. Never are the old towers and walls of Moscow so picturesque as on a starry winter night and one ceases to be disgruntled ... with such beautiful views.

9:30 AM: The Unit meets at the office of the Transportation Manager of the Tsentrosoyuz to arrange for the continuous and exclusive use of one of their auto-trucks ... until such time as our own autos arrive. We wait for a half hour or so, then have a satisfactory interview, the car being promised for the following day. ... We go on to the city Health Department to request statistics on the number, situation and clientele of milk stations in order to be prepared for a rapid distribution of the first consignment of milk which we hear has arrived in Reval.

Anna Haines (left, with scarf) negotiating with Russian officials

It should have been noted above that on the way home from the warehouse the day before, a dog doubtless sniffing lard on A.W.'s coat jumped at him and chewed up a considerable bit of the coat tail. During the Tolstoyan's visit the fragments were pieced together, but by no means inconspicuously. Warehouse nails have done similar damage to A.J.H.'s skirt and galoshes so that we never felt that we quite deserved the title which one translator-stenographer typed at the bottom of an official document, "Society Representatives of Friends."

1:30 PM: Nevertheless in such clothes as we own (Moscow is not critical) we next present ourselves at a theater where we have been invited by the Department of Education to witness a Children's Entertainment. From a box near the stage we get a good view of the audience of more than 600 youngsters, some of whom it is interesting to see garbed in knitted sweaters which we distributed ... only two weeks ago.

During the performance a plainly dressed man with Vandyke beard and small, thick eyeglasses comes into our box ... nodding to A.W. He proves to be Lunacharsky, the Peoples Commissar for Education, and during the next intermission [he] chats very informally about these educational theaters for children ... Soon he withdraws to give ... a short address to the children, whom he greets as "My young friends", telling them that formerly the process of education was considered as task and held up ... as a bugaboo, but that it was his belief that learning new things was a pleasure and that every active mind enjoyed it. Certainly the good behavior of that large group of almost unattended boys and girls ... certified to the success of his attempt to introduce greater freedom into the educational system.

5:30 PM: Supper with the Russian staff as on the preceding day. ... We are busy for several hours with a report ... and then with a telegram for speedier delivery. Sometime after midnight A.W. takes these to the Foreign Office to be censored, if necessary, and delivered to an outward bound courier, as neither of our countries maintains regular mailing connections with Russia.

So pass our days and ends this frivolous account of them. [3]

Soon, a regular exchange of letters was crossing both the English Channel and the Atlantic, by way of a shipping office in Reval, Estonia. Watts and Haines wrote on January 27, 1921:

> We were much pleased to receive a telegram announcing the intention of Ruth Fry and Clement Biddle to visit Moscow. Owing to the disturbed relations between America and Russia ... we were not at first sure that permission could be obtained for [Biddle]. ... We hope to be able to make their visit interesting and inspiring. Especially do we wish to discuss with them the future work of the Friends Service. ... It is essential that they bring the fullest information from the Home Committees as to their desire and ability to meet these opportunities. Our organization and the Joint Distribution Committee (Jewish) are the only relief organizations allowed, or likely to be allowed, to work in Soviet Russia in the near future. We believe that only our organization will be allowed to supply the staff, as well as the material equipment, of hospitals, training schools for nurses, etc. If so much confidence and responsibility is placed upon us we should either make good or get out. [4]

After discussing Soviet plans for a large number of children's sanitariums in the Crimea, and their unwillingness to cooperate with the American Red Cross, she continues.

> It has also been suggested by the authorities here that we attend to all the relief ... [for] English and American prisoners in Moscow (probably about a dozen). At present several different organizations or individuals are attempting this relief with results only indifferently satisfactory to the local authorities. Until we were permitted ... more personnel we felt we must refuse this work, as ... it means the consumption of much time and energy. ... We would be glad however if someone could be sent out especially for this work. ...
>
> Only people who are trained or experienced in the jobs which they will hold should be sent, as there are quite enough new things to

assimilate on one's arrival here without having to learn one's ordinary work. In general the people who will be able to accomplish the most will be those who can win rather than fight their way. One need not be a Communist, but one should be capable of an open mind and a closed mouth. No one of the dreamy parlor-Socialist type should be considered; sensation hunters equally undesirable – it will be a hard business job, no more exciting and considerably more uncomfortable than life at home, but very interesting and entirely satisfying if you like it. [5]

Watts and Haines received a letter from *Narkomindel* (the People's Commissariat for Foreign Affairs) also known as "the Foreign Office," dated April 14, regarding the Soviets' attitude towards the Quaker's work and proposed expansion thereof.

The activities of your organization in Moscow from the time you were enabled to renew them have deserved nothing but appreciation and support from us. The very fact that the *Narkomindel* ... have placed you in conditions ... to conduct your activities speaks with sufficient clarity as to our attitude toward your work. This in itself ... would not lead us to the conclusion of opening wide the doors of Soviet Russia for all kinds of foreign relief societies and organizations that are desirous of doing relief work here. You probably are aware that the overwhelming majority of these organizations are unfriendly towards Soviet Russia and will not fail to utilize every possibility in order to make their activities a source for all kind of intrigues and anti-Soviet propaganda. Moreover we cannot agree with the principles that the relief organizations of the very same capitalistic countries which through their blockade are strangling millions of Russian workers, their wives and children, should attempt with their offered assistance to mask and cover the most horrible features of the inhumane policies of their countries. ...

However, insofar as the proposed assistance will be rendered and go through you, i.e. through people who have really proven their absolute abstinence from politics, and insofar as it will be in the future conducted and rendered in the same spirit in which it was conducted by you for the last year, it will not be hindered in any way by us. [6]

Arthur Watts reported for the team on March 21, "Russia is a wonderful place for conferences and plans, and quite unexpected action which bears no relation to them. This week has been busy with the former, accompanied by a series of the latter." Under the heading "theft of supplies from warehouse" he tells another revealing anecdote about the trials of the relief workers:

On Monday morning we received a telephone message informing us that our warehouse had been broken into during the weekend. ... After taking stock we discovered that we had lost shirts, stockings, petticoats, women's coats, shawls, cotton thread and flannelette to the value of ... one hundred and eleven pounds. On the following day we learned that at five o'clock on Monday morning two cabs had broken down or the horses went lame near the Nicholiafski (sic) Station. When the police went to give a helping hand they discovered several sacks which the occupants said were potatoes but on further examination proved to be clothing. The men ran away but the goods were taken by the police and we were called upon to identify them. They proved to be our supplies or at least part of the goods. ... The escape of the thieves relieves us from having to prosecute though we shall have to go into court in order to reclaim the goods captured by the police.

Watts concludes this report with an update on the administrative situation:

We have at last made definite arrangements for Mr. Khorosh (brother of the Russian who co-operated with Theodore Rigg and Esther White in the earlier mission) to be the manager of our warehouse and we are hoping very shortly to increase our office staff so you will see that we are gradually evolving an organization, which we hope will form the beginning of an extended work. [7]

The weather improved over the next six months, but Anna Haines' May 26, 1921 letter to the AFSC indicates that the famine situation had not:

The past week has not been so crowded with new supplies as the preceding week, but our days have been fully occupied with the distribution of the supplies on hand. Soap, milk and cotton seed oil have all been leaving the warehouse, the first by our own autos and the latter two by transportation provided by the departments or institutions receiving the goods. The courtyard of our warehouse is a very busy place with motor trucks, Ford vans, peasant carts, phaetons and often groups of barefoot children who have come several miles on foot with pitchers and cans to carry away the precious oil. The government ration for the last month was one *funt* (14 oz.) of butter, the only fat provided, per child per month. Adults have received nothing. [8]

Thomas' reply of June 30 reveals some the frustration of the headquarters office, "We are again appealing to you for pictures. It is difficult to draw money out of unwilling pockets without them. We are making the best use of those that have been sent us but we lack those that have a poignant appeal. Pitiful but attractive children's pictures will be worth many times as much as they cost." [9] Returning to the United States to help call attention to the need in Russia, in 1921 Anna Haines spoke before the Russian Famine Fund, a prestigious group with headquarters in New York. They raised funds for distribution by the AFSC, and published Haines' first-hand account of the famine in a small pamphlet entitled *"The Story of a Quaker Woman in Russia"* (see chapter 4). [10]

The politics of medical relief

A persistent goal of all Quaker relief work in Russia during the revolutionary period – and the one that increasingly preoccupied Anna Haines – was to provide medical assistance: health care, supplies and training. When the Quakers arrived in 1916, the public health, sanitation, and medical conditions in Russia were poor, but they grew increasingly worse as a result of WWI, the revolution, civil war, famine, drought, and epidemics of typhus, small pox, cholera, and malaria.

Thus, each of the disasters and tragedies faced by the Quaker relief workers had medical implications. Along with pleas for food, they heard compelling arguments for fighting epidemics, improving sanitation and providing long-term medical care. The first British Quaker teams that came to Russia in 1916 included nurses and doctors, as did the Americans who arrived in Buzuluk in 1917. While in Stockholm in 1919 seeking permission to return to Petrograd with food and medicines, Arthur Watts held long interviews with *Narkomzdrav* (The People's Commissariat of Public Health) and he consistently included medical supplies and health programs in his proposals.[11]

The great famine of 1920-22 brought daunting medical problems in its wake. Dr. Horsley Gantt, one of the leading ARA medical doctors, summarized the health conditions of Russia in 1923-24 after the famine:

> Although 80 per cent of the Russians have probably always been undernourished to the same degree as or even worse than the poor of other countries ... and though the food shortage had become progressively worse since 1916, there was not starvation until the drought and famine years. ... Several other factors accelerated the spread of disease – namely the lack of clothing, dirt, overcrowding, and the refugee movement. ... Owing to the lack of soap and hot water, bathing as a cleansing process was nearly altogether discontinued. ... Overcrowding is still a serious problem. ...The death rate rose from the Russian normal of 25 to 85.
>
> Under these conditions the great epidemics which had begun during the war, and had always been endemic in Russia, reached their maximum. ... Authorities put the total number of deaths from epidemics since 1916 at 8 to 10 million. ...To sum up the situation, we can say that, judged by Western standards, about one half of the population of Russia would today require hospital treatment.[12]

As the famine eased, medical programs began to dominate Quaker programs and plans. The strong relationships with *Narkomzdrav* paved the way for collaborating on sanitation and public health campaigns, establishing clinics for mothers and babies, providing low cost prescription drugs, preventing and treating tuberculosis, cholera and malaria, and building hospitals (see chapter 6).[13]

For Soviet officials and professionals, the struggle to build national health and sanitation policies and to provide rudimentary care to all Russians regardless of circumstance, was a central goal of the revolution. Historians have documented how the origins of early Soviet health policy can be found in the members of the *Pirogov* Society, progressive Russian physicians known as *Pirogovtsi* who worked in the countryside in the 1880s and 1890s.[14] The *Pirogovtsi* developed the tradition of medicine as public service in the populist tradition. Many were personally involved in the revolutionary movement, at least through 1905, while making significant contributions to public health, sanitation, and disease prevention campaigns.

The *Pirogovtsi* included pioneers in such areas as bacteriology, epidemiology, sanitation, and social hygiene. Some had developed innovative plans for a national health ministry under Tsar Nicholas II, and some would become Bolshevik physicians. A commitment to public and preventative health care and a belief in public service, especially in the rural areas, united the *Pirogovtsi* in their opposition to tsarist policy, their development of significant rural health care through the *zemstvo*s, and finally their accommodation to the Bolsheviks. Few *Pirogovtsi* emigrated after the Bolshevik takeover, and after an initial flurry of opposition in 1917-1918, most of them continued their work in public health through the revolutionary period and the 1920s. As Peter Krug has written:

> The members of the *Pirogov* Society in 1917 were not private practitioners but public employees, who saw public employment as the answer to their professional needs. [They] included ... a number of Bolshevik physicians who were to become important figures in Soviet public health administration. The *Pirogov* physicians' initial opposition to Soviet rule was based on their fear of losing control of the central government's public health institutions ... rather than antipathy to socialized medicine. After an initial period of acrimony ... many of the Society's leaders went on to play an important role in the development of Soviet medicine.
>
> The reasons for this development may be found in the fact that the aims of Soviet medicine differed little from those of programs long promoted by the *Pirogov* Society. ... Both *Pirogov* and Bolshevik physicians [recognized] their mutual professional interests in the policy adopted by the Bolshevik party in 1918 of rendering significant support to nonparty technical specialists. [15]

Krug compared the leaders of the *Pirogovtsi* in the revolutionary period with the *Narkomzdrav*:

> The professional experience of ... the leaders stretched back to at least the period of the 1905 revolution, if not considerably further. All had received their medical education in the quarter-century prior to 1905, and many had received at least part of their training at Moscow University ... from 1882 to 1896. Thus, there was ... a great amount of shared experience, including knowledge of both the pre-1905 and post-1905 periods.
>
> Second, the leaders were definitely all public physicians, both by profession and temperament. Many were *zemstvo* physicians in 1917 and nearly all had had close contact with *zemstvo* work in the past, either as employees or consultants. [16]

Following the Bolshevik seizure of power in late 1917, sympathetic physicians such as (Commissar for Public Health) N.A. Semashko began advocating for a national health ministry to centralize policy and combat the epidemics ravaging the countryside. Lenin was cautious at first, but by July 1918 *Narkomzdrav* had been created under Semashko's leadership.[17] At a national congress in the summer of 1918, Semashko clearly articulated

Narkomzdrav's priorities, focusing on the great needs of the rural areas and some of the long-held objectives of the *Pirogovtki*. The first "urgent organizational task" should be to unify Soviet medicine by overcoming bureaucratic divisions in the administration of health care. Second, treatment must be provided to all by qualified professionals free of charge. Finally, sanitation and other social measures aimed at alleviating disease and improving living conditions of the poor should be given greater emphasis. These three concepts – unity, universally available professional care, and preventive medicine through sanitation – remained the cornerstones of Soviet health care. [18]

After 1918, Lenin insisted that all foreign medical assistance to Russia had to be coordinated with *Narkomzdrav* and emphasize social hygiene, disease prevention, sanitation and fighting epidemics. Semashko consistently upheld those priorities, and welcomed foreign (particularly Quaker) assistance whenever he could get it. From Watts's first negotiations in 1919, Quakers enjoyed a special relationship with Semashko and with Dr. Vera Lebedeva, head of the *Narkomzdrav* Department for the protection of motherhood and infancy. Relief supplied by Haines and Watts in 1919 and 1920 formed the cornerstone for collaboration on the nurses' training school into the late 20s.[19] Five Quaker agreements with the Soviets in 1922 -26 emphasize developing hospitals, clinics, and other public health work, once the need for urgent food relief had passed. [20]

Semashko protected his Quaker connections. During the difficult winter of 1920-21, he personally appealed to Lenin for supplies to go to the children's homes, hospitals, and clinics under Quaker jurisdiction.[21] Even in 1925-26, when official Soviet policy favored phasing out and discouraging all foreign assistance, Semashko remained committed to maintaining the Quaker connection. One of the most skeptical AFSC field directors, S. Edgar Nicholson, noted in a letter to Wilbur Thomas in June 1924:

> that the Government really had a friendly attitude toward the Friends. This was voiced by everyone I talked with. ... Of all the Relief Missions in Russia the Quakers are held in the highest esteem and are most trusted. This only emphasizes ... that ... we cannot afford to get too far away from the officials and from the kind of work which the officials are most interested in." [22]

Quaker Medical Work in Buzuluk

With Nancy Babb's medical work in the Totskoye district as a model, during the 1920s Quaker Service increasingly focused on educational programs and establishing sanitariums and clinics, most of which outlasted their agricultural and cottage industry counterparts.[23] In the fall of 1922, the field director in Buzuluk compiled a list of "things to be taken up in Samara" with Bolshevik officials. He included, "medical supplies: 5 hospitals, 2000 beds, 2000 *funts* coal, 10 dispensaries," and "we need sheets and blankets, also 1/2 ration soap for everyone in hospitals and children's homes ... and doctors." [24]

While the Bolshevik leadership generally wanted to decrease the number of foreign relief workers in Russia, they made exceptions for health professionals. For example, Semashko advocated bringing Russian doctors from Moscow and St. Petersburg and having the Quakers augment their salaries. In April 1923, field director Walter Wildman wrote to Wilbur Thomas,

> There is a great need for medical relief. ... The Russians are lacking in efficient and capable personnel as well as supplies and equipment. I believe they will not care for us to do medical work as such unless it is something very specific which they thoroughly approve of. ... They are glad, however, to receive all medical supplies possible." [25]

The Quaker doctors Melville MacKenzie and Elfie Graff worked with Wildman on a comprehensive plan to expand medical work in the Buzuluk area. They recommended bringing in more doctors and nurses, expanding clinics for malaria, tuberculosis and venereal disease, and supplying more drugs and equipment. They urged enlarging the tuberculosis sanitariums for the summer months as a way to keep TB cases from deteriorating. These proposals depended upon increased funding from London and Philadelphia, and an agreement to expand the work utilizing Russian professionals as well as doctors from Moscow who were willing to stay in Buzuluk. Both Ruth Fry and Wilbur Thomas were optimistic in 1923. Walter Wildman's proposal for medical assistance in 1923-24 included:

> 1. Assistance in the repair and further equipment of existing hospitals and sanitariums of a permanent nature and the supplying of medicines and other medical supplies;

> 2. Assistance in the maintenance of *feldsher* points or doctors, when such are desired by the *Oozdrav* and the Society of Friends, and satisfactory *feldshers* or doctors are provided;

> 3. Assistance in the establishment of venereal clinics and the furnishing of all possible inventory for combating the disease,

> 4. The supplying of supplementary food and equipment to institutions combating tuberculosis among adults and children;

> 5. Extension of medical aid to children's homes through local doctors and medical institutions;

> 6. The organization of consultations for mothers and children in existing institutions and at other points mutually agreed upon between the *ooyezd* medical authorities and the Society of Friends;

> 7. The opening of day nurseries during the summer months in rural districts where the need is indicated;

> 8. Assistance to the *oozdrav* in the program for health education and sanitation through use of books and materials;

9. The continuance of the present malaria clinics in Buzuluk and Sorochinskoye and the opening of additional ones;

10. The maintenance of all doctors and nurses brought into the *ooyezd* for the carrying out of the medical program. [26]

The work of combating malaria, cholera, and typhus expanded exponentially throughout the district. [27] By the end of 1924, Quakers ran 44 malaria clinics across a total of 2,000 square miles. They had distributed 85,000 tablets of quinine to a total of 20,000 patients. [28] A British relief worker described the malaria situation in Buzuluk:

> I found peasants prostrate with malaria in my district. This had never existed in the Buzuluk area before, though there were plenty of mosquitoes. It had been brought back by the people who had fled to Tashkent for bread and then returned. ... I was surprised that there were so many fresh cases in the winter, but Dr. Mackenzie explained that this was because of the almost tropical heat of the peasants' huts. "Most of them have water buckets in their houses," he said, "and they make a wonderful breeding place for the mosquitoes left over from the summer." He gave me quinine, and I soon had patients from far and wide who came to me regularly [29]

The Quaker team considered trying to eradicate all mosquito breeding grounds, but the task was overwhelming, especially since the peasants relied on standing pools of water for their cattle and gardens. [30] Instead, they brought in more quinine, opened additional clinics, and broke the epidemic within six months. All field reports from 1923-24 indicate that major work was accomplished in combating malaria, cholera, typhus, and other mini-epidemics. [31]

By the summer of 1924, the ambitious plans of 1923 were faltering. Amidst a decline in funds from the U.S. and Britain the Quakers were over-extended. Feeding programs took longer than anticipated. Misunderstandings with local Russian officials made it difficult to recruit doctors. *Narkomzdrav* reduced its matching contributions and support even as they raised expenses such as rents, fees and salaries for Russian workers. Projects in Moscow, Totskoye and Buzuluk found themselves competing for greatly reduced resources. [32]

Field director Nicholson compounded these challenges with an increasingly pessimistic appraisal of all Quaker work in Russia. During a lengthy visit, he wrote long missives to Philadelphia and London articulating what would increasingly be AFSC's attitude: end relief and reconstruction work in favor of a center in Moscow where Quaker values and concerns would be visible, and search for unity on a single, new, larger, long-term Quaker project. Some favored an Agricultural Training School at Oomnovka while Anna Haines and others advocated a training school for nurses either at Yasnaya Polyana, Tolstoy's home south of Moscow near Tula, or closer to Moscow.

In a January 1924 letter to Wilbur Thomas, Nicholson argued that the famine was over and "continued relief was having a bad effect upon the morale of the people." He observed an "unsympathetic attitude on the part of many officials" and the great absence of "any of the spiritual impressions which I know Friends everywhere are hoping for." Finally, he said that the work was "too costly for the results secured ... covering too large a territory," and therefore impossible to sustain. He wanted to end the current program by the summer of 1924, and have all future work based in Moscow, "which radiates influence to every part of Russia and Siberia." Of the possibilities for a serious "piece of work" in the future, Nicholson favored something medical – but only if it were distinctly Quaker and if funds could be assured. Although it would be a number of years before the final dénouement, his perspective prevailed, and of all the far-reaching schemes for long-term impact in Russia, only Nancy Babb's programs in Totskoye were ever completed.[33]

The Crisis of 1924-25

While Nicholson was expressing those doubts to AFSC in Philadelphia, Semashko and *Narkomzdrav* were also facing major cutbacks and shortages. Late in 1922, AFSC had taken over the fiscal sponsorship of American Medical Aid for Russian Relief, an organization begun during the famine by American liberal and progressive philanthropists and social activists who raised funds and purchased medical supplies requested by *Narkomzdrav*.[34]

Early in 1923, the AFSC also assumed fiscal responsibility for the American Women's Hospital Association (AWHA), which had a small program of clinics and hospitals for babies and young children, under the leadership of Dr. Lebedeva. She was a personal friend of Semashko, and had been one of Anna Haines' first Soviet contacts in 1919.[35] In 1921-22 AWHA was maintaining one entire hospital. By 1923 their support had shrunk to the point that when the Quaker doctor (and AWHA representative) Mabelle C. Phillips visited Dr. Lebedeva in June, she brought along the entire remaining balance of the American charity's funds: a $525 contribution to the maternity institute milk kitchen.[36] By the summer of 1924, the only remaining foreign charities were the American Jewish Joint Distribution Committee (JDC) and the Quakers, who, along with their own projects, were also managing some medical assistance for American Medical Relief and the American Women's Hospital Association.

Narkomzdrav's public health campaigns, epidemiological laboratories and rural clinics suffered from the unwillingness of Soviet medical specialists to fill vacancies in rural areas. Then in 1925-26, a shift of priorities from national to local budgets caused a huge contraction in medical facilities and further reduced care for the peasantry. Semashko stepped up his requests for assistance from both JDC and AFSC, and one of his deputies admitted that "the rural network of physicians' points has one-third the normal bed capacity

[and] forty percent of the normal clinical capability, and specialized care is in a completely rudimentary condition." [37]

Semashko wanted the Quakers to provide money or import high quality specialized equipment for clinics and laboratories. When Wilbur Thomas met with him and Lebedeva in 1923 and 1924, they were not interested in new projects, or allowing Quakers authority over institutions or personnel.[38] Instead, they asked for money to repair buildings, purchase equipment, and advance work that was already planned. As a result in 1924 the Quakers helped *Narkomzdrav* refurbish the old Catherine hospital in Moscow, by supplying beds and new surgical, X-ray, and kitchen equipment.[39] Meanwhile, Nancy Babb was struggling to complete the Totskoye hospital, and turn over all medical work in the Buzuluk area to local leadership. [40]

Groping to find new – identifiably Quaker – programs in Russia in the aftermath of the famine, Quaker leaders in the U.S. and Britain were not satisfied with the prospect of merely sending money and equipment. In the summer of 1925 the AFSC Board of Directors, the Russia Committee, and the newly reorganized Foreign Service Section held a major meeting on the occasion of the return of two Quaker doctors (Graff and Phillips) and the visit of Carl Heath, the new head of the Friends Service Council. Heath was advocating the "Quaker Embassy" concept, but much of the meeting focused on a variety of medical projects. Graff expressed the staff perspective that existing medical projects had made a major contribution and were greatly appreciated by Russian medical authorities who "understood the spirit of goodwill and Friendship that Friends were expressing through their work."

Phillips and Graff outlined four directions for Friends to consider: (1) work in Moscow in close cooperation with *Narkomzdrav*; (2) new projects in Armenia with children in orphanages; (3) Nancy Babb's medical and children's work in the Buzuluk area; (4) some new Quaker project (or joint endeavor with the AWHA) in rural Russia. But the committee, prompted by Carl Heath, wanted a single program based in Moscow, combining public health work with a Quaker presence that would disseminate Friends' philosophy and values. They turned their attention to consideration of a public health and training clinic in Moscow.[41]

Anna Haines' Third Tour, 1925

Anna Haines' return to Russia in the summer of 1925 greatly facilitated Quaker deliberations and explorations. She had gone to the United States in 1922 with a long-range vision, determined to train as an RN, in order to be of more practical assistance to Russia, specifically through nursing education. In March 1925, she wrote:

> When I was in Russia before, doing emergency relief work, I was
> always looking forward to the time when Friends would be released
> from the need of bringing in purely material assistance and could turn

their attention to what seemed to me more permanently constructive help along technical and educational lines. Conversation with a number of Russians who felt that their country should be self-supporting ... but that their greatest need was for teachers in various modern scientific and technical subjects ... who were however sympathetic with their government, corroborated me in my point of view. [42]

Her dream was to establish a western-style training school for nurses. While exploring this plan, she held two jobs: (1) as an unpaid full-time nurse in Dr. Lebedeva's Mothers and Babies Hospital in Moscow; and (2) as the American representative in the Moscow Quaker Centre alongside British Quaker Dorice White. Because of her background and experience, and the confidence of American Quakers in her, Anna Haines functioned as the director of Quaker programs in Russia during the transition year of 1925-26.

At Lebedeva's Moscow hospital Haines was put in charge of one ward, with one part-time student nurse assistant. She quickly began gathering information, contacts, and suggestions, and formulating plans for a model program to improve nurses' training. She arranged for a group of Lebedeva's colleagues to read a number of books from American schools that she had brought along with her. She also made plans to attend a major international conference on nursing and nurses' education in Helskini, Finland, where she hoped to exchange ideas with medical professionals from all over Europe and North America. Along with one of the older instructors at Lebedeva's hospital she developed a presentation on the status of the nursing profession in Russia and new methods for teaching young nurses. She wrote to Philadelphia that this commitment to a joint Russian-American presentation was a "rather big step in a small way in international relations. ... It rather confirms my feeling that peace is after all a by-product of constructive work for better social conditions and not a thing to be too noisily worked for in itself." [43]

Burdened by the long consideration that the Russia Committee (and the AFSC as a whole) had given to the Russia situation in lengthy meetings with Elfie Graff, Mabelle Phillips, and Carl Heath in June and July, Wilbur Thomas wrote to Anna Haines:

> You realize, of course, that some of our Committee have become very critical of the work in Russia. ... The committee came to the conclusion that we must look forward to having a center in Moscow where some work can be done and suitable contacts maintained with the local authorities. The best opportunity seems to be through the medical department and the committee has considered that something on the order of a welfare center would be the best opportunity for service."

He then asked Haines to explore the possibility of getting "a few rooms in one of the more overcrowded sections of the city," to be used for living quarters and "as a public health center." [44]

In August Haines responded with input from the Helsinki conference, *Narkomzdrav* and Dr. Lebedeva. While they agreed that a Quaker public health center was an excellent idea, they considered it "superfluous" in Moscow. "The greater need for such work was in the country or provincial districts," only 50-75 miles away, and Haines promised to explore its feasibility. She also came back from the Helsinki conference filled with ideas for nurses training in Russia. "Perhaps the most valuable experience to me was the opportunity to discuss the nursing situation in Russia as I have come to know it, with the most intelligent and farseeing of the nursing leaders in America." They had agreed:

> It would not be possible to put over a really modern and adequate nursing educational system without sufficient funds to start a training school where the entire Anglo-Saxon plan of curriculum (both theoretical and practical) ... would be under the control of people who understood and were in sympathy with the ideas. [45]

Haines found that her colleagues in Moscow welcomed her enthusiasm and new ideas. She was invited to become an instructor in practical nursing in the hospital's training school, to write a paper on the conference for the local nursing journal, and to give a speech to the medical association. Haines described the complex situation to Thomas:

> I have tried to get the doctor who is in charge of the school to see the advantage of giving the students a general training in adult as well as infant nursing. ... It is the desire of the department to send the graduated nurses to the country where they will often be the only nurse in a large village, but so far he wishes to keep the girls solely interested in baby welfare work. That is to give them a specialized without a basic general training, which is not considered the best approach to scientific nursing for any age. ...
>
> The only thing that would convince the authorities here that they were working on ... a mistaken theory would be a demonstration training school whose graduates would obviously be better fitted to meet the situations in which they would be placed than the girls now being turned out as nurses. ... What is really needed is a whole demonstration plant where the entrance requirements, the hours on duty, the ward supervision, etc, were such as to make good nursing possible. Only some such institution would create the mental and physical environment that would give nursing here a modern, scientific status.
>
> The theoretical training they get here is good, but the girls are too mentally unformed and too dazed by so much that is new. ... They are unable to assimilate and to put into practice what they have been told; nor is the supervision on the ward sufficient to ensure this. One person working alone cannot change this situation very appreciably. ... If ... the Rockefeller Foundation comes to survey the field of nursing education here next year I should like to help them with their investigation. [46]

Haines wrote widely, for AFSC and Friends' publications and for others in the left-liberal community. Her small study, *"Health Work in Soviet Russia"* (published by Vanguard Press in 1926) remains, even in the 21st Century, an informed, sympathetic and critical summary of *Narkomzdrav's* achievements in transforming health care in Russia. [47]

By December, Haines had created a new plan to bridge the gap between the home committee's desire for a model public health and welfare clinic in Moscow, and her conviction that it belonged in a rural area. She recommended opening a clinic in the Leninsky Ooyezd, a rural area immediately adjacent to Moscow – close enough to be under Moscow Provincial control, but where many villages had no medical help of any kind. According to Dorice White:

> The help of Friends in organizing a health centre in this district would be greatly valued by the local people as well as the Moscow Health Department. [It] would have the further advantage of being near enough to Moscow to have frequent visitors and give it publicity for raising funds (along lines similar to the very successful work of Nancy Babb and Dr. Boyanus in Buzuluk and Totskoye)." Haines even arranged to obtain estimates for fixing up a wooden house in Leninsk, with the cooperation of local people. [48]

As her colleagues in Moscow became increasingly enthusiastic about her ideas, Haines' work at the hospital and her discussions with other nurses and doctors also made her more confident about her idea for a full scale western-style training school for nurses. She wrote to Wilbur Thomas in December 1925:

> I can and do teach many details in the practical care of infants and I do more supervision of the work of the students than the other head nurses. Several suggestions which I have made have been adopted in the department; several of the books on nursing which I brought over have been read by one of the head nurses who understands English and who is preparing [a nursing manual] under the orders of a doctor. ... I have been asked to prepare a sort of criticism of the work of the visiting nurses here with comparisons of it and American visiting nursing to be read to a group of doctors and nurses. ... It is a great pity that there is not an English or American Training school for Nurses here just now when so many of their plans are in an uncrystalized state. [49]

By February 1926, Haines knew how to use what she had learned:

> I've gained a very intimate knowledge of the conditions of nursing, the types of nurses, and the problems involved in training schools here, a knowledge which superficial visits of inspection would never have given. I am also beginning to be of some use in explaining our methods in nursing to the doctors here. Last week I had a paper on Visiting Nursing in Russia and America at a meeting of the medical association of the Scientific Institute where about 150 doctors and a few nurses were present. ... Yesterday they told me that they wanted me to bring the same paper and the film to a meeting of the medical association of

the whole city of Moscow. I have written two articles for the Russian Journal for Midwives and Nurses. ...

We have contacts with a good many Moscow doctors now, particularly with those connected with the Department for the Protection of Motherhood and Infancy. Now that some ground in the way of nursing propaganda has been broken it would certainly be an ideal thing if some organization could consider starting a training school along modern lines. . . If this Health department supplied the building and the heating, the most would be approximately $25,000 per year. This plan would be the best way to raise the standard of nursing in Russia. Next to it I believe that the visit of some Russian nurses to America to observe our teaching methods would be the most helpful.[50]

Ultimately, the AFSC rejected the ideas for the Leninsky location. On March 19 Thomas wrote that most of the committee members, and the British Friends, still believed that an investment of new money would only be worthwhile in Moscow. Still, they remained interested in the nurses' training school, and hopeful about raising funds for it. He asked Haines to provide a proposal detailing numbers of foreign personnel, a budget, commitments from *Narkomzdrav* and connections with a medical school or hospital. He asked whether she would be willing to work there if the money were raised.[51] On the strength of those questions Haines proposed to Semashko and *Narkomzdrav*:

The Society of Friends [would] establish ... a training school for nurses — modeled on the lines of the most modern foreign schools. ... At the end of the period of training these nurses would be fitted for positions in hospitals, consultations or ambulatories, as visiting nurses who can teach the prevention of disease in schools and in social organizations, and as midwives for normal cases of labor. They could take part in the health program of a village in the country or an industrial city. ... With the cooperation of the Russian authorities in the matter of housing, the Society of Friends would guarantee the expenses of equipment and of tuition, food, laundry, etc of the training school for a period of five years.[52]

The health ministry referred her plan to Dr. Lebedeva both in her capacity as head of the Department for Motherhood and Infancy and as the person with the closest relationship with Haines. At first, Lebedeva suggested that if the Friends were truly interested in nurses training they should simply contribute money to her own Nurses training center, but Anna Haines persuaded her that the Quaker school would be unique, and argued that a freestanding entity was essential to facilitate fundraising. When Lebedeva gave Friends oral permission to proceed, she offered a number of buildings connected with a scientific institute. Haines estimated that around $22,000 would be required to overhaul the facilities, and procured a written agreement from *Narkomzdrav* for the Society of Friends to open a training school for nurses.[53]

By the end of July 1926, AFSC had prepared some striking fundraising materials, and secured a preliminary pledge of $15,000 from two wealthy donors. Then the AFSC felt compelled to re-evaluate its position. Several committee members expressed displeasure with Wilbur Thomas' persistent focus on the work in Russia (see chapter 5). For example, William C. Biddle offered Thomas his "regrets" that Philadelphia or London had even encouraged Anna Haines or anyone else to make such a proposal. He also reminded Thomas that he had not wanted to encourage Russian officials "that we could undertake an enterprise of any such proportions, [and] we certainly cannot guarantee anything of this kind over a period of five years." [54] Similarly, a cable from London stated, "Committee much interested . . . but regret unable to promise financial support at this time." [55] The AFSC board directed Thomas to write to Anna Haines, saying that while both the Philadelphia and London committees endorsed the idea in principle, they were extremely doubtful about their ability to finance it, and therefore she should withdraw the proposal. Haines was devastated. She urged the committee not to abandon the plan and offered to return home, to speak on behalf of the project and do fundraising. She complained:

> It is a tremendous pity ... to allow the opportunity to open the training school to go by the boards for lack of funds to operate it. The type of nurse ... we think it could produce is greatly needed in Russia, especially in the villages. We are the first foreign organization allowed to establish such an educational institution for Russians. It is a work which could be carried on here in Moscow. ... We are all of us agreed that the only work practicable for Friends is some such piece of technical aid as a demonstration of our friendship toward Russia. ... No stone should be left unturned in the attempt to find funds to carry about the plan for the school. [56]

In a unique contradiction of prevailing Soviet policy, *Narkomzdrav* had presented the Quakers with the opportunity to open the first foreign institute of higher education in Russia in the Soviet period. [55] But within the year, the hesitation and division among AFSC staff and committee members, and the increasing disillusionment of numerous Friends with Wilbur Thomas' leadership, (compounded by disagreements between London and Philadelphia) had doomed Anna Haines' plan. She returned to the United States and remained active with the AFSC – specifically assisting with relief to the coal mining areas of Appalachia during the 1930s – until her death in 1969. Except for Dorice White's lonely years in Moscow, and a brief interest in a medical clinic near Tolstoy's home in 1928, this marked the end of Quaker medical work in Russia. Indeed it was, for all practical purposes, the end of constructive relations between Soviet officials and the Society of Friends for nearly seventy years.

CHAP OF RUSSIA AND
LOCATIONS OF QUAKER SERVICE

8. "A VERY SPECIAL RELATIONSHIP"
RUSSIAN RESPONSES TO THE QUAKERS 1921-27

The Russian reaction to Quaker famine relief and reconstruction programs is another complex story. From Moscow to Samara and Buzuluk, Soviet leaders, village famine committees, and ordinary peasants met Quaker workers with a mixture of enthusiasm and respect, frustration, pragmatism and suspicion.

From the outset, Lenin and the Bolshevik leaders were ambivalent about assistance from foreigners. Concerned that relief was foreign intervention in another guise, the Soviets had resisted wide-scale foreign food relief as early as the Hoover-Nansen proposal of 1919.[1] In the period leading up to the intense famine, the leadership had ignored clear signs of impending catastrophe, such as crop failures and drought, and Lenin only reluctantly allowed Gorky's 1921 appeal to the West.[2] He was determined to keep Western assistance limited, brief, and under Bolshevik control. This approach characterized all government relations with the ARA and other foreign relief organizations through 1923.[3]

From 1921 through 1927 numerous bureaucratic shifts and policy changes resulted in ever-tightening restrictions. "Even in the most desperate famine months of late 1921 and early 1922, the *Politburo* was bitterly divided over the wisdom of allowing relief workers on Soviet soil. ... During ARA's nearly two years in Russia, the greatest bone of contention remained who would manage the distribution of the food and medical supplies from America."[4] From 1921, Olga Kameneva, (wife of Lev Kamenev and sister of Leon Trotsky) provided central *Politburo* oversight, systematically monitoring and documenting all the activities of foreigners involved in relief efforts.[5] Only Lev Kamenev (a prominent moderate among the Bolshevik leadership), Feliks Dzherzhinsky (head of the Cheka, the Soviet secret police and precursor to the KGB), and Lenin himself had more authority than she did. In December 1921, Trotsky and Kamenev were given oversight over both the ARA and other foreign relief organizations, and from the beginning, Cheka agents were placed throughout ARA operations.[6] Once ARA operations wound down, all foreign relief organizations found themselves subject to Olga Kameneva's restrictions, control and reporting requirements.

Special Quaker Relationships

Starting in the summer of 1920, Quakers enjoyed a unique relationship with Bolshevik leaders in the Foreign Ministry, and the Ministries of Education, Supply, and Health. Arthur Watts and Anna Haines had negotiated a remarkable series of agreements with Bolshevik authorities in *Narkomprod* (the People's Commissariat of Food Production), and *Tsentrosoyuz* (the Central Association of Russian Cooperatives) giving the Quakers unprecedented independence and control. By January 1921, they had authorization to distribute relief supplies from the American Red Cross, the American Relief Administration, and the British Save the Children Fund. By May of 1921 another series of agreements enabled Quakers to distribute food and medicine to all Moscow children's homes. This was capped by Anna Haines' visit to the old headquarters in Buzuluk, where Bolshevik authorities allowed Quakers to expand their relief efforts in the area "beyond the Volga" to combat the fast-spreading famine of 1921. All of these efforts preceded the Hoover-Gorky agreement of August 1921, and they would stand the Quakers in good stead in coming years.[7] The London Friends Emergency War Victims Relief Committee noted after its consultation with Arthur Watts in May of 1921, "Facilities for distribution had been given, with an increasing freedom … and seemingly the unit now possessed the confidence of the authorities in a most unusual degree." [8]

Following the Riga Agreement, the AFSC pledged to coordinate its efforts with the ARA, while the British Friends worked loosely under the European Relief Council, headed by Norwegian Polar explorer and philanthropist Fridtjof Nansen. But real interaction with Russian officials occurred in Samara, Buzuluk, and at the village level, rather than in Moscow. In July 1922, when the ARA announced it would terminate its relief efforts, the AFSC was able to negotiate a new, direct agreement with Soviet authorities. In October 1922, Karl Lander, the Soviet liaison with foreign relief organizations, told the Quaker office in Moscow that the government was determined to shift its focus to "regenerating the ruined industries, raising the productivity of agriculture," and shifting the burden of relief to the Russian people and their central and local governments. But he also welcomed the Quakers' continued work and expressed his hope for a speedy conclusion to negotiations for a new agreement.[9]

The Quakers made a commitment to continue their relief in the Buzuluk district and in Moscow, and to expand into a reconstruction phase. This was the most complete and explicit agreement with the Soviet government, setting the pattern for 1923, 1924, 1925 and 1926. New programs included providing up to 1000 horses "free of cost" to the peasants, establishing weaving, spinning and clothing manufacture, and developing hospitals, clinics, and other public health work in the Buzuluk area. The Society of Friends

Quaker Service Moscow Staff in 1922

expressed interest "in the promotion of the social and economic welfare and uplifting of the Russian people" and in "supplementary assistance to children's homes and hospitals and other medical institutions as well as to the agricultural and rural economy.[10] In exchange the Soviet government pledged its cooperation in travel, housing, storage, and communications. All relief was to be distributed "without regard to race, religion, or social or political status." And the Society of Friends would have "power to enter into negotiation and to make contracts with local authorities."[11]

In May 1923, AFSC Executive Secretary Wilbur Thomas and his British counterpart, Ruth Fry, visited Russia. They participated in a series of consultations and negotiations that revealed the Bolshevik authorities' high regard for the Quakers. Ruth Fry reported that she asked "quite frankly" whether the Bolsheviks wanted the Friends to continue, "even if the famine were over," and they said "the Quakers ... were the first people they wanted, as they had always trusted them."[12] Olga Kameneva told Fry that "the Quakers were the foreign organization that [the Bolsheviks] most wished to remain."[13] Fry concluded that the continued help of Friends would be really welcome, for "reconstruction ... rather than emergency relief."[14]

Even amidst the cooperation and goodwill, some problems remained. During 1922-1926 there were many detailed, at times irritating, exchanges with Moscow and Kameneva regarding charges for freight and transport, staff visas, customs duties, tax exemptions for quinine and other medical supplies, and guidelines for importing used clothing and embroidery cotton for the cottage industries. But in almost every case, problems were resolved in the Quakers' favor. Even when all other foreign relief organizations were required to pay all their own expenses, Quakers appealed for, and received, special treatment consistent with earlier agreements. [15]

With few exceptions, throughout the 1922-26 period problems were resolved through the attention to detail and personal intervention of Olga Kameneva. Relief workers admired the long hours she spent checking on conditions and facilitating the flow of food to children's homes. They relied on her skill in untangling the snarls of red tape which so often undermined the effectiveness of their operations.[16] She intervened in small matters and in large ones, exerting considerable pressure on the Ministry of the Interior for the release of a Quaker doctor needed at a malaria clinic in Buzuluk, or an interpreter needed in Sorochinskoye. At a 1923 Berlin Conference on Foreign Relief, Kameneva called Quaker work the "most effective foreign assistance" that Russia received, and she singled out specific medical and agricultural reconstruction projects for more praise than the International Workers Relief Committee.[17]

High-level Bolshevik contacts stood the Quakers in good stead when they ran into difficulties with local officials, especially during the tumultuous famine years of 1921-23. Quaker Service in Buzuluk relied on close cooperation and constant contact with both local government staff and a "Mutual Aid Committee" in each village that determined storage, cooking and feeding sites and most significantly, which families would be fed. They made staffing decisions jointly with Quaker workers. Quaker staff supervised the feeding, maintained liaison with local officials and committees, and carried out all the detail work, particularly plans for new operations. Considering the tremendous geographic area and numbers of villages, feeding points, and medical clinics and the small number of Quaker workers, it is surprising how few conflicts arose.[18]

Nonetheless, Quaker workers experienced many difficulties, ranging from disputes over personnel to disagreements about the scope of the work, the responsibilities of the district committees, the expropriation of relief supplies and funds for personal use, and the inevitable personality conflicts. One observer characterized the AFSC relief work in Sorochinskoye:

> Conflicts over distribution ... can hardly take place as the government already controls this; in the same way financial difficulties are hard to find in view of the fact that the Friends pay all their expenses except house, heat, light and warehouse space. Nevertheless difficulties arise in respect to personnel, etc., so that sessions with the ... district committee and soviet staff are no Quaker meetings.[19]

Quaker, ARA, and Russian archives contain extensive correspondence about minor problems: disagreements over personnel, complaints over misuse of relief supplies, Russian demands for more reports and more statistics, and Quaker requests for equipment, supplies and financial reimbursements. Reports to Moscow, London, and Philadelphia mention "being harassed by various petty obstructions from local officialdom which makes satisfactory work increasingly difficult." Walter Wildman wrote in March 1923, "If things are not just done as local officials desire ... it seems that they are constantly putting obstructions in our way." [20]   He added:

> Some of the work which we would have liked to carry out has been impossible because of the inability of local authorities to render any supplementary assistance which involved additional expense on their part and also because they did not always recognize the immediate value or importance of the proposals. ... Local authorities often dislike or even resent our effort to see a piece of work carried to its ultimate conclusion under our own control and supervision partly because it precludes the possibility of their turning the resultant benefit to their own credit and party ends, and possibly in some particular cases they distrusted our motives.[21]

Edwin Vail also wrote about Quaker relations with local officials and the famine committees during 1922-23. This was a particularly busy time, with much staff turnover, changing priorities, shifts in Soviet bureaucracy, and general confusion. From Sorochinskoye, Vail described thefts from the medical warehouse, expropriation of food supplies, and some officials' infuriating refusal to accept changes in the food distribution lists, even as deaths reduced village populations. He wrote, "The present state of governmental organization allows local officials to get away with a lot. The idealism of the Moscow leaders percolates to the distant quarters very slowly. ... We keep the wires hot to Moscow with our complaints but as soon as one thing is settled another takes its place."[22]

The misappropriation of food meant to save lives caused the most heartfelt agony. Vail wrote about one particularly difficult case:

> Friday ... I went ... to visit a children's home, a hospital, and a famine committee. The manager of the hospital had been in to get my okay for products the day before, and had reported the hospital full. I dropped in and found it less than half full. I went to see the famine committee, but was interrupted by the President of the Soviet who ... presented a written demand that we always should report to him before visiting an institution. I refused to accept any such obligation. Norosky then had a violent argument on his own initiative, which ended in them wanting to arrest him, but they did not dare.
>
> I left with the demand to the President that he withdraw his demand before I would allow any more products to go into the *volost*. The natural presumption is that he has disposed of the products to his own personal benefit. ... I found that everyone is afraid of him and that he controls the hospital, famine committee and children's home. I have recommended ... putting his case before the ... government representative at Sorochy, but who in turn is under the influence of the crooked Sorochy Soviet. We are always working under these handicaps.[23]

A few months later, after taking a vacation, Vail reflected, "now the famine committees cease to give me much worry. I even greet the rascals as if they were saints, and I guess that is about the only way to get them started right."[24]

Arthur Watts and Anna Haines, Theodore Rigg and Esther White had all experienced "petty difficulties with local officials."[25] But problems were ultimately resolved, and Quaker Service maintained goodwill with local officials. At every crossroads, local committees or staff appealed to the Quakers to extend or expand their work.[26] Some officials went out of their way to assist, as one report indicates:

> We are most fortunate to have had the help for the last three weeks of the party instructor for the political district, a man who is full of energy of his convictions and who has given himself and his time without stint to make this cooperation possible. His endorsement of our plans has removed local distrust and made the local government feel that our plans are the plans of Moscow and must be carried out. ... His achievements for us [include] scandals discovered and punished in a constructive way, help in the establishing of the children's homes, help for the hospital and schools, removal of unsatisfactory personnel and committees, helpful advice on local problems.[27]

But as the vision of Quaker Service became more diverse, and Soviet officials exerted greater control over reconstruction, it became clear that foreign organizations, while necessary in the short run, had no long-term place in Russia.

The Arrest of Henry Klassen

Karl Borders was the AFSC Field director in Buzuluk during 1922-23. A quiet, unassuming, thoroughly professional man, he worked hard to make decisions by consensus, in cooperation with the English unit, and with Russian officials. He wrote to Wilbur Thomas:

> I am beginning to appreciate the delightful Quaker fashion of arriving at conclusions by common consent and though such a plan sometimes prolongs our conferences to a very late hour at night, I do feel that we are all going to live happier and more effectively in our work.[28]

The most serious clash between local Soviet authorities and Quaker Service occurred during Borders' tenure. The fact that it was resolved, after a difficult standoff and numerous tense negotiations, is a tribute to his quiet and persistent leadership style.

Henry Klassen, a Russian who spoke both German and English, was one of the interpreters in Sorochinskoye. Soviet authorities tried to force him to resign because he supported Quaker Service in a conflict with the local village committee president. The local government attorney charged Klassen with vague "misdeeds" in conjunction with his interpreting and told him that he could not continue his work, while informing Quaker Service that Klassen was being "removed" and put under bond for trial.

Klassen requested support from Borders who wrote to Philadelphia, "We should not permit our interpreters to be intimidated on general principles." He sought a meeting with the Bolshevik leader to explore the situation and learn the specific charges. Convinced of his integrity and competence, the Quakers agreed to take responsibility for Klassen. They offered him a temporary leave, and the option of living in one of their dwellings until the issue was resolved. The Russian government officials demanded his surrender.[29]

The entire Quaker group in Sorochinskoye met in prayer and concluded that "a large principle of freedom" was involved: their ability to select their own Russian staff and interpreters and to decide who should be guests in Quaker homes. In a meeting with the Bolshevik leadership, Borders continued to press for details of the charges and he threatened to seek an explanation from Moscow. Still, the Bolsheviks insisted that Klassen would have to leave. Quaker Service resolved to appeal to Moscow and informed the local authorities that work in Sorochinskoye would cease unless they were provided with a complete explanation. The judge cited Soviet law permitting the government to remove anyone under indictment from his place of employment and put him under house arrest. The Quakers argued that they operated under separate contract with the government, and therefore the law did not apply and further, they took full responsibility for their employee. The judge replied that if the court did not confine Klassen to his home, he would be put in jail. Borders countered, "we would immediately cease all operations in ... this area and would inform Moscow of our reasons for so doing."[30]

Finally, the judge revealed two charges against Klassen: the "unrightful use of power against the government" in causing the arrest of the local village President and "carrying and flourishing a revolver when in conversation with the President." Quaker staff, present with him on both occasions, knew that the second charge was false, since Klassen was a Mennonite who, like them, utterly rejected the use of force. As for the first, while Klassen's testimony helped cause the dismissal of the President, this was hardly "unrightful use of power" but precisely the kind of truthful witness upon which the Quakers relied.[31]

The Quakers sent telegrams demanding Moscow's intervention, and threatening to halt all relief operations. Suddenly, a new Bolshevik appeared at local headquarters. He "was most understanding and apparently fully appreciated our point of view." He pleaded with Quaker Service not to suspend aid, and assured them that someone would come to Sorochinskoye "to investigate" within a day or two. The relief offices were closed "temporarily" pending a resolution.[32]

The chief Bolshevik official in Buzuluk sent a telegram promising an investigation while "for their protection," armed guards surrounded all Quaker buildings. A few days later the investigator held a five-hour conference with the Quakers, in which he pointed out numerous errors on all sides and sought a resolution. Still, the Quakers would not agree to fire Klassen even if the charges were dropped. They insisted on written charges and a formal trial, or having all charges dismissed, and they offered to resume Quaker Service in Sorochinskoye if either were assured in writing. But if Klassen were found guilty of something which Quaker Service denied, work would again have to be suspended. Finally the Bolsheviks agreed. Klassen resumed work, Quaker Service reopened, and Karl Borders' relationships continued as if nothing had happened. Within two weeks the charges were dropped.[33]

Nancy Babb's Relations with Russian Officials

Nancy Babb's 1921 to 1927 work in Totskoye remains the best example of cooperation and conflict between Quaker Service and local officials. As noted in chapter 6, Babb's success relied on her ability to link her reconstruction plans with the ideas of the local government. Starting in the spring of 1922 she saw how exchanging work for food or material goods, would promote self-reliance throughout the whole village. On all capital projects such as buildings, Babb offered Quaker support on a 50-50 basis with the local government committee: peasants provided labor, the local government provided construction materials and support, and the Quakers provided money, organization, food, and materials that couldn't be obtained locally.[34] By 1923 she was requiring some *volosts* to feed their orphans, or at least to provide bread. In exchange for Quaker rations, she demanded that local governments use their own funds to provide beds and warmer, more sanitary quarters. She noted, "In this way, we have not only saved food but have encouraged a local pride in the homes and mutual aid and friendship between the government and the Quakers. ... This has meant much relief on the constructive basis, and I am confident that in all my plans for relief that I have the full sympathy of the Russian government."[35] Undoubtedly her biggest success in enlisting the cooperation of both peasants and government officials was the construction of the first hospital in Totskoye area.

The extent to which Babb had the support of the peasants, even in opposition to venial officials, is evident in her report on the peasant initiative to challenge and replace the famine committee in Sorochinskoye:

> The [food] distributions in April were the first really completely satisfactory [ones] since the winter work started. The assembly of peasants in Sorochinskoye so successfully created a new feeding list, that ... [they] decided to inaugurate this method in all the villages. Therefore, town meetings were called everywhere and the peasants themselves revised the *pyoks* list. ... Accurate information was gleaned

The main street in Sorochinskoye

in regard to cattle, members of families, invalids, adults capable of work etc. The meeting of the assemblies disclosed the most appalling inaccuracies in the Fall Survey and in one village it was discovered that the committee had added 14 fictitious names ...in order to completely hide their dishonesty. It involved 40 *pyok*s which the committee was keeping for its own private use.

The peasants were enraged and themselves are dealing with the committee. The public reading ... and ...revising [of the list] permits every one in the village to be conversant with all the facts governing the giving of every *pyok*. It is really putting communism into practice by allowing the people to make the decisions, and one hears how this knowledge ... has checked much dishonesty already. These meetings have given splendid opportunity to expound briefly the meaning of the Quakers' presence in Russia and something of their ideals. The most frequently uttered question is "Why did you come?" [36]

But in the end, and despite the cooperation with the Soviet government, from 1925 until 1927 Quaker projects declined precipitously. Even as their work became more established and integrated into local communities, local projects had to cut back because funds from Britain and America were declining.

A proposal for an agricultural training school at Oomnovka reveals some of the tensions at work (see chapter 9 for details). [37] From the outset, the Quakers sought assurance from Bolshevik authorities that the School would be exempt from the education code provision requiring them to teach atheism.[38] But even with such an exemption, the Quakers questioned whether they could function if they couldn't share their convictions or "live out the lives which would be an expression of their beliefs" [39] Madame Kameneva assured them that the Quaker request would be honored if they did not insist on putting it in writing, but the gap could not be bridged, and the school proposal was dropped.

The main street in Buzuluk in 1998

Lasting impact

What lasting impact did Quaker work in rural Russia in the 1920s have on Russian perceptions of western or Quaker relief? In May 1998, David McFadden and Sergei Nikitin made a pilgrimage to Buzuluk, Totskoye, Sorochinskoye, and Mogotovo. In two weeks they met with fifteen survivors of the great famine, in village market places, churches, homes and other locations, sometimes spontaneously, sometimes on the introduction of acquaintances and friends. Almost without exception, these older people not only had vivid memories of the famine and those who brought relief, but they also expressed gratitude for the "Anglo-Americans" and often "Kwakeree" or Quakers and their generous deeds. In the village of Totskoye, David and Sergei saw the hospital that Nancy Babb had built. For five decades it served as the medical center for the village.

Quaker headquarters in Buzuluk had been located in one of the most striking buildings in town – an art nouveau structure built in 1906. In 1988 it had been converted into a busy polyclinic for children. The head Doctor knew about the previous occupants, and she happily led a tour of building, including the Quaker malaria clinic. The Director of the Buzuluk archive invited David and Sergei to write a series of articles which appeared as *"Amerikanskie Kvakerii v Buzuluke"* ("American Quakers in Buzuluk") in the local newspaper, *Rossisskaya Provinsiia* (The Russian Province) in May 1998.

Irina Pavlovna was five years old when famine broke out in 1921. She lived in a village not far from Buzuluk with her grandmother, since her mother had taken the rest of the family to Siberia to try to escape the famine. American Quakers came to the village, brought food, fed the children, and helped them to survive. "God bless the people who sent us food. I will never forget them." [40]

In Sorochinskoye, the headquarters of the American unit in the 1920s, David and Sergei had several conversations with older women who remembered being helped by Quakers. All of them noted that it was not Soviet power that saved them, but American food and personal help.

In Mogotovo, a remote village that was one of the first Quaker war refugee relief sites in 1917, they talked with 80 older school children about Quaker relief and the common interests of Russian and American teenagers. David was deeply touched by the children who asked their unusual visitors "why did you come here?" and "who were the Quakers?" It seemed to him that the Totskoye peasants who had repeatedly asked those questions of Nancy Babb still lingered, acknowledging the Quakers' contributions. [41]

In 1923, Allen Wardwell, from the Commission on Relief, Russian Information Bureau, wrote, "We found evidences everywhere that these efforts have made a deep and lasting impression upon the Russian people as a whole, and have aroused a gratitude which will not die." [42]

9. "TO LIVE QUAKER LIVES"
SERVICE AND PRESENCE; LEGACIES AND LEARNINGS, 1917 - 31

from the revolutions of 1917 through the New Economic Policy (NEP) into early Stalinism and the end of their activities in Soviet Russia in 1931, Quakers held a variety of opinions regarding relief, reconstruction, relations with governments, and expressions of religious belief. Despite their questions and the hardships they endured, they remained until 1931. Why did they leave? One obvious (and partial) answer was the rise of Stalin. The whole explanation is more complex.

As we have noted, British and American Quakers were in Soviet Russia to provide relief first for refugees from WWI, then during the Russian Civil War (1918-1920) and from the great famine of 1921-23. After the famine crisis eased, they offered medical, agricultural and reconstruction programs. In the process, Friends also persisted in their personal and religious witness, and they opened a Quaker Centre in Moscow to facilitate contacts with Russian Tolstoyans and other non-Bolshevik intellectuals and seekers. Their experience demonstrated that coordinating relief efforts, while maintaining cordial relationships with government authorities and at the same trying to manifest Quaker religious values, even under less trying circumstances, was not an easy task.

The controversies about their work shifted with the needs "on the ground." From the beginning (1917-1920) there was debate over "disinterested relief" versus "service with witness." During the intense period of the famine (1921-1923), the urgency of relief efforts predominated. In the post-war, post-famine, context (1924-1926), those who were providing relief and service struggled to balance the work and the role of witness. In 1925-28 some favored "witness and presence in Moscow" while others wanted to concentrate on "concrete reconstruction projects in the provinces." Finally, with the decline of reconstruction projects, by 1928 only a few Quakers and their Tolstoyan friends remained in Moscow, although the debate over "service versus witness" continued until the final exit in 1931.[1]

As a matter of principle, some Quakers emphasized "disinterested relief" (in Arthur Watts' famous phrase), staying out of political controversies, avoiding antagonizing governments (whether Bolshevik, British or American) and scrupulously avoiding any hint of religious proselytizing or propaganda.

Others considered it incumbent upon Friends and their organizations to articulate their values – to publicly express their opposition to war and their support for spiritual seeking, religious freedom and human dignity – even if doing so might jeopardize providing the concrete relief and reconstruction which they were trying to bring to Russia's post-revolutionary chaos and transition.

Once the acute need for relief work had passed, some favored finding concrete, specific projects in medical or agricultural reconstruction in cooperation with government authorities. Others thought the focus should be entirely on a "Quaker Embassy" in Moscow, where spiritual witness and long-term gentle staying power might have greater impact. For two reasons, they couldn't simply do both. First, resources were perennially insufficient to accomplish all the things that British and American committees envisioned. Second, the relationships necessary to build and sustain either relief or presence were largely antithetical to – often to the point of seriously jeopardizing – one another. The political question, "How much cooperation with government authorities would be necessary to accomplish any of these tasks" loomed constantly in the background.

American Friends tended to favor "disinterested relief," but the AFSC continued corresponding with Moscow Centre representatives and discussing the future of Quaker work in Russia with their British counterparts until 1931. The two Quaker Service bodies took great pains to work together. As Rufus Jones repeatedly said, "The Service Committee believes in and desires the fullest cooperation and union of action, wherever possible, with English Friends." [2]

The Beginning – War and Famine, 1917-1920

The earliest years of Quaker work under the Bolsheviks were dominated by revolution, Civil War, and the wrenching disruption of the refugee relief effort begun in 1916 in Moscow and the Volga Valley. [3] But these years also introduced the central questions about work in Russia in such a clear and compelling way that they would never really leave the Quakers' consciousness. A special meeting of the Friends War Victims Relief Committee was held on November 5, 1918, to consider the "spiritual aspects" of Friends work in Russia, particularly in relation to the Russian Revolution. This conference concluded:

> In Moscow today Friends are working under the shadow of Tolstoy and this gives us a point of contact not possessed by others. But we are primarily neither Quakers nor Englishmen and certainly not missionaries who have gone out to impart a faith. We have a faith to share as we learn how to combine field work and field study. ... While our workers should feel there is something bigger behind, there should be no distinction between the material and the spiritual side. [4]

Following the departure of Theodore Rigg and Esther White from Moscow and Petrograd in the winter of 1919, British and American committees held extensive discussions on how to get back into Russia and what the future involvement would be. Former team members met with committees on a regular basis, stressing the "possibilities of service" and the "great value of the work."[5] In March 1920, Hinman Baker made an exploratory trip, bringing 50 tons of supplies for Russian children to Petrograd and Moscow. Then the Friends War Victims Relief Committee received permission for two other British Friends, Arthur Watts and Gregory Welch, to accompany children's relief supplies. Watts became the British anchor of the British-American Quaker relief mission that, in one form or another, remained in Russia until 1931. Welch, on the other hand, remained in Russia only one month, but his experience added to the controversy.

On his return to London Welch argued that – despite their success in distributing relief and negotiating future work with the Bolshevik government – a permanent Quaker relief program was "impossible" because the Soviet government "had no place for philanthropic organizations." Nevertheless, he believed that London Friends should keep Arthur Watts in Russia, so that they could eventually establish a "Quaker Embassy" that would support Tolstoyans and educate any Russians interested in the Society of Friends. If this latter task proved impossible, then Friends should withdraw.[6]

Arthur Watts vehemently disagreed. He argued that numerous Soviet authorities in education, health, and feeding programs genuinely welcomed the Quakers' relief effort, and that the Quaker work *per se* provided a full and sufficient statement of Friends' beliefs. They would be known by their action; nothing else was necessary. In Watts' view, Quakers could stay in Bolshevik Russia only by remaining aloof from all political, religious, or philosophical activity or statements.[7] At first the English committee sided with Welch. They wrote a minute of their philosophy and objectives for presentation to the Russian government. Arthur Watts objected that a statement was not only inappropriate, but it might jeopardize any possibility of a Quaker relief. "The best message we can give to the Russian people at the present time is that there are Christians who are large hearted enough to give disinterested relief."[8]

Under pressure from Watts and the AFSC, the London committee withdrew its statement, but the issue did not go away. Then Watts partially embraced Welch's position, crafting a masterful position of Quaker integrity in a letter to Bolshevik authorities. While he explicitly acknowledged the Quakers' underlying motivation "to come into religious fellowship with people in Russia who share views similar to our own" he promised not to proselytize, but rather to give help wherever it was needed "without attaching any conditions as being allowed to spread the religious views held by the Society of Friends."[9] (See chapter 3 for details.)

Former Quaker headquarters in Buzuluk, now a Children's Clinic

During the height of famine relief activities in the Buzuluk area, English and American Quakers were consumed with the work of raising money, coordinating supplies, recruiting and training workers, and administering a major international relief program. Little time or energy was left to discuss and debate the nature and purpose of work in Russia or the proper balance between relief and witness, service and presence. Even so, there were signs that Friends continued to hold different perspectives. In Buzuluk and in London, they questioned whether to post signs at feeding stations and clinics stating that the Society of Friends was providing the relief, and describing their religious beliefs. They wrestled with the extent to which they should engage the authorities over their right to hire and fire staff.

The Nature of Service

As the overwhelming crisis of famine faded, so did the unity of Friends, both in the field and in the United States. It became harder to raise funds, and debate about the future of the program began to dominate discussions. In the proposal for the Oomnovka agricultural and mechanical training school, Friends had asked the Bolsheviks for an exemption from the requirement to teach atheism – implicitly raising the possibility of instruction in Quakerism.[10] S. Edgar Nicholson, the director of Quaker Service in Buzuluk, wrote to London and Philadelphia that the authorities had denied the exemption, prompting intense discussions. Alice Nike, a member of the Friends Service Council staff in London, wrote to Nicholson in March 1924,

> The chief doubt which Friends felt ... was as to whether any scheme initiated, and to a great extent controlled by the Soviet authorities

would give sufficient freedom to the Friends living in the institution. If we agreed to the scheme ... it is fairly plain that we should have to accept the fact that no religion could be taught to the children under our care. ... The question in our minds was whether, supposing that we felt able to agree to such a condition, our personnel would be allowed sufficient freedom to live out the lives which would be an expression of their beliefs.[11]

The balance of support for service vs. presence was changing among British Friends. A month later, when it was clear that the Friends position was incompatible with that of the Central Soviet authorities, and the Oomnovka training school proposal would not proceed, Alice Nike was not downcast. She wrote to the field staff:

The negotiations which have taken place may have been the means of bringing the mission into more intimate and friendly contact with the officials both in Moscow and Buzuluk. It is certainly all to the good that the question of our religious position should have been so thoroughly ventilated.[12]

But the plan for the school was shelved.

Correspondence between London, Moscow and the rest of the field increasingly focused on propaganda, education, and religion. The Moscow office didn't have enough leaflets about Friends beliefs written in Russian; the "Centre" did not even have a reading room or a regular Meeting for Worship.[13] One British Friend proposed that Quaker staff offer classes in English as a way of interesting Russians in Quaker activities. Materials were translated and sent from London, but it was difficult to raise money or get donations of Quaker books for the library [14] and when E.K. Balls, the head of the Moscow office, discussed the library and the English classes with government authorities, he got a decidedly ambivalent response:

He did not object to our teaching the professors ... English, but said that as a precedent it was a bad thing, and could it not be arranged privately. ... He thinks there will be no difficulties in the way of the library, but was a little wary of anything that might look like Quaker propaganda.[15]

As it turned out, by raising the issues officially, the committee in London forced the Soviet authorities to deny their requests not only for classes in English but for the reading room and library. By the spring of 1925, Friends in Moscow had resigned themselves to a longer, slower, less open process. Balls concluded:

Friends will need to be very patient with the slow development of their work in Russia and be content for some years to come, to be allowed to continue the material aid which we have been able to give in the past few years. Our only possible message work here is to live Quaker lives and by our contacts with everyone around us to continue to inspire the trust and friendship which so far we seem to have succeeded in doing here in Russia. For the continuation of our work here, we must have funds for a clear programme of useful work. [16]

Witness Versus Concrete "Pieces of Work"

From the end of famine relief and direct reconstruction projects, until only the Moscow Centre remained in 1928, contacts with Tolstoyans, Dukobors, and a few Russian Quakers continued, and Meetings for Worship were held infrequently at the Moscow Centre. Several Russian Tolstoyans petitioned London or Philadelphia Friends Meetings, seeking to become corresponding members of the Society of Friends, since their numbers were small and it was politically precarious to consider organizing a Meeting in Moscow. [17]

While some London Quakers urged religious dialogue, the staff and their Russian friends feared that public discussions of religious topics would jeopardize the remaining program. In her September report, Dorice White described the 1926 visit of American YMCA leader, author and evangelist George Sherwood Eddy, saying that arrangements for his three-week stay in Russia were made through the Bureau of Cultural Relations and "they were received everywhere as very distinguished guests." Eddy and his party of twenty stopped by Quaker Centre, and

before leaving Moscow Mr. Eddy made certain criticisms of the policy of the Soviet government, amongst others of the lack of freedom in religion. In answer to this he was told that free discussion on religion in the form of debate was permitted ... and Mr. Eddy was invited to lead a debate on Christianity on the following Sunday. He was joined by Mr. Hekker of Columbia University, who is a resident of Moscow, and a supporter of the seminar for priests of the "Living Church." His opponents who spoke on behalf of Communism were a Moscow professor and an editor of the atheistic paper, *"Bezbozhnik."* Mr. Eddy's speech and the debate were reported widely in the Moscow press, which dealt pretty severely with both Mr. Eddy and his subject.

The debate caused a sensation in the small Quaker community in Russia, reverberating in London and Philadelphia as well. [18]

Throughout 1927 to 1931, Quakers in Russia, Britain and America debated new reconstruction projects, and how to raise the money for them, and how to obtain government permissions and whether to develop the Moscow Centre for a widening circle of Quaker activities. The question of whether Quaker work should focus on Moscow or remain in Buzuluk or another rural area formed a constant subtext.

A Quaker Centre

The idea of a "Quaker Centre" similar to those in Paris and Vienna, where Meeting for Worship could take place along with discussions and outreach, service and volunteer activities, was as old as Friends work in Moscow (1916). But it regained prominence as the focus in London shifted from the Friends War Victim's Relief Committee under the leadership of Ruth

Fry, to the broader mandate of the Friends Service Council led by Carl Heath starting in 1924. Heath was one of the major British advocates for "Quaker Embassies" who wrote and published widely on this concept. As early as 1917, while the war was still raging, Heath and others framed their vision:

> When this present storm of war is passed, we who are Quakers have a plain duty laid upon us, and that is to carry the Quaker message of the direct inner light of the Christ, confirmed of experience and of the transvaluation thereby of human purposes, to every great city in Europe and to every people. It is a great and a far-reaching task and one that, if carried out, will need all the faith, all the courage and all the humility the Society is capable of. [19]

Many years later, in a pamphlet on "The Quaker Centre" and its experience in Europe from 1914 to 1939, Heath continued:

> Everywhere the Quaker Embassy or Centre has acted on the great saying of the Danish leader Kristen Kold, "Men must be enlivened before they can be enlightened." The Centre has not so much preached a doctrine as exemplified an intense life. What has drawn men and women has been the vitality of its friendship and its service. Spiritual intensity is creative ... the essence of renewal of life ... in peace activity, in prison service, in medical, educational and reconstructive work, in lectures and classes and research, and in the spontaneous meetings for worship. [20]

But even the most enthusiastic staff in Moscow found themselves pressed to explain to London why it was so difficult. E.K. Balls wrote to Heath in April 1925, "I am afraid it will be hard to make anything of the Centre here in Moscow, for we have not truly the liberty to do those things which Friends want to do." [21] In every exchange regarding a proposal for a health center or

Quaker Service in Moscow, 1919-1931

nurses' training school, a rural clinic outside Moscow or a provincial hospital in Yasnaya Polyana (see chapter 7), Carl Heath urged the Quaker Embassy concept. He wrote to Dorice White in the Moscow Office in 1925,

> Our work is primarily one of international life, reconciliation and understanding. It is only in a secondary sense that we are concerned for a health centre or health service work. ... What we are aiming at is a ... place where such a touch may be maintained with the heart of Russia as may enable us to really carry out an effort of friendship and comprehension of the men and women who are shaping the destinies of modern Russia. [22]

Indeed, Heath was so committed to this concept that in 1926 he convinced London Friends not to support Anna Haines and the AFSC proposal for the nurses training center, or subsequent plans for rural clinics. His single-mindedness also inhibited London's financial support for the Yasnaya Polyana hospital, which had been proposed by Olga and Alexandra Tolstoy.

With the collapse of these proposals, it became sadly clear that the Moscow office would be lucky to survive, much less to become a Quaker Embassy. By 1928 Dorice White, the last staff member, was referring to her role as "minding the gap" – a thinly veiled reference to the London Underground's warning to riders not to catch one's shoe in the leap from platform to train. Not much else could be done, short of more money, more workers, and a greater engagement in a rapidly changing Soviet Russia. Indeed, by the time Dorice White left in 1931, Friends in London were complaining that the new Commissars in their newly reshuffled bureaucratic posts "knew not the Quakers." They were far less amenable when it came to getting licenses and exemptions, extending leases, and replacing one "piece of work" with another. [23]

Emma Cadbury's Impressions of Soviet Russia

Emma Cadbury – the Quaker who advocated cooperation with both the Soviets and Mr. Hoover in chapter 4 – traveled to the Soviet Union in 1928, and wrote about her impressions. Her optimistic report expresses the hope shared by many people: that Quaker ideals and Soviet models were compatible with one another, and together they might lead to the new, more equitable society that both were seeking. Also embedded within her naive report one finds some of the problems that caused the whole Quaker enterprise in Soviet Russia to founder.

> *In a statement of the points of general agreement on which the Fellowship of Reconciliation was based in the United States, the following assertion is included:*

> *That the love revealed in Christ profoundly reverences personality; strives to create an order of Society which suffers no*

individual to be exploited for the profit and pleasure of another, but assures to each the means of development for his highest usefulness.

For those who accept the truth of this statement and realize the difficulty of [expressing it] even in our individual lives and spheres under the present political and social conditions, there must be peculiar interest in the Union of Soviet Republics which has made a bold effort to create a state which shall insure freedom from exploitation and opportunity for fullness of life at least to that working class which in most countries is the one which suffers most.

Hence it was with quite a thrill ... that I crossed the border from Poland to Russia early last June. ... During my short stay of fourteen days the gigantic size of the territory under Soviet rule and the variety of the peoples living within it were impressed upon me and the almost insuperable difficulty of the task of applying socialist principles in this vast union. On the map the distance from ... the customs station near Minsk to Moscow seems very short but it was ... 47 hours from the Franz Josef Bahnhof in Vienna.

I had rather dreaded the custom house. We had to carry all our luggage in to be examined ... in the large room lined with ... the red-bunting draperies and pictures of Lenin and other "Bolshevist" heroes ... which one found everywhere in Moscow, in hospitals, welfare centers, schools and almost any place of any public importance. An interpreter ... bustled about explaining in English, French or German what we must do. ... The Russian money which I had bought just across the border in Poland must be handed over to the custom's official and only returned when I left the country, as I had already violated the law by buying money outside the country. Here ... could one legally buy rubles – and on leaving the country one must here sell them, or, if there is no more foreign money left in the exchange office ... receive a receipt which can be cashed within two months inside Russia. In Moscow I found that this strict law ... makes it exceedingly difficult both to make payments abroad and to obtain ... cash for a journey beyond the borders. For example, a gentleman whose child was in Riga begged me to let him cash a personal check that he might have it to ... pay her expenses; and a lady traveling to England was very thankful to buy a few pounds. Speculation in foreign exchange is made very risky but proportionately profitable by this regulation. ...

My first afternoon and evening in Moscow were especially remarkable. I ... felt quite comfortable in the care of the Quaker workers, one Russian and one American, who ... were my most helpful caretakers ... throughout my visit. [The Russian] worked ... in one of the villages where the Friends carried on relief work and ... desired to prepare ... for possible help in a training school for nurses which [Anna Haines]... was very anxious to establish. For the past two years [he] attended a course for nurses in Moscow, one condition for which was membership in the Medical Workers' Union. Hence [he has] an intimate knowledge of both country and city conditions and of the points of view of Communist workers, of peasants and of the former aristocracy. ...

After a late dinner a daughter-in-law of Leo Tolstoy took me sight-seeing, first to the book bazaar in one of the central boulevards. ... The booths ... had been put up along both sides of the broad central path, and rough wooden arches at intervals carried sayings in white letters on a red background which my interpreter read me – among them "Religion is the opium of the people" and some good advice about the use of books. ... The subject matter was evidently scientific, political, historical, etc., rather than fiction. The children's books especially interested me and the pictures did convey some meaning.

It was a Sunday afternoon and the Bazaar was evidently a popular promenade. But it was a very different crowd ... from what one meets on Karntnerstrasse [in Vienna]. ... There was no dressing up except that one noted men in clean Russian blouses and girls in fresh cotton dresses such as they might wear during the week to the factory. Many were bare-headed, but ... I saw the red head-kerchiefs of the girls of the Youth Socialist Party which give color to the often drab streets of the city. The general impression was one of equality ... But one seldom if ever saw stylishly dressed people. This may have been partly due to the danger of suspicion of being bourgeoisie. ...

In contrast to this uniformity in ... dress was the notable variety in the people. Looking into their faces one distinguished many types of men and women, their character standing out the more clearly because not veiled by the accident of wealth as indicated by dress. Moreover there was an evident variety of race and nationality suggesting the many peoples belonging within the Soviet Union. ...

Day by day ... came new appreciation of the ideals and the achievements of the new regime, as I visited various interesting institutions for the welfare of the people and talked with enthusiastic workers, and fresh appreciation also of the art and culture of the old regime as revealed in museums and churches, and in the guarded speech of those who had known and loved it. Even these [people] saw much good in the present masters of Russia, and one was filled with admiration for their self-sacrificing dedication to the service of the people in cooperation with the Soviet officials, with magnanimous forgiveness for unspeakable suffering and loss through the revolution.

The market, Moscow, 1927

In Moscow ... the stability and permanence of the present government seemed unquestioned, and one had a strong sense that the industrial proletariat was really ruling and was taking its responsibility most seriously, with freedom to criticize the highest officials for any failure to promote the good of the people.

The men who were re-plastering the [Quaker] Center building were doing their job very carelessly and very slowly, but I found that they were peasants who had come to the city for work and that such workers were not very loyal. The department for social welfare ... told me it was very difficult to provide work for these people ... [because there] was not sufficient building material. ... Rumor reached us of a rather ugly attempt at riot by the unemployed. But Russia is by no means the only country where unemployment is a very serious problem and they claim to be including foreign as well as homeborn unemployed as recipients of their dole of food.

I understood that the rooms in the art gallery where the ikons are displayed were closed to the public, and that attendance at church by teachers and others ... of public influence might endanger their positions. ...

There was a possibility that Friends could be of help in connection with a new hospital which is being built by the government as a memorial to Leo Tolstoy, in this year of the centennial of his birth, at Yasnaya Polyana. ... In connection with this I spent a few days at this *most interesting place. ... His daughter, Alexandra Tolstoy, lives here much of the time and is keenly interested in the community life. She took us to visit two schools. ... [One] takes especially the boys and girls of intellectual promise and prepares them for the University while the one ... a few miles away keeps those children whose development seems most likely to be promoted by training of the hand as well as the brain. The spirit of freedom is very evident and the children are conscious of their responsibility to their community. ...*

In the country, however, one has uncomfortable doubts about the present working of the new government, and realizes that it is primarily a workers' government and is of, rather than by, the peasants. The sickle is subordinate to the hammer. There is much loyalty among the peasants, but already on the train ... we heard outspoken complaint of their economic situation. The militia were forcing them to sell their grain and they obtained bread only by ration, sometimes standing in line for hours at the bakers. ...

One watches with interest to see what will happen. A student of Social and Political Science once said to me, "In Russia for the first time Socialist theories have had a full chance to be tried out. Where the experiment has shown them impractical new methods are adopted." Already this Socialist government has proved itself capable of a big readjustment. One may hope it is living enough to do so again and again.

For, taken all in all, the Soviet government in Russia is a great challenge to our so-called Christian order, and while passing examination on what we feel is wrong it stirs the hope that there is a chance of a better day when "no individual will be exploited for the profit and pleasure of another, but to each will be assured the means of development for his highest usefulness!" [24]

Why did the Quakers finally leave Soviet Russia in 1931? The simplest answer is that they had nothing left to do, short of an undeveloped idea for a Quaker Centre, and stalled or failed proposals for various health programs. Finally, their lease was not extended. But this masks other factors including the government's hostility to religion. When Clarence Pickett and Carl Heath replaced Wilbur Thomas and Ruth Fry, both of whom had visited Russia regularly, the Russia work lost its dynamic supporters at the Quaker organizations in America and England. Energy and fundraising were focused on different priorities, and no one wanted to re-fight the early battles, or to articulate, as either Gregory Welch or Arthur Watts had done, a clear compelling vision for Quaker service in Russia. That would not occur again until 1949.

10. CONCLUSION
UNDERSTANDING THE QUAKERS

*I*n 1951, the liberal theologian and WWII pacifist Harry Emerson Fosdick published *Rufus Jones Speaks to Our Time*. After noting that "so luminous a personality cannot be printed" he compiled an invaluable anthology from Jones' fifty-seven books and too many articles, speeches, sermons, editorials and other writings to enumerate. He also gave us yet another brief overview of the early years of the American Friends Service Committee. Thus Fosdick describes an extraordinary moment in the history of the AFSC when, in 1938, the 65-year-old Rufus Jones participated in the delegation to Gestapo headquarters in Berlin, seeking to rescue Jews and others from Nazi persecution and "to enquire whether there is anything we can do to promote human welfare and to relieve suffering." Fosdick asserts:

> Those who suppose that the Quakers were or are discouraged because such attempts ... did not solve the international problem or prevent the Second World War *do not understand the Quakers* [emphasis added]. The *war* did not solve the world's problem either, but left more and worse problems than were here before. The Quakers have a long view ... [1]

What understanding can our 'long view' draw from the experience of Quakers in revolutionary Russia? The questions posed by Arthur Watts and Gregory Welch, Nancy Babb and Anna Haines and later by David McFadden and Sergei Nikitin remain as fresh and compelling today as they were then. What is the proper role of American and British Quakers who are committed both to providing "a cool glass of water" and to religious witness as a way of conveying deeply held values? How can people of goodwill genuinely alleviate humanitarian tragedies, negotiate with both revolutionary and democratic governments, and maintain a balance between assisting individuals and working to transform unjust systems? In order to put "faith into practice," is it necessary to testify to one's deeply felt beliefs at every important turn? Or is it enough to build the hospital, feed the hungry, and make sure the Quaker star is stenciled on all the warehouses, milk crates, and medical supplies? How do you go about protecting staff and fellow workers, and defending your principles to authorities at home and in the field, while seeking financial and organizational support from Quakers and non-Quakers in order to sustain the work?

Some insights can be drawn from two books that were published while we were writing this one. Samantha Power's Pulitzer Prize winning *A Problem from Hell; America and the Age of Genocide*, describes governments – and specifically successive United States governments – making decisions and failing to make decisions, claiming to "not know" or "not fully appreciate" what was already being reported in the mainstream press. She shows them acting indifferent and failing to act in time, as horrific *genocidal* slaughters were taking place around the world. In her work we see how regularly even well intentioned governments, whether democratically elected or self-appointed, whether progressive or repressive, make political and diplomatic decisions for questionable gains. All too often a short-term alliance, an arms deal, the promise of a seat at the United Nations, a wink or a look in the other direction resulted in the deaths of hundreds of thousands of civilian men, women and children.

Powers offers a few shining examples of heroism buried in the horror, where individual acts of courage could and did make a difference. For example, Canadian Major General Romeo Dallaire was the commander of the UN peacekeeping forces in Rwanda at the height of the violence in April 1994. Power tells us that under his leadership, some soldiers from the UN Assistance Mission for Rwanda (UNAMIR),

> ... scoured Kigali, rescuing Tutsi, and later established defensive positions in the city, opening their doors to the fortunate Tutsi who made it through roadblocks to reach them. One Senegalese captain, Mbaye Daigne, saved 100 or so lives single-handedly. Some 25,000 Rwandans eventually assembled at positions manned by UNAMIR personnel. The Hutu were generally reluctant to massacre large groups of Tutsi if foreigners (armed or unarmed) were present. It did not take many UN soldiers to dissuade the Hutu from attacking. At the Hotel des Mille Collines, ten peacekeepers and four UN military observers helped to protect the several hundred civilians sheltered there for the duration of the crisis. [2]

But shortly thereafter, bowing to pressures from member states, the UN withdrew from Rwanda, and the slaughter resumed.

David Rieff's "*A Bed for the Night; Humanitarianism in Crisis*" takes its title from an astute poem by Bertolt Brecht about a solitary man on a wintry New York street corner, who offers beds to homeless people. Brecht asserts:

> It won't change the world
> It won't improve relations among men
> It will not shorten the age of exploitation
> But a few men have a bed for the night
> For a night the wind is kept from them
> The snow meant for them falls on the roadway. [3]

Rieff's concerns are narrower than Samantha Power's. Looking at humanitarian aid workers since the 1990s in Bosnia, Rwanda, Kosovo and Afghanistan, he shows how their advocacy for human rights and their increasing dependence on ever-larger governmental, non-governmental and even military organizations has compromised their effectiveness. When aid organizations receive funding from governments, the choice of where and to whom aid will be delivered inevitably has political consequences. Rieff praises humanitarian aid workers for being personally willing to enter conflict situations in order to save lives, and critiques their naiveté at believing that American power "really did have the potential of making the world safe for democracy." [4] The biggest problem arises when relief workers condone the use of military force to protect not only civilians at risk of genocide but themselves as well. As with Vietnam, some people end up justifying bombing a village in order to save it.

Unfortunately, Rieff focuses his analysis on the largest humanitarian relief organizations (the International Red Cross, CARE, Medecins Sans Frontieres) and only briefly mentions the AFSC. He does note that AFSC was different from most relief groups operating in Southeast Asia during the American war in Vietnam. Specifically, since it did not rely on USAID for funding or staff, AFSC was able to publicly criticize U.S. policy.

What does all this tell us about those – in revolutionary Russian and since then – who lived according to their values, drained swamps, provided food and medical relief, built schools and community centers and hospitals? Did they save lives? Did they make a difference? Could they have done more, or done it differently? There can be little doubt. The clear message that emerges from their genuine material contributions and their philosophical, religious and political struggles is that *individuals, and small groups of them, do make a difference,* particularly by remaining true to their conscience, by adhering to nonviolent principles and by rigorously avoiding entanglements with governmental agendas. In a world so torn by violence and conflict, it matters that some people are willing to take humanitarian action, to express their deeply held convictions, to offer a cool glass of water and to reflect on its meaning.

One Does What One Can

Steve Cary was a gentle giant in the field of humanitarian service who worked in and for the American Friends Service Committee for fifty years until his death in 2002. His career took him to many of the disaster- and war-torn lands where Quaker relief workers were reconstructing homes and clinics, binding wounds and sharing their faith. Then when he came home he described his deeply moving experiences. Steve was fond of telling a story that he said encapsulated the meaning of Quaker Service.

There's a man riding along a dirt road in the country, and he looks down from his horse and he sees a little bird lying in the dirt on his back with his feet in the air. He's so curious about this that he gets off his horse and walks back and says, "Little bird, what are you doing lying there in the dust on your back with your feet in the air?" And the little bird says, "The sky is falling and I'm trying to hold it up." The man bursts out laughing, "Why that's the dumbest thing I ever heard in my life. What does a little bird like you think you can do about the sky falling?" And the little bird looks up and says, "One does what one can. One does what one can."

FOOTNOTES

Abbreviations used in footnotes:
AFSC FSR = AFSC Archives, Philadelphia, Foreign Service, Russia
AFSC SEF = AFSC Archives, Philadelphia, Special Executive Files (Wilbur
    Thomas' records)
AJH = Anna J. Haines
FHL-L = Friends Historical Library, Friends House London
FHL-SC = Friends Historical Library, Swarthmore College
FSC = Friends Service Council, London
FSC RU = Friends Service Council Russia Unit
GARF = Government Archive of the Russian Federation
NB = Nancy Babb
RMJ = Rufus M. Jones
RMJ-HC = Rufus M. Jones Papers, Haverford College
SPC = Swarthmore Peace Collection, Swarthmore College
TSKAKP = Central Committee Archive of the Communist Party of the USSR [pre
    1989].
WARVICREL = Friends War Victims Relief Committee, Friends House London
WKT = Wilbur K. Thomas

NOTES FOR INTRODUCTION

1. Rufus M. Jones, *A Service of Love in War Time: American Friends Relief Work in Europe, 1917-1919* (New York: The Macmillan Company, 1920), p. xi
2. Ibid. p. xi
3. J. William Frost, "Our Deeds Carry our Message: The Early History of the American Friends Service Committee" Quaker History, Vol. 81, Spring 1992, No. 1, Friends Historical Association, p. 39
4. Ibid. p. 39
5. Richenda Scott, *Quakers in Russia* (London: Michael Joseph, 1964) p. 151

NOTES FOR CHAPTER 1:
A PERSONAL OVERVIEW, BY SERGEI NIKITIN

1. Annual Report, WARVICREL, 1916-17
2. Ibid.
3. Rigg, Chronicles of a Relief worker at Buzuluk, 1916-1918, FHL-L
4. Rigg to Cadbury, June 3, 1917, AFSC FSR, 1917
5. AJH to AFSC, October 10, 1917, AFSC FSR, 1917
6. Annual Report 1917, AFSC FSR, 1917
7. Emilie Bradbury Diary, AFSC FSR, 1918
8. Miscellaneous letters from Russia workers, AFSC FSR, 1917
9. Emilie Bradbury Diary, June 28, 1918, AFSC FSR 1918; Rigg papers FHL-L
10. Buzuluk newspaper clipping and translation, AFSC FSR, 1918
11. Rigg Papers, FHL-L
12. Ibid.

13. Nancy Babb Papers, Hoover Institution on War, Revolution and Peace, Stanford University, California
14. Lenin to V.V. Kuibyshev, September 19, 1921 Lenin on the United States (New York: International
Publishers, 1970) pp. 549-550
15. Arthur Watts report to London and Philadelphia, March 1921, AFSC FSR, 1921
16. Welch report on journey to Russia, June-August 1929, WARVICREL,
17. Quoted in J.W.C. Chadkirk, "Revolution and Relief: Quaker Famine Relief in the Samara Province of
Russia, 1916-1923," unpublished paper, 1994.
18. Watts to Nuorteva, October 18, 1920, AFSC FSR, 1920
19. Quoted in J.W.C. Chadkirk, "Revolution and Relief: Quaker Famine Relief in the Samara Province of
Russia, 1916-1923," unpublished paper, 1994.
20. Hurley to AFSC, July 1922, AFSC FSR, 1922
21. AFSC publicity materials, AFSC FSR, 1922
22. WKT report on a trip to Russia, 1923, AFSC SEF
23. Edwin Vail Papers, Hoover Institution on War, Revolution and Peace, Stanford University, California

NOTES FOR CHAPTER 2:
"WHAT IF THE EMPEROR OF RUSSIA SHOULD WANT A PERSON?"

1. Richenda Scott, *Quakers in Russia* (London: Michael Joseph, 1964) p. 34.
2. Ibid. p 39
3. Ibid. p 42
4. Ibid. p 54
5. Ibid. p 57
6. Ibid. p 59
7. Ibid. p 60-79
8. Ibid. p 130
9. Ibid. p 131
10. Ibid. p 131-132
11. On the 1890s famine, see George S. Queen, "America Relief in the Russian Famine of 1891-92," Russian Review 14:2 (April, 1955): 140-150 and Richard S. Robbins, Famine in Russia, 1891-1892: *The Imperial Government Responds to a Crisis* (New York, 1975).
12. Orlando Figes, *A People's Tragedy; A History of the Russian Revolution* (New York: Viking, 1997) p 178.

NOTES FOR CHAPTER 3:
"WE ASSIST THE CHILDREN AND CIVILIANS IN ALL COUNTRIES, IRRESPECTIVE OF THEIR FORM OF GOVERNMENT"

1. For overviews of this story, see J. O. Greenwood, *Friends and Relief* (New York, 1975), 116-125 and Michael Asquith, *Famine: Studies in Relief* (Oxford, 1943).
2. AJH to Henry Cadbury, October 14, 1917, AFSC Foreign Service, Russia, (AFSC FSR), 1917. Haines' appointment as the American representative, and her letters home to Philadelphia, remain a crucial link in the developing story of relations between the American and British Quakers and the Bolsheviks. This correspondence can be found in the AFSC Russian Relief files, 1917-1923.
3. Robert Tatlock, "First Year of American Friends War Relief Service," June 1, 1917, to May 31, 1918, AFSC Publications Archives.
4. Theodore Rigg to Ruth Fry, December 18, 1917, AFSC FSR, 1917.
5. AJH to Cadbury, December 31, 1917, AFSC FSR, 1917
6. Notes on the back of an envelope, November 30, 1917, Rufus M. Jones Papers Haverford College (HC), Box 53.
7. John Rickman to mother, March 22, 1918, Biddle Mss, Series 5, Box 8, FHL-SC.
8. Marriage Certificate, Lydia Lewis and Richard J. Rickman, March 20, 1918, Biddle Mss, series J, FHL-SC. For a popular contemporary account, see Lydia Lewis Rickman, "Commonplaces in Buzuluk, Atlantic Monthly (March, 1919)
9. Vincent Nicholson to AJH, June 13, 1918, AFSC FSR, 1918.
10. GH Pearson to Ruth Fry, September 21, 1918, AFSC FSR, 1918.
11. "Mission to Moscow: the Experiences of Two Relief Workers in the First World War," by T. Rigg and E. M. White, unpublished mss. AFSC FSR, 1919; copy of certificate given Theodore Rigg by G. Chichernin, Peoples Commissar for Foreign Affairs, 18 June 1918, AFSC FSR, 1918.
12. David W. McFadden, *Alternative Paths; Soviets and Americans, 1917-1920* (New York: Oxford University Press, 1993) 153-159; George F. Kennan, The Decision to Intervene (New York: W. W. Norton, 1984) [1958] 457-469.
13. Anna Haines waited as long as she could to hear from Philadelphia before writing Vincent Nicholson in December, 1918, informing him that the remains of the Buzuluk group had joined the American Red Cross in Omsk. AJH to Nicholson, December 30, 1918, AFSC FSR, 1918.
14. Rigg to Fry, June 9, 1918, AFSC FSR, 1918.
15. Rigg to Fry, August 21, 1918, AFSC FSR, 1918. See also "Mission to Moscow," AFSC FSR, 1918.
16. Rigg to Fry, September 24, 1918, AFSC FSR, 1918; See also "Mission to Moscow," p. 24.
17. Rigg to Fry, November 22, 1918; AFSC FSR, 1918; See also "Mission to Moscow," p. 13.
18. White to Scattergood, October 1, 1918, AFSC FSR, 1918; See also "Mission to Moscow," p. 13.
19. Rigg to Fry, August 21, 1918, AFSC FSR, 1918
20. White to Pearson, October 2, 1918, AFSC FSR, 1918.
21. Rigg to Fry November 22, 1918, AFSC FSR, 1918.

22. Phillips to AFSC, December 21, 1918, AFSC FSR, 1918.
23. "Mission to Moscow," p 30.
24. Henry Cadbury, draft report of the Russian Committee of AFSC, November 21, 1918, AFSC FSR, 1918
25. Fry to AJH, March 27, 1919, AFSC FSR, 1919.
26. Lucy Biddle Lewis to Lydia Rickman, April 26, 1919, Biddle-Timbres Papers, FHL-SC.
27. See WKT to AJH, April 24, 1919, AFSC FSR, 1919; Fry to AJH, March 27, 1919; AFSC FSR, 1919; Nuorteva to Bryant, John Reed Papers, Harvard University.
28. For an excellent discussion of the politics of the blockade, see Norman H. Gaworek, "From Blockade to Trade: Allied Economic Warfare Against Soviet Russia, June 1919 to January 1920," Jahrbucher fur Geschichte Osteuropas 23 (1975): 36-69.
29. Colby to AFSC, July 20, 1920, AFSC FSR, 1920.
30. State Department to Vincent Nicholson, Acting Secretary AFSC, August 17, 1920, AFSC FSR, 1920. For more detailed discussions of Colby and his policies, see Ronald Radosh, "John Spargo and Wilson's Russian Policy, 1920," Journal of American History LII (December, 1965): 548-560; Daniel M. Smith, Aftermath of War: Bainbridge Colby and Wilsonian Diplomacy, 1920-1921 (Philadelphia, 1970); Linda Killen, "Dusting Off an Old Document: Colby's 1920 Russian Policy Revisited," Newsletter of Society for Historians of American Foreign Relations 22, No. 2 (June 1991): 32-41; and McFadden, Alternative Paths, 330-335.
31. Welch to AFSC, July 20, 1920, AFSC FSR, 1920.
32. Watts to Friends War Victims Relief Committee (WARVICREL), July 21, 1920.
33. Report by Gregory Welch on Journey to Russia, June 22 to August 28, 1920, AFSC FSR, 1920, pp. 4-5.
34. Watts to WARVICREL, July 21, 1920, AFSC FSR, 1920.
35. Lucy Biddle Lewis to WKT, September 20, 1920, AFSC FSR, 1920.
36. WKT to Fry, October 19, 1920, AFSC FSR, 1920.
37. Watts to Nuorteva, October 18, 1920, AFSC FSR, 1920.
38. Watts to WARVICREL, October 21, 19209, AFSC FSR, 1920.
39. AJH to WKT, November 10, 1920, AFSC FSR, 1920.
40. Albright to Libby, Report on Reval Conference, November 24, 1920, AFSC FSR, 1920.
41. AJH to WKT, December 23, 1920, AFSC FSR, 1920.
42. AJH to WKT, December 30, 1920, AFSC FSR, 1920.
43. Nuorteva to Watts, January 1921, AFSC FSR, 1920.

NOTE FOR CHAPTER 4:
A FIRST-HAND ACCOUNT OF THE FAMINE

This chapter is excerpted from an undated pamphlet called "The Story of a Quaker Woman in Russia; Address by Anna Haines, An American Quaker who has been in charge of the Quaker relief work in Russia for over a year." The pamphlet was issued by the Russian Famine Fund, 15 Park Row, New York, n.d. [1922]. AFSC FSR, 1922.

NOTES FOR CHAPTER 5:
"WHY DON'T YOU WORK LIKE THE QUAKERS DO?"

1. See also Thomas C. Kennedy, *British Quakerism, 1860-1920: The Transformation of a Religious Community* (Oxford, 2001), pp. 157-210 on the relationship between Rufus Jones and the "renaissance" of British Quakerism.

2. There are two biographies of Rufus Jones. By far the best, despite the more than 40 years since its publication, is Elizabeth Gray Vining's sympathetic study of the Quaker leader, grounded in the Rufus Jones Papers at Haverford: *Friend of Life: the Biography of Rufus M. Jones* (London: Michael Joseph, 1958). Cecil Hinshaw's *Rufus Jones: Master Quaker* (1951) was published too soon after Jones's death to take advantage of the Papers of either Jones or his contemporaries.

3. RMJ to Charles Taylor, February 21, 1911, Rufus Jones Papers, Haverford College (RMJ-HC), Box 53. See also RMJ, The Trail of Life in the Middle Years, p. 36, and Mary Hoxie Jones, "RMJ," p. 35. RMJ, "The Challenge of the Closed Door, "Commencement Address, Sidwell Friends School, 1926, RMJ-HC, Box 74.

4. See RMJ to Harry Kates, November 26, 1924, RMJ-HC; RMJ Diary, September 30, 1923, RMJ-HC, Box 63.

5. RMJ Diary August 19, 1925, RMJ-HC, Box 63.

6. RMJ to Charles Jenkins, June 14, 1927, RMJ-HC

7. Editorial, Present Day Papers, Vol. I, No. 9, September 1914.

8. Mary Hoxie Jones, *Rufus M. Jones*, p. 48-51 and Rufus Jones, A Service of Love in Wartime (New York: Macmillan, 1920). For the scholarly account of the formation and early years of the AFSC, see Frost, "Our Deeds Carry our Message."

9. Ibid. See also Thomas Kennedy, pp. 183-210.

10. See RMJ mss on British-American cooperation (n.d. 1919), RMJ-HC. The importance of RMJ in British American consultation can be measured by the voluminous correspondence in RMJ-HC both with British leaders and with British Friends. On the Fry-Jones relationship, see Fry to RMJ, May 7, 1919; Fry to RMJ May 1, 1920; Fry to RMJ April 9, 1920; Fry to RMJ March 19, 1924, all RMJ-HC.

11. RMJ, "A Way of Life and Service," Oberlin College (pamphlet), 1939, 25-26.

12. Cadbury Family Papers, Quaker Collection, Haverford College.

13. WKT to RMJ, August 5, 1921, RMJ-HC.

14. WKT, "Food and Friendship for the Russian People," mss for speech, December 12, 1922, Thomas Papers, FHL-SC.

15. Homer Morris to WKT, March 27, 1922, AFSC FSR, 1922.

16. WKT, "Food and Friendship for the Russian People," Thomas Papers, FHL-SC. For the speeches that Thomas gave, see AFSC SEF. One indication of Thomas's commitment to the issue of Russia is that he kept a special Executive Secretary notebook of key correspondence, which until recently was stored separately in the archives. For the ten-year period in which he was Executive Secretary, most of that correspondence concerned Russia.

17. WKT to Wildman, December 1, 1922, AFSC FSR, 1922.

18. George Nash, *The Life of Herbert Hoover, Vol. 1: The Engineer, 1874-1914* (New York: W.W. Norton, 1983) p. 573

19. David Burner, Herbert Hoover, A Public Life (New York, Alfred A. Knopf, 1979) p. x.
20. Henry Scattergood to RMJ, July 23, 1919, RMJ-HC Box 18
21. WKT to RMJ, June 19, 1920, RMJ-HC.
22. WKT to RMJ, January 29, 1921, RMJ-HC; and Perrin Galpin, ARA to RMJ, October 20, 1921, RMJ-HC
23. Bernard Patenaude, The Big Show in Bololand: The American Relief Expedition to Soviet Russia in the Famine of 1921 (Stanford, 2002)
24. Harold H. Fisher, The Famine in Soviet Russia, 1919-1923: The Operations of The American Relief Administration (New York, 1927); Herbert Hoover, An American Epic: Famine in Forty five nations: The Battle on the Front Line, 1914-1923, 3 vols. (Chicago, 1961); Benjamin Weissman, Herbert Hoover and Famine Relief to Soviet Russia, 1921-1923 (Stanford, 1974); see also Weissman, "Herbert Hoover's 'Treaty' with Soviet Russia, August 20, 1921," Slavic Review 28 (1969): 276-288. For the documents, see "Gorky Appeals to American People for Aid, July 13, 1921, Hoover's Response July 23, 1921, and the Riga Agreement on Aid for Russia, August 20, 1921, in Harold J. Goldberg, ed., Documents on Soviet-American Relations, Vol. 1: Intervention, Famine Relief, International Affairs, 1917-1933 (Gulf Breeze, Fl: Academic International Press, 1993), 198-200, 208-211.
25. For the basic documents, see Nansen Proposal on Famine Relief, April 3, 1919; Allied Reply, April 17, 1919 and Soviet Response, May 7, 1919 all in Goldberg, v. 1, 190-194. For a detailed discussion of the politics of the Hoover-Nansen proposal, see McFadden, 244-263.
26. AJH and Watts to WKT, January 27, 1921, AFSC SEF, 1921.
27. Chicherin to Watts, April 14, 1921, AFSC SEF, 1921.
28. For the text of these agreements and the story of their negotiation, see exchange of letters between Friends International Service and Tsentrosoyuz, December 28, 1920; AJH to WKT, December 23, 1920; AJH and Watts to WKT, December 30, 1920; Nuorteva to Watts, January 4, 1921; AJH to WKT, January 13, 1921; Watts to Chicherin, April 7, 1921; Watts to Chicherin, April 13, 1921; Chicherin to Watts, April 14, 1921; AJH to WKT, May (nd), 1921, all AFSC FSR, 1920, 1921.
29. Watts to WKT, August 12, 1921, AFSC SEF, 1921.
30. WKT to AJH, August 6, 1921. This committee became known as the "All America Fund for Russian Famine Relief." See also WKT to AJH, August 18, 1921, AFSC SEF, 1921. For the background of the fundraising see AJH to WKT, May 26, 1921; WKT to AJH, June 30, 1921; AJH to WKT, July 13, 1921; WKT to AJH, August 6, 1921, all AFSC SEF, 1921.
31. Watts to WKT, January 5, 1921, AFSC SEF, 1921
32. Watts to WKT, January 20, 1921, AFSC SEF, 1921.
33. Hoover to WKT, January 26, 1921, RMJ-HC.
34. WKT to James Norton, enclosed in letter to RMJ, July 22, 1921, RMJ-HC.
35. For the best short account of the negotiations, drawn from ARA archives, see Weissman, "Herbert Hoover's Treaty" 276-288.
36. WKT to RMJ, August 18, 1921, RMJ-HC.
37. Pantenaude pp 39-46.
38. WKT to RMJ, August 18, 1921, RMJ-HC.
39. Ibid.
40. WKT to AJH and Watts, August 18, 1921, AFSC SEF, 1921.

41. See Riga agreement, Goldberg, pp. 208-211 and Weissman, "Herbert Hoover's Treaty"
42. Memorandum of discussion, joint meeting of Executive Board and Russia Committee, August 23, 1921, AFSC Administrative files, 1921.
43. Ibid.
44. Ibid.
45. The American Jewish Joint Distribution Committee (JDC) was founded in 1914 to coordinate distribution of charity from several Jewish organizations. The Orthodox community (generally descendants of Eastern Europeans) had created the "Central Committee for the Relief of Jews Suffering Through the War," while Reform (generally German) Jews had created the American Jewish Relief Committee and socialist Jews had created the Peoples' Relief Committee. The JDC, which would continue providing financial and material relief well into the Second World War, was always at least partially non-sectarian (as in the work in Russia) both on principle and as a strategic decision. [See Yehuda Bauer, *My Brother's Keeper; A History of the American Jewish Joint Distribution Committee 1929-1939* (Philadelphia, Jewish Publication Society of America, 1974) and Yehuda Bauer, *American Jewry and the Holocaust, The American Jewish Joint Distribution Committee, 1939-1945* (Detroit, Wayne State University Press, 1981)]
46. Confidential Memorandum of Discussion of meeting of European Relief Council by James A. Norton for AFSC, August 24, 1921, AFSC SEF, 1921.
47. Fisher, The Famine in Soviet Russia, p. 459
48. RMJ-WKT to WARVICREL, August 24, 1921, AFSC FSR, 1921; RMJ draft report in James Norton to RMJ August 24, 1921, RMJ-HC. See also "Program agreed to by all organizations composing European Relief Council, August 24, 1921," AFSC FSR, 1921.
49. Wildman to AFSERCO, August 25, 1921, AFSC FSR, 1921.
50. WARVICREL to AFSERCO, August 27, 1921, AFSC FSR, 1921
51. WKT to Fry, September 16, 1921, AFSC SEF
52. WKT to AJH and Watts, September 17, 1921, AFSC Gen files 1921
53. AJH to WKT, September 20, 1921, AFSC SEF, 1921; AJH to AFSERCO September 15, 1921, AFSC FSR, 1921.
54. Watts to AFSC September 24, 1921, AFSC FSR, 1921.
55. Watts to AFSC September 30, 1921, AFSC FSR, 1921.
56. Watts to WKT, October 28, 1921, AFSC SEF, 1921
57. Watts to AFSC October 28, 1921, AFSC SEF 1921
58. NB to WKT November 10, 1921 AFSC SEF 1921.
59. Ruth Fry to WKT December 1, 1921, AFSC FSR, 1921.
60. Agreement between the Religious Society of Friends of England and America (Quakers) and the Peoples Commissariat for Food Supplies (*Narkomprod*), RSFSR, September 16, 1921, AFSC FSR, 1921; A. Eiduck, RSFSR Plenipotentiary to Arthur Watts, December 21, 1921, AFSC FSR, 1921.
61. Confidential Memorandum of discussion of meeting of European Relief Council by James A. Norton for AFSC, August 24, 1921, AFSC, SEF, 1921
62. WKT cable to RMJ August 25, 1921, RMJ-HC.
63. WKT to James Norton for RMJ, August 25, 1921, RMJ-HC
64. RMJ to James Norton, August 25, 1921, AFSC Administrative files, 1921
65. Gannett to Norton, September 5, 1921 in Norton to RMJ, September 7, 1921, RMJ-HC.

66. Hoover to RMJ, September 10, 1921, AFSC Executive Committee files
67. Hoover to RMJ, September 10, 1921, RMJ-HC.
68. RMJ to Hoover, September 16, 1921, RMJ-HC.
69. Hoover to RMJ, September 21, 1921, AFSC SEF
70. Hoover to RMJ November 1, 1921, RMJ-HC.
71. RMJ to Hoover, January 2, 1922, RMJ-HC.
72. WKT to AFSC Executive Board, January 3, 1922, AFSC SEF.
73. RMJ to Hoover, January 4, 1922, RMJ-HC; Hoover to RMJ, January 6, 1922, RMJ-HC
74. Minutes, AFSC Executive Board and Russia Committee, January 9, 1922. AFSC Minutes
75. WKT to Hoover, February 9, 1922, AFSC SEF.
76. Hoover to RMJ, February 13, 1922, RMJ-HC.
77. RMJ to Hoover February 14, 1922, RMJ-HC.
78. Draft, RMJ to Hoover, February 24, 1922, RMJ-HC.
79. WKT to RMJ, February 16, 1922, RMJ-HC, Box 21.
80. Evans to WKT, January 7, 1922, Thomas Papers, FHL-SC.
81. William C. Biddle to RMJ, February 10, 1922, RMJ-HC.
82. "Hoover Sabotages Russian Relief," New York Call, February 26, 1922, Thomas Papers, FHL-SC.
83. Rhoads to Hoover, March 13, 1922, Thomas Papers, FHL-SC.
84. Rhoads to New York Call, March 13, 1922, Thomas Papers, FHL-SC
85. Agreement between the government of the Russian Socialist Federative Soviet Republic (RSFSR) and the Society of Friends of England and America October 25, 1922; K Lander on behalf of RSFSR William Albright and Walter Wildman, for the Society of Friends, AFSC FSR, 1922. For further details on this agreement and an analysis see Michael Asquith, Famine: Relief Work in Russia, 1921-1923 (Oxford, 1942), 29-32.

NOTES FOR CHAPTER 6:
"WHO WISHED FOR FOOD HAD TO WORK"

1. NB Diary, Babb Papers, Hoover Institution on War, Revolution and Peace, Stanford University
2. Nancy Babb files, AFSC personnel files
3. NB letter to WKT February 14, 1925, AFSC personnel files
4. Edward Thomas, Quaker Adventures (New York: Fleming H. Revell Company, 1928) pp. 104-108
5. Ibid. p 110
6. Report for Totskoye District, September 1922, Babb Papers, Hoover, Box 1
7. See Hurley to Karkhlin, July 18, 1922, Samara Archives f 79, op 1, del 22; Report on Buzuluk Ooezd GARF f 1058, op 1, del 548; January 1923; Babb Papers, Hoover, folder 2
8. NB to Wildman, February 5, 1923, AFSC personnel files, 1921-1927.
9. Report of District Supervisor, Totskoye, nd (1922), AFSC FSR, 1922.
10. Gamaleyevka District Report, June, 1923, Babb Papers, Hoover, Box 1
11. Totskoye District report, September 1922; Babb Papers Hoover, Box 1.
12. NB Totskoye District report, October 1923, AFSC FSR, 1923.
13. NB Totskoye District report, October 1924, Babb Papers, Hoover, Box 2

14. Harry Timbres report for Quakers workers conference, August 21, 1922, Babb Papers, Hoover, Box 23. See also Dorothy North report, January 1923, Hoover Babb Papers, Box 2
15. Jessica Smith, February 1923, Jessica Smith Papers, Hoover.
16. Edwin Vail, Gamaleyevka report, November 1922, Edwin Vail Papers, Hoover.
17. Totskoye District report, January 1923, AFSC FSR, 1923
18. Jessica Smith Papers, Hoover, 1923.
19. NB, Totskoye District report, January 1923, AFSC FSR, 1923.
20. NB, Totskoye District report, October 1922, Babb Papers, Hoover, Box 2
21. Minutes, Conference of Quaker workers, Sorochinskoye, December 26, 1922, Babb Papers, Hoover, Box 2
22. NB, Totskoye District Report, December 1922, AFSC FSR, 1922.
23. Minutes, District Supervisors Meeting, Sorochinskoye, January 31, 1923, Babb Papers, Hoover, Box 1
24. Dorothy North to NB, January 25, 1923, Babb Papers, Hoover, Box 2
25. Minutes, Message Committee, AFSC, January 20, 1925, AFSC Minutes
26. NB Totskoye District report, September 1922, AFSC FSR, 1922. See also Dorothy North, Gracheevka, January 1923, Babb Papers, Hoover, Box 2
27. Timbres report on Sorochinskoye, August 21, 1922, Babb Papers, Hoover, Box 2
28. Hurley to Karkhlin, July 18, 1922, Samara Archives, f. 79, op 1, del 22.
29. Edwin Vail, Gamaleyevka report, August, 1922, Vail Papers, Hoover
30. NB, Totskoye District report, October 1922, Babb Papers, Hoover, Box 2; NB report for Totskoye District October 1924, Babb Papers, Hoover, Box 2; NB notes, 1925, Babb Papers, Hoover, Box 2; Edwin Vail report Gamaleyevka November 1922, Vail Papers, Hoover
31. Edwin Vail, Gamaleyevka report, January 1923, Vail Papers, 1923.
32. NB, Totskoye report, October 1925, Babb Papers, Hoover, Box 2
33. NB, Totskoye report, October 1926, Babb Papers Hoover Box 2
34. NB, report of District Supervisor, Totskoye, 1923, AFSC FSR, 1923
35. Karl Borders to WKT, November 6, 1922, AFSC FSR, 1922.
36. Edwin Vail, Gamaleyevka District report, August 1922, Edwin Vail Papers, Hoover
37. Kenworthy to WKT, March 17, 1922, AFSC FSR, 1922
38. Report of Conference of Friends International Service, American Unit, Sorochinskoye, November 13, 1922, AFSC FSR, 1922.
39. NB to AJH, September (nd) 1922, Babb Papers, Hoover, Box 2
40. Conference of Quaker workers, November 1922, AFSC FSR, 1922.
41. NB, Totskoye District report, October 1923, Babb Papers, Hoover, Box 2.
42. Wildman to RMJ, January 24, 1923, RMJ-HC, HC
43. Agreement between ODK and town of Orenburg, February 26, 1923, AFSC FSR, 1923.
44. Alfred Smaltz to WKT, July 18, 1923, AFSC FSR, 1923.
45. Proposal from Quaker Service to the Department of Agriculture, May 31, 1923, AFSC FSR, 1923
46. Smirnoff, Latsiz, Karassev, for the Peoples Commissariat of Agriculture to the Society of Friends Quakers from England and America, June 7, 1923, AFSC FSR, 1923. See also Wildman to Ruth Fry, June 12, 1923, AFSC FSR, 1923.
47. Smaltz to WKT July 18, 1923, AFSC FSR, 1923

48. Ibid.
49. NB Totskoye District report, October 1922, Babb Papers, Hoover, Box 2
50. Parry Paul's unpublished manuscript, Parry Paul Papers. FHL-SC
51. Edwin Vail, Gamaleyevka District report, August 1922, Babb Papers, Hoover, Box 1. See also Totskoye District Report, January 1923, AFSC FSR, 1923
52. Report of Russian relief dispensed from Totskoye for Year October 1923 to October 1924, Babb Papers Hoover, Box 1
53. Annual Report Mother and Baby Clinic, 1924, Babb Papers, Hoover, Box 1
54. Report of Russian relief dispensed from Totskoye for year October 1923 to October 1924 AFSC FSR, 1924. For additional detail on the scope of Quaker medical work, see Chapter 7.
55. Buzuluk medical report January 1923, GARF f 1058, op 1, del 548(2).
56. Minutes of joint Meeting, January 7, 1925, AFSC Minutes
57. NB Report, January 7, 1925, Babb Papers, Hoover
58. V. K. Boyanus, List of lectures with the mothers of Totskoye village, 1925-1926, Babb Papers, Hoover, Box 2
59. Dorice White to WKT, December 9, 1925, AFSC SEF
60. NB to WKT, July 12, 1925, AFSC SEF, 1925
61. Ruth Fry Diary, January 3, 1925, Ruth Fry Papers, FHL-SC
62. NB to WKT, January 15, 1926, AFSC SEF, 1926\
63. NB to WKT, March 28, 1926, AFSC SEF, 1926
64. NB to WKT, October 22, 1926, AFSC FSR, 1926
65. NB Mss, "How I built the Hospital" Babb Papers, Hoover, Box 2
66. Letter from Totskoye medical staff to NB, April 30, 1927, AFSC Personnel Files, 1921-1927
67. Sergei Nikitin, "Quakers and the Great Russian Famine," Quaker Life (January – February 1998) p 5-7. David McFadden and Sergei Nikitin, "We Remember:" Russian Famine Survivors Tell of Quaker Aid" Friends Journal (December 2000) p 16.

NOTES FOR CHAPTER 7: "THE DAYS OF OUR LIFE"

1. For more information about Anna Haines see Edward Thomas Quaker Adventures and Richenda Scott Quakers in Russia.
2. AJH to WKT, November 25, 1920 AFSC FSR 1920
3. AJH, "The Days of Our Life," AFSC FSR 1920
4. Watts and AJH to WKT, January 27, 1921, AFSC SEF
5. Ibid.
6. Chicherin to Watts, April 14, 1921, AFSC FSR, 1921
7. Watts and AJH to WKT, March 21, 1921, AFSC FSR, 1921
8. AJH to WKT, May 25, 1921, AFSC FSR, 1921
9. WKT to AJH, June 30, 1921, AFSC FSR, 1921
10. AJH, "The Story of a Quaker Woman in Russia" (New York, 1922).
11. Watts, "Conditions in Soviet Russia," November 23, 1919, WARVICREL July 2, 1921, p. 143
12. Horsley Gantt, A Medical Review of Soviet Russia (London, 1924) reprint from British Medical Journal, 1924, 12-16.

13. For details on the Nancy Babb's medical projects see chapter 6 and Nancy Babb personnel files, AFSC personnel files, 1917-1927.
14. Margaret Trott, "Soviet Medicine and Western Charity 1917-1927," PhD. dissertation, University of Virginia, 1994, 25-26; Peter Krug, "Russian Public Physicians and Revolution: the Pirogov Society, 1917-1920," Ph.D. dissertation, University of Wisconsin, 1979; John F. Hutchinson, Politics and Public Health in Revolutionary Russia, 1890-1918 (Baltimore: Johns Hopkins, 1990); Susan Gross Solomon and John F. Hutchinson, Health and Society in Revolutionary Russia (Bloomington: Indiana University, 1990. In the latter book, see particularly John F. Hutchinson, "Who Killed Cock Robin? An Inquiry into the Death of Zemstvo Medicine," 30-27; and Neil B. Weissman, "Origins of Soviet Health Administration, Narkomzdrav, 1918-1928," 97-120.
15. Krug, ii.
16. Krug, 71.
17. Krug, 177; Trott, 232, 234, 86; On Lenin's caution, see Hutchinson, 175-179; and on collaboration between Pirogovtsi and Bolshevik physicians in Narkomzdrav, see Hutchinson 185-188.
18. Weissman, 97.
19. For evidence of the special esteem with which Semashko held the Quakers, see for example, Norah Meade of the ARA, ARA Russia Unit Papers, Hoover, 1923, Francesca Wilson, In the Margins of Chaos, 155, and William Haskell, Memoirs, 149-155.
20. Quaker service proposals to M. Karkhlin, government representative for foreign organizations for Samara, July 16, 1923, AFSC FSR, 1923; Lander to Branson, June 19, 1923 and Lander to Branson, June 27, 1923, Central Executive Committee RSFSR decree, September 7, 1923, GARF f. 1058, op 1, del 548. See also Kameneva to Quaker Service, September 12, 1923, AFSC FSR, 1923. For agreements of 1924, 1925, 1926 see Society of Friends to Committee for Relations with Foreign Relief organizations, July 16, 1924; agreement August 15, 1925; Agreement June 1926, all in AFSC FSR, 1924, 1925, 1926.
21. As Lenin reportedly reassured Semashko, "My dear Semashko. . . the Quakers are only for you" (Lenin to Semashko August 12, 1921, Leninskie Sbornik XXXVI: 287. For details of the Quaker sponsorship and work with Semashko, see McFadden, "The Haines-Watts Mission. . . ." See also Margaret A. Trott, "Soviet Medicine and Western Charity, 1917-1927,"Ph.D. Dissertation, University of Virginia, 1994, 147.
22. S. Edgar Nicholson to WKT, June 26, 1924, AFSC FSR, 1924.
23. Report of Russian Relief, Buzuluk, 1923-24; Report of Russian Relief, Totskoye, 1923-24; AFSC FSR, 1924; Babb Papers Hoover, Box 1; Ruth Fry Diary, Jan 3, 1925, Fry Papers, SPC.
24. Homer Morris Collection, Box 16, Earlham College Library
25. Wildman to WKT, April 4, 1923, AFSC FSR, 1923.
26. Wildman to President of Foreign Relief Commission, September 12, 1923, AFSC FSR, 1923.
27. MacKenzie to Ruth Fry, June 9, 1923, Ruth Fry Papers, SPC; AFSC general files, 1923; GARF f 482, op 16, del 152; f 3385, op 1 del 7(1). Totskoye report 1923-24, in Babb Papers, Hoover, Box 2.

28. Report of Russian Relief, Totskoye, October 23, 1924 attached to Minutes, AFSC Russian Committee, January 7, 1925, see also reference to Quaker anti-malaria work in GARF fond 3385, op 1, del 80.
29. Francesca Wilson, In the Margins of Chaos (London: John Murray, 1946), p. 150. See also MacKenzie, Medical Relief, 10.
30. Edwin Vail Journal, May 28, 1923, Edwin Vail Papers, Hoover
31. See Edwin Vail, Gamaleyevka report, August 1923, Edwin Vail Papers, Hoover; report of district supervisor, Totskoye, 1923, AFSC FSR, 1923; Dorothy North Grachkeeva report, 1923, AFSC FSR, 1923.
32. Wildman to WKT, September 15, 1923; see also Elfie Graff to Dr. Lovejoy, copy to WKT, AFSC FSR, 1924. See also new collective agreement between ODK and Russian workers union, February 1925, AFSC FSR 1925.
33. S. Edgar Nicholson to WKT, January 22, 1924, AFSC FSR, 1924.
34. Serving on the General Committee of American Medical Aid, for example, were Paxton Hibben, Bishop Paul Jones, A. J. Muste, John Dewey, Jerome Davis, Sidney Hillman, Oswald Garrison Villard, Albert Rhys Willians, and John Haynes Holmes. Armand Hammer was a major contributor. See acknowledgement form, American Medical Aid for Russia, AFSC files.
35. American Women's Hospital correspondence, AFSC FSR, orgs 1922-1923.
36. M.C. Phillips to Esther Lovejoy, Americans Women's Hospital correspondence, Ibid.
37. Quoted in Weissman, "Origins of Soviet Health Administration," p. 113. See also Trott, "Squabbles in the Walled City: Soviet Officialdom and Western Medical Charity, 1920-1925,"unpublished paper presented at the AAASS conference, November 18, 1999, pp. 13-15. For a discussion of Narkomzdrav's difficulties in maintaining medical services in the face of budget cutbacks, reluctance of local soviets, and unwillingness of doctors to relocate in the rural areas, see Weissman, 110-113.
38. See for example, WKT to Alice Davis, May 3, 1923, AFSC FSR 1923.
39. Julia Branson (Moscow) to WKT, January 21, 1924, AFSC FSR, 1924.
40. See chapter 6.
41. Minutes, Foreign Service Section, AFSC, June 30, 1925; Minutes, AFSC July 23, 1925.
42. AJH to E. K. Balls, March 16, 1925, AFSC FSR, 1925.
43. AJH to WKT, June 27, 1925, AFSC FSR, 1925. See also AJH to WKT, June 6, 1925, and AJH to WKT, June 20, 1925.
44. WKT to AJH, July 3, 1925, AFSC FSR, 1925.
45. AJH to WKT, August 8, 1925; AJH to WKT August 26, 1925; AFSC FSR, 1925.
46. Ibid.
47. For other examples of Anna Haines' writing see "A Russian Inventory," American Friend, February 18, 1926, American Friend, November 25, 1927, and "Progress in Health Work in Russia, American Friend, December 1, 1927.
48. Dorice White to WKT, December 9, 1925, AFSC FSR, 1925.
49. AJH to WKT, December 18, 1925, AFSC FSR, 1925.
50. AJH to WKT, February 11, 1926, AFSC FSR, 1926
51. WKT to AJH, March 19, 1926, AFSC FSR, 1926.
52. Proposal by the Society of Friends to the Commissar of Narkomzdrav, Dr. N.A. Semashko, May 12, 1926, AFSC FSR, 1926; AJH to WKT May 12, 1926 AFSC FSR, 1926.

53. AJH to WKT, June 26, 1926, July 6, 1926; July 19, 1926, and Peoples Commissariat for Health Agreement with Society of Friends for Nurses Training Center, July 19, 1926, all AFSC FSR, 1926.
54. Biddle to WKT, June 17, 1926, AFSC FSR, 1926.
55. Heath to WKT, August 25, 1926, AFSC FSR, 1926
56. AJH to WKT, July 30, 1926, AFSC FSR, 1926
57. For discussion of Soviet decision to completely phase out foreign relief work, see Trott, and Weissman. For further consideration of AFSC fundraising etc, see WKT to Dorice White, October 26, 1927; and Fred Tritton to WKT, July 6, 1927 AFSC FSR 1927.

NOTES FOR CHAPTER 8:
"A VERY SPECIAL RELATIONSHIP"

1. For the basic documents, see "Nansen Proposal on Famine Relief," April 3, 1919; Allied reply April 17, 1919 and Soviet response, May 7, 1919, all in Goldberg, 190-194. For a detailed discussion of the politics of the Hoover-Nansen proposal, see McFadden, 244-263,
2. Goldberg, 198-200; 208-211.
3. An excellent overview of the Soviet approach to the famine can be found in Charles M. Edmondson, "The Politics of Hunger: the Soviet Response to Famine, 1921," Soviet Studies XXIX, No. 4 (October 1977: 506-518.
4. Margaret Trott, "The Brief Heyday of an Early Soviet Bureaucrat: Olga Kameneva and Foreign Famine Relief, 1922-1926," unpublished paper presented to the Great Lakes History Conference, October 4, 1996.
5. Ibid. 5, 9, 12-13. The story of the ARA's relations with Kamenev and Dzherzhinski particularly in overcoming a key transportation crisis of 1922, is found in both in Fisher and more vividly in the unpublished memoirs of William N. Haskell, the Director of Russian operations of the ARA, Haskell Papers, Hoover; and also Haskell to Herter, March 6, 1923. For outside confirmation of Kameneva's importance see Allen Wardwell Graham R. Taylor and Allen T. Burns, "The Russian Famines, 1921-22, 1922-23, Summary Report," Commission on Russian Relief of the National Information Bureau, New York, 1923.
6. TSKAKP (B), f 17, op 84, del 224, December 31, 1921; Cheka report on ARA activity, September 27, 1921
7. For the texts of these agreements and their negotiations, see exchange of letters, Friends International Service and Tsentrosoyuz, December 28, 1920; AJH to WKT, December 23, 1920; AJH and Watts to WKT, December 30, 1920; Nuorteva to Watts, January 4, 1921; AJH to WKT, January 13, 1921; Watts to Chicherin, April 7, 1921; Watts to Chicherin, April 13, 1921; Chicherin to Watts April 14, 1921; AJH to WKT, May (nd) 1921; all AFSC FSR, 1920-21.
8. Minutes of General Committee, WARVICREL, May 3, 1921, FHL-L
9. Lander to Norment, October 15, 1922 AFSC FSR, 1922.
10. Quaker Service proposals to M. Karkhlin, government representative for foreign organizations for Samara, July 16, 1923; AFSC FSR, 1923; Wildman to WKT, June 7, 1923; Lander to Branson, June 19, 1923; Lander to Branson, June 27, 1923; Central Executive Committee RSFSR decree, September 7, 1923; Wildman to WKT, September 15, 1923; Kameneva to Quaker Service,

September 12, 1923; all AFSC FSR, 1923. See also Julia Branson to Karl Lander, March 27, 1923, GARF f. 1058, op 1, del 548. See also Edwin Vail Diary June 17, 1923, Vail Papers, Hoover. For agreement of 1924, 1925, 1926, see Society of Friends to Committee on Relations with Foreign Relief Organizations, July 16, 1924; Agreement August 15, 1925; Agreement June 10, 1925, agreement between Samara Gubernia and Quaker Service, June 1926, all AFSC FSR, 1924, 1925, 1926.

11. Agreement between the government of the Russian Socialist Federated Soviet Republic (RSFSR) and the Society of Friends of England and America October 25, 1922, AFSC FSR 1922.

12. Ruth Fry, "Second Journey to Russia," May 2, 1923, Ruth Fry Papers, SPC.

13. Ibid. May 5, 1923.

14. Minutes of Special conference, WARVICREL, 5, 22-23, FHL-L. These conclusions from the visit of 1923 were repeated in 1924-25. See Ruth Fry, "Journey to Russia," 1924-25, December 24, 1924, January 9, 10, 15, 21, 22, 1925.

15. See for example Wildman to Lander regarding uses of bales of clothing, January 24, 1923, GARF f. 1058, op 1, del 548; Branson to Lander regarding transport duties, June 5, 1923, GARF f. 1065, op 3, de3l 64 (3); Stevens to Veller, regarding the release of quinine, February 19, 1924; GARF f. 1065, op 3, del 64(2); S. Edgar Nicholson to Veller, April 16, 1924 re: DMC cotton; Stevens to Veller and Ball to Veller regarding adjustment of freight rates and social security tax, GARF f. 1065, op 3, del 1924.

16. Trott, "Kameneva," p. 6

17. For Kameneva's speech in Berlin, see GARF, f. 3385, op 1, del 17. See also Norah Meade, report on trip to Berlin, July 17, 1923; ARA Russian unit, Berlin, ARA Papers, Hoover Institute; Ruth Fry "Journey to Russia," 1924-25; interview with Kameneva Ruth Fry Papers, SPC; Kameneva letter to interior ministry, GARF 3395, op 1, del 56; E.K. Balls to Alice Nike, December 18, 1924; FSC RU 1 from Moscow, 1923-31; Friends Service Council Archives, FHL-L.

18. In Famine: Studies in Relief, pp.40-41, Michael Asquith cites three reasons for this: (1) English and American Quakers operated as international rather than national organizations; (2) Quakers were generally understood and respected as to stay out of politics and religious proselytizing; (3) the long history of Quaker relief work dating to the 1890s was a clear benefit.

19. Fleming report, March 1923, ARA Russia Unit, Relief Organizations – Quakers – Hoover Institute.

20. Wildman to WKT, March 10, 1923, AFSC FSR, 1923.

21. Wildman to Kenworthy, June 4, 1923, AFSC FSR, 1923.

22. Edwin Vail Journal, February 4, 1923, Vail Papers, Hoover Institute

23. Ibid. Feb 11, 1923.

24. Ibid. May 18, 1923.

25. For evidence of these difficulties, see WKT to Wildman, November 17, 1922; AFSC FSR, 1922; Wildman to WKT, March 10, 1923; Wildman to WKT March 1, 1923; Kenworthy to Wildman, April 25, 1923; AFSC FSR, 1922-23.

26. See appeal from Buzuluk Pomgol to Quakers to continue their work, Buzuluk to Quaker Service, June 23, 1922; Ponomarev Buzuluk Pomgol report, May 1922, Buzuluk Archives, f. 536, op 1; Ruth Fry, "Journey to Russia," 1924-1925; Richard Kilbey to Veller, September 13, 1923, GARF f. 23385, op 1, del 55.

27. Katherine Amend report, Garkova outpost, June 1923, Vail Papers
28. Borders to WKT, September 22, 1923, AFSC SEF, 1922.
29. Karl Borders, "Klassen's Case," in Borders to WKT, November 12, 1922, AFSC SEF.
30. Ibid.
31. Ibid.
32. Ibid. pp. 5-6
33. Ibid. pp. 8-9
34. See Hurley to Karkhlin, July 18, 1922, Samara Archives, f 79, op 1, del 22; Report on Buzuluk ooezyd, GARF f. 1058, op 1, del 548; January 1923; 1924 NB report, Hoover Babb Papers, Box 2
35. NB to Wildman, February 5, 1923, AFSC Personnel files 1917-1927.
36. Babb Papers, Hoover, Box 1
37. For a complete description of the Oomnovka proposal, see Louise Edelman to Carl Heath, February 23, 1924 FSC RU/1 Friends Service Council Records, FHL-L.
38. S. Edgar Nicholson to Alice Nike, March 21, 1924, FSC RU 1 FHL-L
39. S. Edgar Nicholson to Kameneva, March 20, 1924, Kameneva to S. Edgar Nicholson March 27, 1924, S. Edgar Nicholson to Kameneva March 27, 1924, GARF f. 3385, op 1, del 56. For the aftermath and further Quaker discussion, see Alice Nike to Edgar Nicholson, April 25, 1924 FSC RU 2, FHL-L.
40. Articles from the Rossisskaya Provinsiia, May 1988,
41. Sergei Nikitin, "Quakers and the Great Russian Famine" Quaker Life (January-February 1998) pp. 5-7.
42. Allen Wardwell et al, Summary Report, Commission on Relief, National Information Bureau

NOTES FOR CHAPTER 9: "TO LIVE QUAKER LIVES"

1. British records on Quaker work in Russia are concentrated in the records of the Friends War Victims Relief Committee (WARVICREL), 1916-1923, and the Friends International Service and Friends Service Council (1923-1931) as well as the family papers of Gregory Welch and Theodore Rigg and others, all housed in Friends House London (FHL-L); and the papers of Ruth Fry, in the Swarthmore Peace Collection (SPC) at Swarthmore College.
2. RMJ, draft statement of cooperation with English Friends, nd (1919), RMJ-HC,
3. For the story of British Quaker refugee relief starting in 1916, see chapters 1 and 3
4. Minutes of a special meeting to consider the spiritual aspect of the work, particularly in relation to the Russian Revolution, November 5, 1918, WARVICREL Records, 1918, FHL-L.
5. Esther White, quoted in minutes of special meeting of Russia subcommittee of Russia and Poland Committee, WARVICREL March 4, 1919, FHL-L.
6. Report by Gregory Welch on journey to Russia, June 22 to August 28, 1920, copies in both AFSC FSR, 1920 and WARVICREL Records FHL-L. For the longer story of Gregory Welch's experience in Russia and his perspectives on Quaker service there, see Welch, "Excursion into Russia," 192 pp. mss, FHL-L.

7. Watts to WARVICREL July 21, 1920, WARVICREL Record FHL-L.
8. Watts to WARVICREL October 21, 1920, WARVICREL FHL-L.
9. Watts to Nuorteva Foreign commissariat, October 18, 1920, WARVICREL records.
10. S. Edgar Nicholson to Alice Nike, March 21, 1924, FSC/RU 1 FSC Record, FHL-L.
11. Alice Nike to S. Edgar Nicholson, March 14, 1924, FSC/RU2, FSC, FHL-L.
12. Alice Nike to S. Edgar Nicholson, April 25, 1924, FSC RU 2, FSC, FHL-L.
13. Alice Nike to S. Edgar Nicholson, February 15, 1924, FSC RU 2; Alice Nike to E.K. Balls, 11/7/24, FSC RU 2, FHL-L.
14. Alice Nike to E.K. Balls, January 9, 1925, FSC RU 2, FHL-L.
15. E.K. Balls to Alice Nike, February 9, 1925, FSC RU 1, FHL-L.
16. E.K. Balls to Carl Heath April 17, 1925, FSC RU 1, FHL-L.
17. See for example E.K. Balls to Carl Heath March 25, 1925 concerning the petition of Sergei Golitsin for membership, FSC RU 1. See also E.K. Balls to Carl Heath March 6, 19825, FSC RU 1, FHL-L.
18. See Alice Nike to Dorice White, September 2, 1926; Izvestia 24 August 1926 and Eddy Papers as well as Dorice White Moscow Center Report in a letter to WKT, September 2, 1926, AFSC-SEF.
19. Carl Heath, "Quaker Embassies," 1917; Carl Heath, "The Quaker Centre," London, Friends Service Council, 1939.
20. Carl Heath, "The Quaker Centre"
21. E. K. Balls to Carl Heath, April 29, 1925, FSC RU 1, FHL-L.
22. Carl Heath to Dorice White September 8, 1925 FSC RU 2, FHL-L.
23. Dorice White to Alice Nike February 13, 1930, FSC RU 1, FHL-L.
24. Emma Cadbury "Impressions of Soviet Russia," Cadbury Family Papers, Quaker Collection, Haverford College.

NOTES FOR CHAPTER 10: CONCLUSION

1) Samantha Power, *A Problem from Hell; America and the Age of Genocide.* (New York: Basic Books, 2002) p. 503
2) Ibid. p. 368
3) David Rieff, *A Bed for the Night; Humanitarianism in Crisis.* (New York: Simon & Schuster, 2002) no page number.
4) Ibid. p. 114

GLOSSARY

AFSC
The American Friends Service Committee was founded by Quakers in 1917 initially to provide alternative service opportunities for conscientious objectors to WWI; in 2004 it carries out peace, justice, relief and development programs throughout the United States and around the globe.

American Relief Administration (ARA)
The U.S. government funded semi-autonomous relief agency for post-WWI Europe, which was later expanded to Soviet Russia, 1921-1922.

Bolshevik
The left wing of the Russian Social Democratic Party derived its name from the 1903 split between the Bolshevik (majority) faction and the Menshevik (minority) faction. They maintained the "Bolshevik" name until it was subsumed by "Communist" in the early 1920s. The key principle of the party was its loyalty to V. I. Lenin and later, other party leaders.

Cheka
The "All-Russian Extraordinary Commission for Struggle Against Counter-Revolution and Sabotage" was actually the Soviet secret police, and the precursor to the NKVD and KGB.

Cossacks
Nomadic horsemen of the Russian steppes who traditionally served as a buffer between Russia and its neighbors to the south and east; Cossacks opposed the Bolshevik revolution in 1918 and generally sided with its opponents during the Civil War.

Czechoslovaks
Troops of the newly emerging state of Czechoslovakia who fought Germany and Austria-Hungary in the latter stages of World War I. They were caught up in Russian revolution as they were cut off from the western front in Germany and tried to make their way through Siberia to Vladivostok, where they became part of the anti-Bolshevik forces in the Civil War, 1918-1920.

Dessiatine
A unit of land equal to approximately 2.7 acres.

Feldshers
These physicians' assistants with training roughly equal to a practical nurse were very common and important medical personnel in rural Russia in the late Tsarist and early Soviet period.

Friends International Service
British Friends organization (of which British Quakers in Russia were a part) which superseded the Friends War Victims Relief Committee (WARVICREL) in the aftermath of WWI.

Friends War Victims Relief Committee (WARVICREL)
The original British Friends organization for relief work during WWI, which sponsored the original Friends Mission to Russia in 1916.

Funt
Approximately 14 ounces.

Gorky Appeal
The writer Maxim Gorky's 1921 public appeal by for western relief in the Great Russian famine. Negotiations following his appeal led to the Riga agreement, also known as the "Hoover-Gorky agreement."

Gubernia
Equivalent to a county or province, it would have been subdivided into volosts.

Hicksites
Beginning early in the 19th century, these "unprogrammed" followers of Elisha Hicks focused on the Inward Light, as opposed to Orthodox Quakers who relied more on the Bible and Christian teachings as a guide to individual conscience.

Joint Distribution Committee (JDC)
The American Jewish Joint Distribution Committee was founded in 1914 to coordinate distribution of charity from several Jewish organizations. [See footnotes for chapter 6.]

Milliard
Million

Moujik or mouzhik
A Russian peasant man

Narkomindel
The Peoples' Commissariat for Foreign Affairs

Narkoondel
The People's Commissariat for Justice

Narkomprod
The Peoples' Commissariat for Food Production

Narkomzdrav
The Peoples' Commissariat for Public Health

ODK
Obshestvo Druzhei Kwakeree: The Society of Friends (Quakers); the Russian acronym for Quakers

Ooezdem
Bolshevik government of ooyezd

Ooyezd
Administrative district, roughly equivalent to a town or rural district.

Oozdocom
Bolshevik official in charge of ooyezd

Oozdrav
Bolshevik health committee at local level

Orthdox Quakers
(See Hicksites, above) During the "Great Separation" starting in the late 1820s, these unprogrammed Orthodox Friends relied on the Bible and Christian teachings as the principle guide to individual conscience.

Pirogov Society/Pirogovtsi
Russian association of mostly rural physicians in the late Tsarist period; they worked to promote public health, improve medical care and education. Many participated actively in the reform and revolutionary years, and often became part of the Bolshevik medical cadres of the 1920s.

Politburo
Executive committee of the Bolshevik Central Committee

Pood, pud
Russian unit of weight, equivalent to 16.38 kg or 36 pounds

Pyok
Food ration of indeterminate size

Riga Agreement
Agreement between the United States and Soviet Russia which allowed American relief workers to distribute famine relief under the auspices of the American Relief Administration (ARA), 1921-22

RSFSR
Russian Socialist Federated Soviet Republic: the Soviet Russian government, 1917-1923

Russian Famine Fund
Organization of moderates and liberals primarily in New York that raised funds to relieve the famine in Soviet Russia, 1921-1923.

Sorochy
Familiar name for Sorochinskoye, one of the centers for American Quaker famine relief and reconstruction, 1922-25

Soviet
A council or body of delegates representing a local community, province, county, state or nation. Village or town soviets constituted the basic governmental unit; the Supreme Soviet held ultimate authority.

Soviet Russia
Short term for RSFSR

Soviet Union
Government of Soviet Russia, Ukraine, Kazakhstan, Belarus and others starting in 1923, also known as the Union of Soviet Socialist Republics or USSR.

Tolstoyan
These followers of the great novelist and pacifist Leo Tolstoy formed scattered groups of spiritual seekers, vegetarians and pacifists during the years following Tolstoy's death in 1905. Led by Vladimir Tchertkov, Tolstoy's secretary and promoter, they flourished between 1916 and 1927 while Soviet policy encouraged religious and philosophical alternatives to the Russian Orthodox Church. By the late 1920s, they were subjected to persecution and a major crackdown occurred in 1928.

Tsentrosoyuz
The central association of Russian cooperatives

Tsar (or czar)
Autocrat of the Russian empire, from the 16th century until 1917

Union of Soviet Socialist Republics (USSR)
See: Soviet Union

Volost
Rural Township and administrative center, similar to a US County seat

Zemstvo
Following the Great Reforms of Alexander II (1855-1866), an elected county or town assembly responsible for local health, education and agriculture. It was active in organizing for further reform and change in Russia, particularly during the Revolution of 1905 and was replaced by soviets in 1917.

SELECTED CHRONOLOGY, QUAKER SERVICE IN REVOLUTIONARY RUSSIA, 1916-1931

1916

April	four British Quakers arrive in St. Petersburg
August	the first (British) Quaker unit begins work in Buzuluk and Mogotovo
Autumn	Disastrous Russian offensive undermines support for Tsar
December	Rasputin's assassination in Petrograd further undermines Tsar's government

1917

	Quakers open orphanage, several hospitals and centers for refugees
February	(March, new style) Massive street demonstrations in Petrograd Soldiers mutiny; government loses control Tsar Nicholas II abdicates; he and his family held under house arrest
March	Provisional government is formed; Soviet of workers, soldiers and peasants formed to balance government
April	Lenin returns to Petrograd from abroad New laws eliminate restrictions on religious practice, speech, and press State control of bread is established
August	Holy Synod is abolished and patriarchate is reestablished Royal family exiled to Tobolsk
October	Six American Quakers arrive to join Friends Unit in Buzuluk
November	Provisional Government flees; Bolsheviks form Soviet government
December	Formation of the Cheka Finland and Poland become independent Decree on Peace, Decree on Land, Decree on Bread

1918

January	Constituent Assembly convenes and is dispersed Quakers report from Buzuluk: "Beyond a certain amount of lawlessness. . . everything is quiet. . . and we are treated with the utmost respect by Bolshevik representatives here.
February	Beginning of opposition to Bolsheviks in South, North, and Siberia Laws establish separation of church and state; Church property transferred to state ownership Germany resumes war with the Russian Soviet Republic, taking land and ports
March	Brest-Litovsk Peace Treaty between Germany and Russia The Allies including American troops, land at Murmansk Bolsheviks move capital from Petrograd to Moscow Quakers close hospitals at Mogotovo and Andrieyevka Compulsory military service re-established

June	Theodore Rigg visits Petrograd and Moscow
July	Rigg and Esther White move to Moscow to work for children's colonies
	Tsar Nicholas II and his family are killed by Bolsheviks in Yekaterinburg
August	Soviets recognize independent Poland
	Failed assassination attempt on Lenin by Socialist Revolutionaries
October	Quaker relief workers leave Buzuluk;
	Some work with Red Cross in Siberia while others return to the US and Britain

1919

January	Paris Peace Conference
	Negotiations between Quakers and U.S. government and between Quakers and Bolsheviks
	Secret U.S. government mission to Bolsheviks (Bullitt)

1920

April	Poland invades Russia
June	Arthur Watts and Gregory Welch visit Soviet Russia to assess opportunities for Quaker Service
October	Polish-Soviet War ends
November	Anna Haines arrives in Moscow to work with Arthur Watts distributing food, medicine, and clothing.

1921

	Beginning of New Economic Policy (NEP)
March	Bolshevik sailors at Kronstadt revolt against government; suppressed
	Bolsheviks adopt New Economic Policy enabling foreign trade and limited free market economy
August	Famine in the Volga region
	Anna Haines and others travel to Samara to assess the situation
September	British Quakers return to Buzuluk to begin food distribution for famine victims
December	First American Quakers join the unit in Buzuluk

1922

April	Stalin named General Secretary of the Communist party
	Thirty three British and fourteen American Quakers are working in Samara district
May	Quakers are feeding most of the starving people in Buzuluk

| October | Under new agreement with Soviet authorities, Quakers bring in tractors and horses, and expand relief work to reconstruction |
| December | Establishment of Union of Soviet Socialist Republics (USSR) |

1923

Nancy Babb's work in Totskoye grows to include cultivating 1,800 acres, maintaining 44 clinics, with the help of 11,000 Russians.

1924

January	Death of V.I. Lenin
	Quakers continue medical work in Buzuluk; make plans for school in Oomnovka
June	Quakers open prenatal clinic in Sorochinskoye

1925 — Trotsky sent into exile to Kazakhstan

1926 — Nancy Babb's hospital completed
Stalinist struggle against the "United Opposition" of Trotsky and Zinoviev; defeat of opposition and expulsion from the communist Party.

1927 — Nancy Babb leaves Russia for the United States

1928 — Stalin defeats the "right Opposition" of Bukharin, Rykov, and Tomsky; becomes individual dictator.

1929 — Beginning of Stalin Revolution: first Five year Plan adopted; wholesale collectivization of peasants; end of New Economic Policy.
Tolstoy Jubilee, Yasnaya Polyana
Soviet crackdown against all religious practice
Dorice White, Quaker Centre Moscow, only foreign worker in Russia

1929 — Trotsky sent into foreign exile

1930 — Dorice White goes to Ireland for holidays and is not allowed to return

1931 — Lease on Quaker Centre Moscow not renewed; end of Quaker presence for nearly thirty years.

KEY STAFF AND VISITORS, QUAKER SERVICE IN RUSSIA
1916 - 31

William Albright
Katherine Amend
Grace Arnold
Nancy Babb
A. E. Backhouse
Hinman Baker
Richard Reynolds Ball
E.K. Balls
Natalie Balls
Margaret Barber
Florence Barrow
Harrison Barrow
Karl Borders
Emilie Bradbury
Neville Bradley
Julia Branson
E. W. Brooks
Joseph Burtt
Charles R. Buxton
Emma Cadbury
William Cadbury
E. St. John Catchpool
Ethel Christie
Cuthbert Clayton
Charles Colles
Tom Copeman
Albert P.I. Cotterell
Nadia Danilevski
Alice Davis
Dorothy Detzer
Cuthbert Dukes
Robert Dunn
Louis Edelman
Marvin Edelman
Dr. Elliott
Amelia Fabriszewski
Dora Fox
Elsie Fox
J. Tylor Fox
Ruth Fry
Horsley Gantt

*Estelle Hewson modeling
Russian peasant blouse,
Minsk, 1922*

Dr. Elfie Graff
Bertha Graveson
Mrs. Haden-Guest
Anna Haines
Henry Hamilton
T. D. Heald
Carl Heath
Anne Herkner
Estelle Simms Hewson
Cornell Hewson
Norah Hill
Weston Howland

Beulah Hurley
Frank Keddie
Murray Kenworthy
C. Gordon Lewis
Frederick Libby
Wilfrid Little
Melville MacKenzie
Herbert Manning
Edith Morris
Homer Morris
S. Edgar Nicholson
Caroline Norment
Gertrude Ostler
Mary Pattison
Parry Paul
Muriel Payne
George Pearson
Mabelle C. Phillips
Kathryn Price
Marjorie Rackstraw
John Rickman
Lydia Lewis Rickman
Theodore Rigg
Sir Benjamin Robertson
Ernest Rowntree
Elizabeth Saramatnikova
Frank Shaw
Alfred Smaltz
Jessica Smith
Harry Stevens
Anna Louise Strong
Robert Tatlock
Margaret Thorpe
Wilbur Thomas
Violet Tillard
Harry Timbres
Rebecca Janney Timbres
Edwin Vail
Arthur Watts
Frank Watts

Gregory Welch
Annie Wells
Miriam West
Dorice White
Esther White
Phillip Wickstead
J. Cuthbert Wigham
Walter Wildman
Cornelia Young

Cornell Hewson in his
"Russian uniform," Minsk,
1922

BIBLIOGRApby

BOOKS

Abrams, Ray H. Preachers Present Arms: A Study of the War-Time Attitudes and Activities of the Churches and Clergy of the United States, 1914-1918. New York: Round Table Press, 1933.

Abramovitch, Raphael. The Soviet Revolution, 1917-1939. New York, 1962.

Abramson, Rudy. Spanning the Century: the Life of W. Averell Harriman, 1891-1986. New York, 1992.

Acheson, Judy. Young America Looks at Russia. New York: Frederick Stokes, 1932.

Addams, Jane. Peace and Bread in Time of War. New York: Macmillan, 1922.

Ahlstrom, Sydney. A Religious History of the American People. New Haven: Yale University Press, 1972.

Alloit, Stephen. John Wilhelm Rowntree, 1860-1905. York, England: Sessions Book Trust, 1994.

American-Russian Chamber of Commerce. Russia: the American Problem. New York, n.d. [1920].

Andres, Enrike. The NEP: Its Origin and Goal. Moscow, 1969.

Andreyev, Olga Cherov. Cold Spring in Russia. Ann Arbor, 1978.

Angell, Norman. After All: the Autobiography of Norman Angell. New York: Farrar, Straus and Cudahy, Inc., 1952.

Anweiler, Oscar. The Soviets: the Russian Workers, Peasants and Soldiers Councils, 1905-1921. New York, 1974.

Arnold, David. Famine, Social Crisis and Historical Change. Oxford: Basil Blackwell, 1988

Asquith, Michael. Famine: Quaker Work in Russia, 1921-1923. London, 1943.

Atkinson, Dorothy. The End of the Russian Land Commune, 1905-1930. Stanford,1983.

Avrich, Paul. Kronstadt, 1921. Princeton, 1970.

[Babine, Alexis]. A Russian Civil War Diary: Alexis Babine in Saratov, 1917-1922. ed. Donald J. Raleigh. Durham, NC: Duke University Press, 1988.

Bacon, Margaret Hope. Let This Life Speak: the Legacy of Henry J. Cadbury. Philadelphia: University of Pennsylvania Press, 1987.

Bacon, Margaret Hope. The Quiet Rebels: the Story of Quakers in America. Basic Books, 1969.

Baker, Ray Stannard. What Wilson Did at Paris. Garden City, NY: Doubleday, 1919.

Ball, Alan. Russia's Last Capitalists: the Nepmen, 1921-1929. Berkeley: University of California Press, 1987.

Bane, Suda Lorena and Ralph Haswell Lutz, eds. Organization of American Relief in Europe, 1918-1919. Stanford, 1943.

Barbour, Hugh, Christpher Densmore, Elizabeth H. Moger, Nancy C. Sorel, Alson D. Van Wagner, and Arthur J. Worrall, ed. Quaker Cross Currents: Three Hundred Years of Friends in the New York Yearly Meetings. Syracuse University Press, 1995.

Bauer, Yehuda. *My Brother's Keeper; A History of the American Jewish Joint Distribution Committee 1929- 1939*. Philadelphia, Jewish Publication Society of America, 1974.

Bauer, Yehuda. *American Jewry and the Holocaust, The American Jewish Joint Distribution Committee, 1939-1945*. Detroit, Wayne State University Press, 1981.

Beatty, Bessie. *The Red Heart of Russia*. New York, 1919.

Bechhofer C. E Roberts. *Through Starving Russia: Being the Record of Journey to Moscow and the Volga Provinces in August and September 1921*. London, 1921.

Benjamin, Philip S. *The Philadelphia Quakers in the Industrial Age, 1865-1920*. Philadelphia: Temple University Press, 1976.

Benson, Jane. *Quaker Pioneers in Russia*. London, 1902.

Berkman, Alexander. *The Bolshevik Myth: Diary, 1920-1922*. New York, 1925.

Berkman, Alexander, ed. *Letters from Russian Prisons*. New York, 1925.

Best, Gary Dean. *The Politics of American Individualism: Herbert Hoover in Transition, 1918-1921*. Westport CT, 1975.

Bethell, Nicholas. *The Last Secret*. New York: Basic Books, 1974.

Billikopf, Jacob and Maurice B. Hexter. *Jewish Situation in Eastern Europe including Russia and the Work of the Joint Distribution Committee: Joint Report as Delivered at the National Conference of the United Jewish Campaign and the Joint Distribution Committee*. Chicago, 1926.

Boettke, Peter J. *The Political Economy of Soviet Socialism: the Formative Years, 1918-1928*. Boston, 1990.

Bogen, Boris David. *Born a Jew*. New York: Macmillan, 1930.

Borders, Karl. *Village Life Under the Soviets*. New York 1927.

Bose, Turim Chandra. *American-Soviet Relations, 1921-1933*. Calcutta, 1967.

Brinton, Anna, ed. *Then and Now: Quaker Essays: Historical and Contemporary*. Philadelphia: University of Pennsylvania Press, 1960.

Brinton, Howard H. ed. *Byways in Quaker History*. Wallingford, Pendle Hill, 1944.

Brinton, Howard H. *Friends for Three Hundred Years*. New York: Harper and Brothers, 1952.

British Friends Council. *Some Notes on Social Conditions in Soviet Russia*. London, 1925.

Brock, Peter. *Freedom from Violence*. Toronto: University of Toronto, 1991.

Brock, Peter. *Pacifism in the United States from the Colonial Era to the First World War*. Princeton: Princeton University Press, 1908.

Brock, Peter. *The Quaker Peace Testimony, 1660 to 1914*. London, 1990.

Bronner, Edwin B., ed. *American Quakers Today*. Philadelphia: Friends World Committee, 1966.

Bronner, Edwin B., *The Other Branch: London Yearly Meeting and the Hicksites, 1827-1912*. London, 1975.

Brovkin, Vladimir. *Behind the Front Lines of the Civil War, 1918-1922*. Princeton, 1994.

Brown, William A., Jr. *The Groping Giant: Revolutionary Russia as Seen by an American Democrat*. New Haven: Yale University Press, 1920.

Bullitt, Orville H., ed. *For the President: Personal and Secret Correspondence between Franklin D. Roosevelt and William C. Bullitt.* Boston, 1972.

Burner, David. *Herbert Hoover: A Public Life.* New York, Alfred A. Knopf, 1979.

Byrd, Robert O. *Quaker Ways in Foreign Policy.* Toronto, 1960.

Byrnes, Robert F. *Awakening American Education in the World: the Role of Archibald Cary Coolidge, 1866-1924.* South Bend: University of Notre Dame, 1982.

Carr, E. H. *The Foundations of a Planned Economy, 1926-1929.* London 1971.

Carr, E. H. *Socialism in One Country.* London, 1964.

Carter, Paul A. *The Decline and Revival of the Social Gospel: Social and Political Liberalism in American Protestant Churches, 1920-1940.* Ithaca, 1956.

Carter, Paul A. *The Spiritual Crisis of the Gilded Age.* DeKalb: Northern Illinois Press, 1971.

Carroll, E. Malcolm. *Soviet Communism and Western Opinion, 1919-1921.* Chapel Hill, 1965.

Cauthen, Kenneth. *The Impact of American Religious Liberalism.* New York: Harper and Row, 1962.

Chaiainov, A.V. *The Theory of Peasant Economy,* ed. Daniel Thommer. Homewood Ill, 1966.

Chamberlin, William Henry. *Soviet Russia: a Living Record and a History.* Boston: Little Brown and Company, 1930.

Chambers, Clarke A. *Seedtime of Reform: American Social Service and Social Action, 1918-1933.* Minneapolis: University of Minnesota Press, 1963.

Chatfield, Earle Charles. *For Peace and Justice: Pacifism in America, 1914-1941.* Knoxville, TN, 1971.

Child, Richard Washburn. *Potential Russia.* New York, 1916.

Craig, Robert H. Religion *and Radical Politics: an Alternative Christian Tradition in the United States.* Philadelphia: Temple University Press, 1992.

Curtiss, John Shelton. *The Russian Church and the Soviet State, 1917-1950.* Boston, 1953.

Curtis, Susan. *A Consuming Faith: the Social Gospel and Modern American Culture.* Baltimore, 1991.

Danilov, V. P. *Rural Russia under the New Regime.* trans. and with an introduction by O. Figes. London, 1988.

Davies, R. W., Mark Harrison, and S. G. Wheatcroft, eds. *The Economic Transformation of the Soviet Union, 1913-1945.* Cambridge: Cambridge University Press, 1994.

Davis, David Brion. *Revolutions: Reflections on American Equality and Foreign Liberations.* Cambridge, Ma, 1990.

DeBenedetti, Charles. *Origins of the Modern American Peace Movement, 1915-1929.*

DeBenedetti, Charles. *The Peace Reform in American History.* Bloomington: Indiana University Press, 1980.

Degras, Jane, comp. ed. *Soviet Documents in Foreign Policy, vol. 1, 1917-1924*. London, 1951.

Dennis, Alfred P., Stanley High, *Maurice Hindus, and Anna Louise Strong, Russia in Transition: An American Symposium*. New York: Foreign Policy Association, 1925.

Detzer, Dorothy. *Appointment on the Hill*. New York 1948.

Dewey, John. *Impressions of Soviet Russia and the Revolutionary World*. New York, 1932.

Doak, Frances Renfrow. *Mary Mendenhall Hobbs*. Greensboro, NC, np, 1955.

Dorn, Jacob H. *Washington Gladden: Prophet of the Social Gospel*. Columbus: Ohio State University Press, 1966.

Dubie, Alain. Frank A. Golder: *An Adventure of a Historian in Quest of Russian History*. Boulder: East European Monographs, 1989.

Dukes, Paul. *Red Dusk and the Morrow*. New York, 1922.

Dunn, Stephen P. and Ethel Dunn. *The Peasants of Central Russia*. New York, 1967.

Duranty, Walter. *I Write as I Please*. New York: Simon and Schuster, 1935.

Duranty, Walter. *Russia Reported*. London, 1934

Dyck, Harvey. *A Mennonite in Russia: the Diaries of Jacob P. Epp, 1851-1880*. Toronto: University of Toronto Press, 1991.

Dyck, J. P. ed. *Troubles and Triumphs, 1914-1924: Excerpts from the Diary of Peter J. Dyck*. Manitoba, 1981.

Eddy, Sherwood. *Eighty Adventurous Years: An Autobiography*. New York, 1955.

Eddy, Sherwood. *The Kingdom of God and the American Dream: the Religious and Secular Ideals of American History*. New York: Harper and Brothers, 1941.

Eddy, Sherwood. *.A Pilgrimage of Ideas, or The Reeducation of Sherwood Eddy*. New York, 1934.

Eddy, Sherwood. *Russia's Challenge*. 1927.

Eddy, Sherwood. *Russia Today*. 1930.

Ellis, Ethan. *Frank B. Kellogg and American Foreign Policy, 1925-1939*.

Figes, Orlando. *Peasant Russia, Civil War: the Volga Countryside in Revolution, 1917-1921*. Oxford England, 1989.

Figes, Orlando, *A Peoples Tragedy: the Russian Revolution, 1891-1924*. New York, 1998.

Filene, Peter G. *Americans and the Soviet Experiment, 1917-1933*. Cambridge, Mass, 1967.

Finkelstein Lewis, ed. *American Spiritual Autobiographies*. New York: Harper and Brothers, 1948.

Fischer, Louis. *Men and Politics: an Autobiography*. New York, 1941.

Fisher, Harold H. *The Famine in Soviet Russia, 1919-1923: The Operations of the American Relief Administration*. New York, 1927.

Fitzpatrick, Sheila, et al. *Russia in the Era of NEP: Explorations in Soviet Society and Culture*. Bloomington, 1991.

Fitzpatrick, Sheila. Stalin's *Peasants: Resistance and Survival in the Russian Village after Collectivization.* New York, 1994.

Fodor, Alexander. *A Quest for a Nonviolent Russia: the Partnership of Leo Tolstoy and Vladimir Chertkov.* University Press of America, 1992.

Fodor, Alexander. *Tolstoy and the Russians.* Ann Arbor: Ardis, 1984.

Foner, Philip S. *Impact of the Bolshevik Revolution on American Radicals, Liberals, and Labor.* New York, 1967.

Forbes, John. *Friends and Russian Relief, 1917-1927.* Philadelphia, 1952.

Forcey, Charles Budd. *The Crossroads of Liberalism; Croly, Weyl, Lippmann, and the Progressive Era, 1900-1923.* New York, 1961.

Forcey, Charles Budd. *Forty Years for Peace: a History of the Fellowship of Reconciliation, 1914-1954.* New York: Fellowship of Reconciliation, 1954.

Fosdick, Henry E. *The Living of These Days.* New York: Harper and Brothers, 1956.

Fosdick, Henry E. *Rufus Jones Speaks to Our Time; An Anthology.* New York: The Macmillan Company, 1951.

Fox, Richard. *Storming Heaven.* New York: Harcourt Brace, 1928.

Freeze, Gregory. *The Parish Clergy in Nineteenth Century Russia: Crisis Reform, Counterreform.* Princeton, 1983.

Frith, Francis. *William Pollard, William Edward Turner. A Reasonable Faith: Short Essays for the Times.* London: Macmillan, 1884.

Fry, Anna Ruth. *A Quaker Adventure; the Story of Nine Years' Relief and Reconstruction.* New York: Frank Maurice, 1927.

Fry, Anna Ruth. *Three Visits to Russia, 1922-1925.* London, 1942.

Gardner, Virginia. *"Friend and Lover:" the Life of Louise Bryant.* New York: Horizon Press, 1982.

Gelfand, Lawrence E, ed. *Herbert Hoover. The Great War and Its Aftermath, 1914-1923.* Iowa City, 1979.

Gidney, James B., ed. *Witness to Revolution: Letters from Russia, 1916-1919,* by Edward T. Heald. Kent, Ohio, 1972.

Gill, G. J. *Peasants and Government in the Russian Revolution.* London, 1979.

Glad, Betty. *Charles Evans Hughes and the Illusions of Innocence: a Study in American Diplomatic History.* Urbana, Ill: University of Illinois, 1966.

Golder, Frank, Samuel Harper and Alexander Petrunkevich. *The Russian Revolution.* Cambridge: Harvard University Press, 1918.

Golder, Frank and Lincoln Hutchinson. *On the Trail of the Russian Famine.* Stanford, 1927.

[Golder, Frank]. *War, Revolution and Peace in Russia: the Passages of Frank Golder, 1914-1927.* Comp. and ed Terence Emmons and Bertrand M. Patenaude. Stanford, 1992.

Goldman, Emma. *My Disillusionment in Russia.* London, 1924.

Goldman, Emma. *My Further Disillusionment with Russia.* Garden City, NY, 1925.

Gorer, Geoffrey and John Rickman. *The People of Great Russia: A Psychological Study.* London, 1945.

Gorrell, Donald K. *The Age of Social Responsibility: The Social Gospel in the Progressive Era, 1900-1920.* Macon, GA, 1988.

[Gote, Iu. V.] *Time of Troubles: the Diary of Iurii Vladimirovich Gote,* Moscow, July 8, 1917 to July 23, 1922. Trans, ed and intro. Terence Emmons. Princeton, NJ, 1988.

Greenwood, John Omerod. *Quaker Encounters: Friends and Relief.* York, England, 1975.

Gregg, John P. *General Report of the American Relief Administration, Saratov, 1921-23.* U.S. Government, ARA, 1923.

Golkin, Arline. *Famine: a Heritage of Hunger: a Guide to the Issues and References.* Claremont: Regina Books, 1987.

Grubb, Edward. *The Evangelical Movement and its Impact on the Society of Friends.* Leominster, England, 1924.

Haines, Anna. *Health Work in Soviet Russia.* New York: Vanguard Press, 1928.

Hall, Willis H. *Quaker International Work in Europe Since 1914.* Chambery, 1938.

Hamilton, Henry W. *The Aftermath of War: Experiences of a Quaker Relief Worker on the Polish-Russian Border, 1923-1924.* Dayton: Merryside House, 1982.

Hamm, Thomas D. *The Transformation of American Quakerism: Orthodox Friends, 1800-1907.* Bloomington: Indiana University Press 1988.

Handy, Robert T. *A History of the Churches in the United States and Canada.* New York: Oxford University Press, 1976.

Handy, Robert T., ed. *The Social Gospel in America, 1870-1920.* New York: Oxford University Press, 1966.

Harper, Paul V., ed. *The Russia I Believe In: Memoirs of Samuel N. Harper, 1902-1941.* Chicago, 1945.

Harper, Samuel N. *Civic Training in Soviet Russia.* Chicago, 1927.

Harper, Samuel N. *The Hardships of Our Co-Religionists in the German Volga Colonies.* Pokrovsk, 1921.

Harriman, W. Averell. *America and Russia in a Changing World.* New York, 1971.

Harrison, Margaret E. *Marooned in Moscow: The Story of an American Woman Imprisoned in Russia.* New York, 1921.

Harrison, Margaret E. *Unfinished Tales from a Russian Prison.* New York, 1923.

Hibben, Paxton. *Reconstruction in Russia: an Address before the Forum of the Community Church of New York City, Easter Sunday, 1925.* New York, 1925.

Hiebert, P.C. and Orrie Miller. *Feeding the Hungry: Russia's Famine, 1919-1925.* Scottsdale, PA, 1929.

Hindus, Maurice. *Broken Earth.* New York, 1926.

Hindus, Maurice. *Humanity Uprooted.* New York, 1929.

Hindus, Maurice. *Red Bread.* New York, 1931.

Hinshaw, David. *Rufus Jones: Master Quaker.* New York: G. P. Putnam Sons, 1951.

Hirst, Margaret F. *The Quakers in Peace and War*. London: Swarthmore Press, 1923.

Hopkins, C. Howard. *The Rise of the Social Gospel in American Protestantism, 1865-1915*. New Haven, 1940.

Hopkins, C. Howard. *The Social Gospel: Religion and Reform in Changing America*. Philadelphia: Temple University Press, 1976.

Hocking, Ernest, Chair, and the Committee of Appraisal. *Rethinking Missions: a Laymen's Inquiry after One Hundred Years*. New York: Harper and Brothers, 1932.

Holder, Charles Frederick. *Quakers in Great Britain and America: the Religious and Political History of the Society of Friends from 17th to 20th Century*. New York, 1913.

Hole, Allen D. *The Place of the Quaker Message in Modern Life*. Richmond, Indiana: Central Book and Tract Committee, 1909.

Holmes, John Haynes. *I Speak for Myself*. New York, 1959.

Hoover, Herbert. *The Memoirs of Herbert Hoover: the Cabinet and the Presidency, 1920-1933*. New York: Macmillan, 1952.

Howe, Herbert Barber. *Yorkshire to Westchester, A Chronicle of the Wood Family*. Rutland, Vermont, 1948.

Hullinger, Edwin Ware. *The Reforging of Russia*. New York, 1925.

Hutchinson, William R. *The Modernist Impulse in American Protestantism*. Cambridge: Harvard, 1976.

Ingersoll, Jean M. *Famine in Russia, 1921-22, Famine in Bechuanaland, 1965*. Hudson Institute, New York, 1965.

Ingle, H. Larry. *Quakers in Conflict: The Hicksite Reformation*. Knoxville: University of Tennessee Press, 1986.

Irwin, Will. *Herbert Hoover: a Reminiscent Biography*. New York: The Century Company, 1928.

Isichei, Elisabeth. *Victorian Quakers*. Oxford: Clarendon, 1970.

Jackson, William M. *The Higher Criticism and the Relation of Its Result to Quakerism*. Philadelphia: Young Friends Association, 1895.

Jay, Allen. *Autobiography of Allen Jay, Born 1831 Died 1910*. Philadelphia, John C. Winston, 1910.

Johnson, Donald. *The Challenge to American Freedom: World War I and the Rise of the ACLU*. Lexington, KY, 1963.

Johnson, Robert David. *The Peace Progressives and American Foreign Relations*. Cambridge and London, 1995.

Jonas, Gerald. *On Doing Good*. New York: Charles Scribners Sons, 1971.

Jones, Lester. *Quakers in Action: Recent Humanitarian and Reform Activities of American Quakers*. New York: Macmillan, 1929.

Jones, Louis Thomas. *The Quakers of Iowa*. Iowa City: Clio, 1914.

Jones, Mary Hoxie. *Rufus M. Jones*. London: Friends Home Service Committee, 1955.

Jones, Mary Hoxie. *Swords into Ploughshares: An Account of the American Friends Service Committee, 1917-1937*. New York, Macmillan, 1937.

Jones, Mary Hoxie, ed. *Thou Dost Open Up My Life: Selections from the Rufus Tones Collection.* Wallingford: Pendle Hill, 1963.

Jones, Rufus. *American Friends in France, 1917-1919.* New York: Russell Sage Foundation, 1943.

Jones, Rufus. *The Boy Jesus and His Companions.* New York, 1922.

Jones, Rufus. *A Boy's Religion from Memory.* London. Headley Brothers, 1903.

Jones, Rufus. *A Call to What is Vital.* New York: Macmillan, 1948.

Jones, Rufus. *The Double Search: Studies in Atonement and Prayer.* Philadelphia: John C. Winston, 1906.

Jones, Rufus. *A Dynamic Faith.* London: Headley Brothers, 1901.

Jones, Rufus. *The Eternal Gospel.* New York: Macmillan, 1938.

Jones, Rufus. *Finding the Trail of Life.* New York: Macmillan, 1926.

Jones, Rufus. *The Later Periods of Quakerism.* London: Macmillan, 1921. 2 vols. 1931.

Jones, Rufus. *Practical Christianity.* Philadelphia, 1899.

Jones, Rufus. *Quakerism: a Spiritual Movement.* Philadelphia: Philadelphia Yearly Meeting, 1963, 1935.

Jones, Rufus. *Rethinking Religious Liberalism.* Boston: Beacon Press, 1920.

Jones, Rufus. *A Service of Love in Wartime.* New York: Macmillan, 1920.

Jones, Rufus. *A Small Town Boy.* New York: Macmillan, 1941.

Jones, Rufus. *Social Law in the Spiritual World.* Philadelphia: John C. Winston, 1904.

Jones, Rufus. *The Trail of Life in College.* New York: Macmillan, 1929.

Jones, Rufus. *The Trail of Life in the Middle Years.* New York: Macmillan, 1934.

Jones, Stinton. *Russia in Revolution: Being the Experience of an Englishman in Petrograd during the Upheaval.* London,1917.

Jones, T. Canby. *Thomas Kelly As I Remember Him.* Wallingford, PA: Pendle Hill, 1989.

Josephson, Harold. *James T. Shotwell and the Rise of Internationalism in America.* Rutherford, NJ: Farleigh Dickinson, 1975.

Kahoe, Walter. ed. *Clarence Pickett: A Memoir.* 1966.

Kameneva, Olga Davydovna. *Kak proletarii vsekh stran pomogaiut golodaiushchim Rossii.* Moscow, 1923.

Keep, John L. H. *The Russian Revolution: A Study in Mass Mobilization.* London, 1976.

Kelly, Richard M. *Thomas Kelly: A Biography.* New York: Harper and Row, 1966.

Kenez, Peter. *Civil War in South Russia, 1918: the First Year of the Volunteer Army.* Berkeley and Los Angeles, 1971.

Kenez, Peter. *Civil War in South Russia, 1919-1920: the Defeat of the Whites.* Berkeley and Los Angeles 1977.

Kennedy, Thomas C., *British Quakerism, 1860-1920: The Transformation of a Religious Community.* Oxford, 2001.

Kenworthy, Leonard S., ed. *Living in the Light: Some Quaker Pioneers of the Twentieth Century.* Kennett Square, Pa, 1984.

Kerensky, Alexander. *The Catastrophe: Kerensky's Own Story of the Russian Revolution*. New York: D. Appleton, 1927.

Kingston-Mann, Esther, and Timothy Mixter, eds., *Peasant Economic Culture and Politics of European Russia, 1800-1921*. Princeton, 1991.

Kingston-Mann, Esther. *Lenin and the Problem of Marxist Peasant Revolution*. Oxford, 1985.

Klippenstein, Lawrence. *Mennonite Pacifism and State Service in Russia: a Case Study of Church-State Relation, 1789-1939*. University of Minnesota, 1939.

Koch, F. C. *The Volga Germans in Russia and the Americas from 1763 to the Present*. Philadelphia, 1977.

Kuklick, Bruce. *The Rise of American Philosophy*. Cambridge, MA, 1860-1930. New Haven: Yale University Press, 1977.

Lamont, Corliss and Margaret Lamont. *Russia Day by Day: A Travel Diary*. New York, 1933.

Lamont, Thomas W. *Across World Frontiers*. New York, 1951.

Lasch, Christopher. *American Liberals and the Russian Revolution*. New York, 1962.

League of Nations. *Records of the Second Assembly*. Geneva, 1921.

League of Nations. *Report on Economic Conditions in Russia with Special Reference to the Famine of 1921-1922 and the State of Agriculture*. Ser 2, No.6 Geneva 1922.

Leavitt Moses A. *The JDC Story: Highlights of JDC Activities, 1914-1952*. New York, 1953.

Leggett, George. *The Cheka: Lenin's Political Police, 1917-1922*.Oxford, 1981.

Lewin, Moshe. *Russian Peasants and Soviet Power*. London, 1968.

Liggett, Walter. *The Rise of Herbert Hoover*. New York, 1932.

Lih, Lars. *Bread and Authority in Russia, 1914-1921*.

Link, Eugene P. *Labor-Religion Prophet: The Life and Times of Harry F. Ward*. Boulder, Co, 1984.

Long, James W. *From Privileged to Dispossessed: the Volga Germans, 1860-1917*. Lincoln: University of Nebraska, 1988.

Longshore, Thomas Elwood. *The Higher Criticism in Theology and Religion Contrasted with Ancient Myth and Miracles as Factors in Human Evolution, and Other Essays on Reform*. New York: C. P. Somerby, 1892.

Lord, Robert. *Some Problems of the Peace Conference*. Cambridge, 1922.

Lyons, Eugene. *Herbert Hoover: A Biography*. Garden City: Doubleday, 1947.

Lyons, Eugene. *Our Unknown Ex-President*. Garden City, NY: Doubleday, 1948.

Mackenzie, F.A., *Russia before Dawn*. London, 1923.

Male, D. J., *Russian Peasant Organization before Collectivization*. Cambridge, 1971.

Malle, Silvane. *The Economic Organization of War Communism, 1918 - 1921*. Cambridge, 1985.

Maude, Aylmer. *The Life of Tolstoy: The Later Years*. New York, 1910.

May, Henry F. *The Protestant Churches and Industrial America*. New York: Harper Brothers, 1949.

McCullagh, F. *The Bolshevik Persecution of Christianity*. London, 1927.

McElroy, Robert W. *Morality and American Foreign Policy: the Role of Ethics in International Affairs*. Princeton, 1992.

Melgounov, Sergey Petrovich. *The Red Terror in Russia*. London, 1926.

Millar, James R. ed. *The Soviet Rural Community*. Urbana, 1971.

Moore, R. Laurence. *Religious Outsiders and the Making of America*. New York: Oxford University Press, 1986.

Murray, Robert K. *Red Scare: a Study in National Hysteria, 1919-1920*. Minneapolis, 1955.

Nansen, Fridtjof. *La Famine en Russie: Conference Faite par Ie Dr. Nansen*. Paris, 1922.

Nash, George B. *The Life of Herbert Hoover: the Engineer, 1874-1914*. New York, W. W. Norton, 1983.

Nash, George B. *The Life of Herbert Hoover: the Humanitarian, 1914-1917*. New York: W. W. Norton, 1988

Nash, George B. *The Life of Herbert Hoover: Master of Emergencies. 1917-1918*. New York, 1996.

Nearing, Scott. *Education in Soviet Russia*. New York, 1927.

Nearing, Scott. *Glimpses of the Soviet Republic*. New York, 1926.

Noble, David. *The Paradox of Progressive Thought*. Minneapolis: University of Minnesota Press, 1958.

Noble, David. *The Progressive Mind, 1890-1917*. Minneapolis: Burgess Publishing, 1981.

O'Neill, William L. *The Last Romantic: A Life of Max Eastman*. New York: Oxford, 1978.

Orr, E.P. *Quakers in Peace and War, 1920-1967*. Sussex, England, 1974.

Osborne, Byron Lindley. *The Malone Story: the Dream of Two Quaker Young People*. Canton, Ohio, 1970.

Parks J.D. *Culture, Conflict, and Coexistence: American-Soviet Cultural Relations, 1917-1958*. Jefferson, Mo., 1983.

Payne, Muriel. *Plague, Pestilence, and Famine*. London, 1923.

Pearson, Diane. *The Summer of the Barshinskeys*. New York, 1984.

Perrini, Carl. *Heir to Empire: United States Economic Diplomacy. 1916-1923*. Pittsburgh, 1969.

Perry, R. B. *Thought and Character of William James*. Cambridge: Harvard University Press, 1948.

Peterson, H.C. and Gilbert C. File. *Opponents of War, 1917-1918*. Madison, 1957.

Pethybridge, Roger. *One Step Backwards, Two Steps Forward: Soviet Society and Policy in the New Economic Policy*. Oxford, 1990.

Phillips, William. *Ventures in Diplomacy*. Boston: Beacon press, 1952.

Pickett, Clarence. *For More than Bread*. Boston, 1953.

Poole, Ernest. "The Dark People:" Russia's Crisis. New York: Macmillan, 1918.

Poole, Ernest. *The Village: Russian Impressions*. New York, 1919.

Porter, Anna. *A Moscow Diary*. Chicago, 1926.

Power, Samantha, *A Problem from Hell; America and the Age of Genocide*. New York: Basic Books, 2002

Preston, William, Jr. *Aliens and Dissenters: Federal Suppression of Radicals 1903-1933*. Cambridge, 1963.

Pusey, Merle J. *Charles Evans Hughes*. New York: Macmillan, 1951.

Pusey, Merle J. *Quakers around the World*. London: FWCC, 1994.

Radkey, Oliver H. *The Agrarian Foes of Bolshevism: Promise and Default of the Russian Socialist Revolutio*naries. New York, 1958.

Radkey, Oliver. The *Sickle under the Hammer: Russian Social Revolutionaries in the Early Months of Soviet Rule*. New York, 1973.

Radkey, Oliver. *The Unknown Civil War in South Russia: a Study of the Green Movement in the Tambov Region, 1920-1921*. Stanford, 1976.

Raleigh, Donald. *Revolution on the Volga*. Ithaca: Cornell University Press, 1986.

Ransome, Arthur. *Russia in 1919*. New York, 1919.

Rhodes, Benjamin D. *James P. Goodrich: Indiana's Governor Strangelove*. Selinsgrove, Pa: Susquehanna University Press, 1996.

Riasanovsky, Nicholas V. *Russia and the West in the Teachings of the Slavophiles: a Study of Romantic Ideology*. Cambridge, MA, 1952.

Rickman, John. *An Eye Witness from Russia*. London, 1919.

Rieff, David. A Bed for the Night, Humanitarianism in Crisis, New York: Simon & Schuster, 2002

Roberts, Arthur O. *The Association of Evangelical Friends*. Newberg, Or: Barclay Press, 1975.

Roberts, Nancy L. *American Peace Writers, Editors, and Periodicals: a Dictionary*. Westport: Greenwood Press, 1991.

Robinson, JoAnn. *Abraham Went Out: a Biography of A. J. Muste*. Philadelphia, 1981.

Robbins, Richard G., Jr. *Famine in Russia, 1891-1892: the Imperial Government Responds to a Crisis*. New York, 1975.

Roginskij, A. B., ed. *Vospominanija Krestijan-tolstovtsev, 1910-1930-egodv*. Moscow: Kniga, 1989.

Rosenberg, James N. *On the Steppes: a Russian Diary*. New York, 1927.

Ross, Dorothy. *The Origins of American Social Science*. Cambridge: Cambridge University Press, 1991.

Ross, Edward Alsworth. *The Russian Soviet Republic*. New York and London, 1923.

Rowntree, John Wilhelm. *Essays and Addresses*. ed. Joshua Rowntree. London: Headley Brothers, 1905.

Russell, Elbert. *The History of Quakerism*. New York: Macmillan, 1912.

Russell, Elbert. *Jesus of Nazareth in the Light of Today*. Philadelphia: John C. Winston, 1909.

Russell, Elbert. *Quaker: An Autobiography*. Jackson, TN, 1956.

Russell, Francis. *The Shadow of Blooming Grove: Warren G. Harding in His Times*. New York: McGraw Hill, 1968.

Russian Relief: *Hearings before the Committee on Foreign Affairs House of Representatives, 67th Congress Second Session, on HR 9459 and HR 9548 for the Relief of the Distressed People of Russia. December 13 and 14, 1921.* (Washington, 1921)

Scott, James. C. *The Moral Economy of the Peasant.* New Haven, 1976.

Scott, James. C. *Weapons of the Weak: Everyday Forms of Peasant Resistance.* New Haven, 1985.

Scott, Richenda. *Quakers in Russia.* London: Michael Joseph, 1964.

Selleck, George. *Quakers in Boston.* Boston: Friends Meeting at Cambridge, 1976.

Semashko, N.A. *Health Protection in the USSR.* London: Viktor Gollanza, 1925.

Sen, Amartya. *Poverty and Famines; an Essay on Entitlement and Deprivation.* Oxford, 1981.

Shanin, Teodor. *The Awkward Class.* Oxford, 1972.

Sharp, Evelyn. *In the Volga Valley.* London: Friends Relief Committee, 1922.

Sheinis, Zinovy. *Maxim Litvinov.* trans. Vic Shneierson. Moscow, 1990

Siegel, Katherine A. S. *Loans and Legitimacy: The Evolution of Soviet American Relations, 1919-1933.* Lexington: University of Kentucky Press, 1996.

Siegelbaum, Lewis. *Soviet State and Society Between the Revolutions, 1918-1929.* Cambridge, 1992.

Smith, Jessica. *Women in Soviet Russia.* New York: Vanguard Press, 1928.

Smith, R. E. F. *Bread and Salt: a Social and Economic History of Food and Drink in Russia.* Cambridge: Cambridge University Press, 1984.

Smith, Richard Norton. *An Uncommon Man: The Triumph of Herbert Hoover.* High Plains Publishing, 1984.

Solomon, Susan Gross, and John F. Hutchinson. *Health and Society in Revolutionary Russia.* Bloomington: Indiana University Press, 1990.

Solomon, Susan Gross, and John F. Hutchinson. *Some Notes on Social Conditions in Soviet Russia.* London: Friends Council, 1925.

Sorokin, Pitirim. *Russia and the United States.* New York: E. P. Dutton, 1944.

Steinberg, Mark, ed. *Maxim Gorky, Untimely Thoughts.* New Haven: Yale University, 1995.

Steveni, William Barnes. *Europe's Great Calamity: The Russian Famine- an Appeal for the Russian Peasant.* London, 1922.

Steveni, William Barnes. *Through Famine-Stricken Russia.* London, 1892.

Strauss, Lewis. *Men and Decisions.* New York: Doubleday, 1962.

Strong, Anna Louise. *I Change Worlds.* New York, 1937.

Strong, Tracy. Right in Her Soul: the Life of Anna Louise Strong. New York: Random House, 1983.

Surface, Frank M. and Raymond L. Bland. *American Food in the World War and Reconstruction Period.* Stanford, 1931.

Swan, Jane. *The Lost Children: A Russian Odyssey.* Carlisle, Pa: South Mountain Press, 1989.

Szasz, Ferenc Morton. *The Divided Mind of American Protestantism, 1880 1930*. University of Alabama Press, 1982.

Talbert, Roy J. *Negative Intelligence: The Army and The American Left, 1917-1941*. Jackson, Mississippi, 1991.

Taniuchi, Y. *The Village Gathering in Russia in the mid-1920s*. Birmingham, 1968.

The Mennonites in Russia, 1917-1930. Selected Documents Winnepeg, 1975.

Thomas, Edward. *Quaker Adventures*. New York: Fleming H. Revell Company, 1928

Thompson, Dorothy. *The New Russia*. New York, 1928.

Thompson, John M. *Russia, Bolshevism, and the Versailles Peace*. Princeton, 1966.

Toews, J.B. *Czars, Soviets, and Mennonites*. Newton, 1982.

Toews. J.B. *Lost Fatherland: Mennonite Emigration from Soviet Russia, 1921-1927*. Scottsdale, 1967.

Tolstoi, L.N. *My Religion*. New York: Thomas Cromwell and Co., 1885.

Tolstoy, Alexandra. *I Worked for the Soviet*. New Haven: Yale, 1934.

Tolstoy, Alexandra. *Tolstoy: A Life of My Father*. New York: Harper, 1953.

Tolstoy, Alexandra. *Out of the Past*. New York: Columbia, 1981.

Trueblood, Elton. *The People Called Quakers*. Harper and Row, 1966.

United States Congress, House of Representatives. *Russian Relief: Hearings before the Committee on Foreign Affairs on HR 9459 and HR 9548, 67th Congress, Second Session* 1921.

United States Department of State. *Russia: The Volga River and the Caspian Sea: Confidential Report*. Washington D.C. 1919.

Villard, Oswald Garrison. *Fighting Years: Memoirs of a Liberal Editor*. New York, 1939.

Vining, Elizabeth Gray. *Friend of Life: the Biography of Rufus M. Jones*. London: Michael Joseph, 1958.

Viola, Lynne. *Peasant Rebels under Stalin: Collectivization and the Culture of Peasant Resistance*. Oxford, 1996.

Walicki, Andrzcj. *The Controversy over Capitalism: Studies in the Social Philosophy of the Russian Populists*. South Bend, Indiana, 1988.

Weeks, Charles, Jr. *An American Naval Diplomat in Revolutionary Russia*. Annapolis, 1993.

Weisbrod, Marvin. *Some Form of Peace*. New York: Viking, 1968.

Weissman, Benjamin M. *Herbert Hoover and Famine Relief to Soviet Russia, 1921-1923*. Stanford, 1974.

Wicksteed, A. *Life Under The Soviets*. London, 1928.

White, Colin. *Russia and America: the Roots of Economic Divergence*. London, 1987.

White, Dorice. *Ten Years in Soviet Russia*. London: Russian Affairs Committee Friends Service Council, 1933.

White, Ronald C. Jr. and C. Howard Hopkins, eds. *The Social Gospel: Religion and Reform in Changing America*. Philadelphia: Temple University Press, 1976.

White, Stephen. *The Bolshevik Poster*. New Haven, 1988.

White, Stephen. *The Origins of Détente: Genoa Conference and Soviet-Western Relations, 1921-1922*. Cambridge, 1985.

Wiebe, Robert H. *The Search for Order, 1877-1920*. New York: Hill and Wang, 1967.

Wilson, Francesca M. *In the Margins of Chaos: Recollections of Relief Work*. New York: Macmillan, 1945.

Wilson Joan Hoff. *Herbert Hoover: Forgotten Progressive*. New York: HarperCollins, 1975.

Wood, James. *The Distinguishing Doctrines of the Society of Friends*. New York: Friends Book and Tract Committee, 1898.

Wortman, Richard. *The Crisis of Russian Populism*. Cambridge, 1967.

Wrezin, Michael. *Oswald Garrison Villard: Pacifist at War*. Bloomington: Indiana University press, 1965.

Yarrow, Clarence. *Quaker Experience in International Conciliation*. New Haven, 1978.

Yoder, John H. *Nevertheless: Varieties of Religious Pacifism*. Scottsdale, 1971.

Zelie, John Sheridan. *The Russian Relief Work of the Federal Council of Churches*. New York, 1922.

ARTICLES AND PERIODICALS

Allen, Ronald H. "Report of the Work of the ARA in Samara," *ARA Bound Documents* VI: 528 (Stanford: Hoover Institution on War, Revolution and Peace).

ARA Bulletin, SER 2, 5 VOLS. New York, 1921-26. Hoover Institute Archives, Stanford

Baranchenko, V.E. "Karl Lander", *Voprosy Istorii*, No. 1 (1971): 200-204

Barbour, Hugh and Michael Berkel, "Liberals, Mystics, and Rufus Jones," in Hugh Barbour, et al, eds, *Quaker Crosscurrents*. Syracuse University Press, 1995, 222-226.

Barbour, Hugh and Thomas D. Hamm, "James Wood and the Five Years Meeting," in Hugh Barbour, et al, eds, *Quaker Crosscurrents*. Syracuse University Press, 1995, 210-214.

Bassuk, Daniel E. "Rufus Jones and Mysticism" *Quaker Religious Thought* 7/4 (Summer, 1978).

Beeukwes, Henry. "American Medical and Sanitary Relief in the Russian Famine, 1921-23," *ARA Bulletin* 45 (April, 1926).

Billikopf, Jacob. "Present Day Russia Conditions as Viewed by an Impartial Observer," *Annals of the American Academy of Political and Social Science* CXXXII (July, 1927); 32-36.

Berk, S. "The Democratic Counter-Revolution: Komuch and the Civil War on the Volga," *Canadian-American Slavic Studies* Vol. 7 (1973).

Bolshakov, A. M. "The Soviet Countryside, 1917-1924," in R.E.F. Smith, ed, *The Russian Peasant*. London, 1977.

Bolshakov, A. M. "Brainin Reaffirms Faith in Russian Colonization," *American Hebrew* CXX (November 12,1926): 35

Bolshakov, A. M. "Bread and Intervention" *Freeman* III (August 17, 1921): 533.

Brinton, Howard H. "Friends for Seventy Five Years." *Bulletin of the Friends Historical Association* 49 (Spring, 1960: 13-15.

Brinton, Howard H. "The Revival Movement in Iowa: a Letter from Joel Bean to Rufus M. Jones," *Bulletin of the Friends Historical Association* 50 (Fall, 1961): 102-110.

Brock, Peter "Vasya Bozdnyakov's Dukhobor Narrative," *Slavonic and East European Review* 43 No 100 (December, 1964) and No 101 (June, 1965).

Brooks, Jeffrey. "The Press and its Messages: Images of America in the 1920s and 1930s." in *Russia in the Era of NEP: Explorations in Soviet Society and Culture,* ed. Sheila Fitzpatrick, Alexander Rabinowitch, and Richard Stites. Bloomington, 1991.

Brooks, Sidney. "Russian Railroads in the National Crisis," *ARA Bulletin,* Ser 2, No 42 (November, 1923, 1-91.

Browne, Lewis. "Around the World with a Portable." *American Hebrew* CXX (November 26, 1926): 79, 84.

Cadbury, Henry. "His very name Rufus was Congenially Unusual," *Haverford College Horizons* v 4, No 2 (December 1962).

Cantor, Milton. "The Radical Confrontation with Foreign Policy: War and Revolution, 1914-1920," in *Dissent: Explorations in the History of American Radicalism,* ed. By Alfred F. Young. DeKalb, Ill, 1968.

Carter, J. Roger. "The Quaker International Centre in Berlin, 1920-1942," *Journal of Friends Historical Society* 56 (No. 1) (1990): 15-31.

Chaianov, A. V. "Chto Znachet golod dlia zemle deniia," *Pomoshch* 1 (August 16,1921).

Chamberlin, William Henry. "Missionaries of American Techniques in Russia," *Asia* XXXII (July-August 1932); 422-427,460-463.

Channon, J. "Tsarist Landowners after the Revolution: Former Pomeshchiki in Rural Russia During NEP," *Soviet Studies* 39, No.4 (1987).

Cherniavsky, Michael. "Old Believers and the New Religion" in Michael Cherniavsky, ed., *The Structure of Russian History: Intepretive Essays.* New York, 1970, 140-188.

Colton, Ethan T. "With the YMCA in Revolutionary Russia," *Russian Review* 14(April, 1955), 128-139.

Davis, Donald E. and Eugene P. Trani. "The American YMCA and the Russian Revolution," *Slavic Review* 33 (September, 1974): 469-491.

Davis, Jerome. "The System of Government in Soviet Russia," *Current History* XXVII (December, 1927): 382.

DeBenedetti, Charles ,"Alternative Strategies in the American Peace Movement in the 1920s," in Charles Chatfield, ed., *Peace Movements in America.* New York, 1973.

Dorn, Jacob. "The Social Gospel and Socialism: a Comparison of the Thought of Frances Greenwood Peabody, Washington Gladden and Walter Rauschenbusch," *Church History* 62 (March, 1993): 82-100.

Edelhertz, Bernard. "The Russian Oasis," *American Hebrew* CSSII (March 30, 1928: 722, 732.

Edmundson, Charles M. "The Politics of Hunger: the Soviet Response to Famine, 1921," *Soviet Studies* 29 (October, 1977).

Edmundson, Charles M "An Inquiry into the Termination of Soviet Famine Relief Programs and the Renewal of Grain Export,1922-23," *Soviet Studies* 33 (July, 1981).

Ellingston, James R. "Report on Senator Brookhart's Visit to Russia," *ARA Bound Documents III:* 516-553 (Stanford: Hoover Institution on War, Revolution and Peace.

Endy, Melvin B., Jr. "The Interpretation of Quakerism: Rufus Jones and His Critics," *Quaker History* (Spring, 1981), 21.

Evans, Grant. "The Accursed Problem: Communists and Peasants," *Peasant Studies* 15 (1988): 73-102.

Figes Orlando. "Collective Farming and the 19th Century Russian Land Commune, a Research Note" *Soviet Studies,* 38, No.1 (1986).

Figes Orlando. "The Village and Volost Soviet Elections of 1919" *Soviet Studies* 40, No.1 (1988).

Figes Orlando. "V. P. Danilov on the Analytical Distinction Between Peasants and Farmers," in T. Shanin, ed, *Peasants and Peasant Societies.*

Fisher, Harold. "Frank Alfred Golder," *The Journal of Modern History* 14 (June, 1929): 253-255.

Frick, Stephen. Various pieces in the *Journal of the Friends Historical Society,* Vols. 52 and 53, (1970, 1974 and 1975).

Frierson, Cathy. "Crime and Punishment in the Russian Village: Rural Concepts of Criminality at the End of the Nineteenth Century," *Slavic Review* 45 (1986)

Frost, J. William. "Our Deeds Carry our Message: the Early History of the American Friends Service Committee," *Quaker History* 81 (1992): 3-51.

Giffen, Frederick C. "James Putnam Goodrich and Soviet Russia," *Mid-America* 71 (October 1989): 153-174.

Giesinger, Adam. "The Volga German Refugees of 1921-1922," *The Journal of the American Historical Society of Germans from Russia* 5 (Fall, 1982).

Goodrich, James P. "The Evolution of Soviet Russia," *International Conciliation* No. 185 (April 1923): 205-235.

Goodrich, James P. "Impressions of the Bolshevik Regime," *Century* (May, 1922), 55-65.

Goodrich, James P. "The True Communists of Russia," *Current History* (September, 1922): 927-32.

Gorky, Maxim. "On the Russian Peasantry," in R.E.F. Smith, ed, *The Russian Peasant, 1920 and 1984.* London, 1977.

Gregory, P. "Grain Marketings and Peasant Consumption in Russia, 1885-1913," *Explorations in Economic History,* Vol. 17 (1980).

Gregory, P. "Russian Living Standards during the Industrialization Era, 1885-1913," *Review of Income and Wealth* Vol. 26 (1980).

Gregory, T.T.C. "Overthrowing a Red Regime," *World's Work* XLII (June, 1921): 153-164.

Gregory, T.T.C. "Stemming the Red Tide," *World's Work* (April, 1921).

Haskell, William N. "How we Fed the Starving Russians." *Plain Talk* (July, 1948): 15-19.

Hindus, Maurice. "Ford Conquers Russia," *Outlook* CXLVI (June 29, 1927): 280-282.

Hodgson, Robert H. "Memoirs of an Official Agent: Trading with Russia, 1921-23" *History Today* 4 (August, 1954): 522-28.

Hopkins, George. "The Politics of Food: the United States and Soviet Hungary, March-June, 1919" *Mid-America* 55 (1973): 245-270. ,

Jones, Rufus M. "The Background and Objectives of Foreign Missions," *Crozer Quarterly* (April, 1933).

Jones, Rufus M. "Christ and Modern Thought," *American Friend* 10th Month 7, 1897. 933.

Jones, Rufus M. "Friends and the Present Hour." *American Friend* (December 16,1920).

Jones, Rufus M. "History of the American Friend," *American Friend* (July 13, 1944) 267.

Jones, Rufus M. "The New Quakerism," *American Friend* (November 3,1910) 695-696.

Jones, Rufus M. Judaism on the Russian Prairies," *American Hebrew* CXIX (September 3, 1926): 451.

Kagdan, Allan L. "American Jews and the Soviet Experiment: The Agro-Joint Project, 1924-1937," *Jewish Social Studies* 43:2 (Spring, 1981): 153-64.

Kahan, Arcadius. "Natural Calamities and their Effect upon the Food Supply in Russia,"]*ahrbucher fur Geschichte Osteuropas* 16 (1968): 353-377.

Kasinec, Edward. "Alexis V. Babine (1866-1930): a Biographical Note," in *Slavic Books and Bookmen: Papers and Essays.* New York, 1984, 73-77.

Kennedy, Thomas C. "Fighting about Peace: The No-conscription Fellowship and the British Friends Service Committee, 1915-1919" *Quaker History* 69/1 (Spring, 1980).

Kennedy, Thomas C. "The Quaker Renaissance and the Origins of the Modern British Peace Movement, 1895-1920," *Albion* 16,3 (Fall, 1984): 243-272.

Kennan, George F. "Our Aid to Russia: a Forgotten Chapter." *New York Times Magazine,* July 19, 1959.

Landfield, Jerome. "The Relief of Starving Russians." *American Review of Reviews* (September 1921): 267-271.

Libbey, James K. "The American-Russian Chamber of Commerce," *Diplomatic History* 9 (Summer, 1985): 233-248.

Libby, Frederick J. "The Open Mind for Russia," *American Friend* IX (February 17, 1921): 132.

Lih, Lars T. "Bolshevik Razverstka and War Communism," *Slavic Review* 54 (1986).

Long, J. "Agricultural Condition in the German Colonies of Novouzensk District, Samara, 1864-1914," *Slavonic and East European Review* 57 No 4 (1979).

Long, James W. "The Volga Germans and the Famine of 1921," *Russian Review* 51 (October, 1992): 510-525.

Malone, J. Walter. "Russia and Her Retribution." *Soul Winner* (May 18, 1905), p. 277.

Meyer, Maxim. "A Different Kind of Internationalism, 1921-1991: the Great hunger 70 Years Later," *XX Century and Peace* (February, 1991): 34-38.

Miller, Robert Moats. "The Attitudes of the Major Protestant Churches of America towards War and Peace, 1919-1929," *The Historian* 19 November, 1956).

Mills and Nuelson. "The Truth about Soviet Russia: The Bolsheviks and The Churches," *Zion's Herald* C (December 20, 1922): 1610.

Mills and Nuelson. "Mr. Hoover: Feed Russia!" *The Nation* CXII 9 (February 16, 1921): 255.

Mills and Nuelson. "Mr. Hoover's Ultimatum to Russia." *World Tomorrow* IV (August, 1921): 228-229.

Murray, Robert K. "Herbert Hoover and the Harding Cabinet," in *Herbert Hoover as Secretary of Commerce: Studies in New Era Thought and Practice,* ed. by Ellis W. Hawley. Iowa City, 1981.

Oliver, John. "J. Walter Malone: The American Friend and an Evangelical Quaker's Social Agenda," *Quaker History* 80, # 2 (Fall, 1991): 63-84.

Patenaude, Bertrand M. "Peasants into Russians: the Utopian Essence of War Communism," *Russian Review* 54 (October, 1995): 552-570.

Patenaude, Bertrand M. "The Strange Death of Soviet Communism: the 1921 Version" in *Reexamining the Soviet Experience: Essays in Honor of Alexander Dallin.* Ed. David Holloway and Norman Naimark. Boulder, Co, 1996.

Pasvolsky, Leo. "The Underlying Economic Factors in the Russian Situation," *Annals AAPSS* 114 (1924): 56-61.

Pethybridge, R. W., "Railways and Press Communications in Soviet Russia in the early NEP period. *Soviet Studies* 38 (April, 1986): 194-206.

Queen, George S. "American Relief in the Russian Famine of 1891" *Russian Review* 14:2 (April, 1955): 140-150.

Radek, Karl. "The Famine and the Capitalist World," *Living Age* 31 (October 29,1921): 287.

Raleigh, Donald J. "Revolutionary Politics in Provincial Russia: the Tsaritsyn 'Republic' in 1917", *Slavic Review* 40, No.2 (1981): 194-209.

Reimer, A. "Russian Mennonite Nonresistance in World War I and Its Aftermath," *Journal of Mennonite Studies*, 1993: 135-148.

Rhodes, Benjamin. "Governor James P. Goodrich of Indiana and the 'Plain Facts about Russia'" *Indiana Magazine of History* 85 (March, 1988): 1-30.

Rickard, Edgar and W. L. Brown. "Successful Accomplishment of ARA Work in Russia," *ARA Bulletin* 27 (August, 1922).

Russell, Elbert. "The Principle of Progressive Revelation in Scripture." *American Friend* (January 25,1900, 77-79).

Scott, Richenda C. "Authority or Experience: John Wilhelm Rowntree and the Dilemma of 19th Century British Quakerism," *Journal of the Friends Historical Society* XLIX No. 2 (April 1960), 75-95.

Serbyn, Roman. "The Famine of 1921-1923: a Model for 1932-1933?" in *Famine in Ukraine: 1932-1933*. ed. Roman Serbyn and Bohdan Krawchenko. Edmonton, Canada, 1986.

Senn, A. "P.I. Biryukov, A. Tolstoyan in War Revolution and Peace," *The Russian Review* 32, No.3 (July, 1973).

Simms, James V. "Impact of the Russian Famine, 1891-92, Upon the United States," *Mid-America* 60: 3 (October, 1978): 171-184.

Simms, James V. "The Status of Russian Relief," *The Survey* XLIV (June 26, 1920):431.

Taylor, Graham. "The Bolshevism of Professor Ward" *The Survey* (March 29, 1919), 921.

Villard, Oswald Garrison. "Russia from a Car Window: V: The Soviets and the Human Being" *The Nation* CXXIX (December 4, 1929): 654-657.

Wacker, Grant. "The Holy Spirit and the Spirit of the Age in American Protestantism, 1880-1910," *Journal of American History* 72 (June, 1985): 45-62.

Waters, Elizabeth, "The Female Form in Soviet Political Iconography, 1917-1932," in Barbara Evans Clements, et al, ed., *Russia's Women: Accommodation, Resistance Transformation*. Berkeley, 1991.

Watts, Arthur J. "The Care of Children in Soviet Russia," *Soviet Russia* (March 5,1921).

Weissman, Benjamin. "Herbert Hoover's 'Treaty' with Soviet Russia, August 20, 1921," *Slavic Review* 28 (1969): 276-288.

Wheatcroft, S. "Famine and Epidemic Crisis in Russia, 1918-1922: the Case of Saratov," *Annales de Demographie Historique* (1983): 329-351.

Wilson, Roger C. "We Shall Never Thrive upon Ignorance": J.J. Gurney: the Service of John Wilhelm Rowntree, 1893-1905" in *A Quaker Miscellany for Edward H. Milligan*. Ed. David Blamires, Jeremy Greenwood and Alex Kerr. Manchester, 1985, 155.

Yakovlev, Alexey. "The ARA Men and Their Work in a Russian Province, 1921-1922." ARA, 1922.

Zeiger, Susan. "Finding a Cure for War: Women's Politics and the Peace Movement in the 1920s," *Journal of Social History* (Fall, 1990).

Zelnick, Reginald E. "Wie es eigentlich gegessen: Some Curious Thoughts on the Role of Borsch in Russian History," in John M. Merriman, ed., *For Want of a Horse: Choice and Chance in History.* Lexington, MA, 1985.

UNPUBLISHED ACADEMIC PAPERS

Barton, Betty L. "The Fellowship of Reconciliation: Pacifism, Labor, and Social Welfare, 1915-1960," Ph.D. dissertation, Florida State University, 1974.Caffrey, Augustine J. "The Affirmation Mysticism of Rufus Matthew Jones." DST dissertation, Catholic University of America, 1967.

Chavez, Leo Eugene. "Herbert Hoover and Food Relief: an Application of American Ideology." Ph.D. dissertation, University of Michigan, 1976.

Claussen, Martin Paul. "American-Soviet Relations and the Russian Famine, 1921-1923," Ph.D. dissertation, George Washington University, 1976.

Cooper, Wilmer A. "Rufus M. Jones and the Contemporary Quaker View of Man," Ph.D. Dissertation, Vanderbilt University, 1956.

Dixon, Warren Adams. "Revolution, Reconstruction and Peace: Herbert Hoover and European Food Relief, 1918-1919," MA. Thesis, University of Wisconsin, Madison, 1964.

Edmondson, Charles Milton, "Soviet Famine Relief Measures, 1921-1923," Ph.D. dissertation, Florida State University, 1970.

Engerman, David Charles. "Economic and Cultural Aspects of Early American-Soviet Relations." M.A. thesis, Rutgers University, 1993.

Fallows, T. S. "Forging the Zemstvo Movement: Liberalism and Radicalism on the Volga, 1890-1905," Ph.D. dissertation, Harvard 1981.

Krug,Peter. "Russian Public Physicians and Revolution: the Pirogov Society, 1917-1920," Ph.D. dissertation, University of Wisconsin, 1979

Majid, Anouar. "Granville Hicks and the Dilemma of American Radicalism," Ph.D. dissertation, Syracuse University, 1991

Minear, Mark E. "The Richmond Conference of 1887" M.A. thesis, Earlham School of Religion, 1984. .

Owen, Thomas C. "Radical and Reactionary Critics of Capitalism in Russia, 1890-1921: Xenophobia and the Russian Revolution" paper delivered to the American Association for the Advancement of Slavic Studies, November, 1992.

Patenaude, Bertrand Mark. "Bolshevism in Retreat: the Transition to the New Economic Policy," Ph.D. dissertation, Stanford University, 1987.

Propas, Frederick, "The State Department Bureaucratic Politics and Soviet American Relations, 1918-1938." Ph.D. dissertation, UCLA, 1982.

St. John, Jacqueline. "John F. Stevens: American Assistance to Russian and Siberian Railroads, 1917-1922," Ph.D. dissertation, University of Oklahoma, 1969.

Thomas, Wilbur. "The Social Service of Quakerism." Ph.D. dissertation, Boston University, 1914.

Traini, Eugene P. "Herbert Hoover and the Russian Revolution, 1917-1920," paper presented at the seminar marking the 100th anniversary of the birth of Herbert Hoover, West Branch, Iowa, 1974.

Trott, Margaret. "Soviet Medicine and Western Charity 1917-1927," PhD. dissertation, University of Virginia, 1994

Weissman, Benjamin M. "The American Relief Administration in Russia, 1921-1923: a Case Study in the Interaction between Opposing Political Systems," Ph.D. dissertation, Columbia University, 1968.

OTHER UNPUBLISHED PAPERS AND DOCUMENTS

American Friends Service Committee, Foreign Service Records, 1917-1931, AFSC Archives, Philadelphia

American Friends Service Committee, Russia Committee Records, 1917 - 1924. AFSC Archives, Philadelphia

American Friends Service Committee, Executive Board Minutes, 1917 - 1931, AFSC Archives, Philadelphia

American Red Cross, Papers, Washington D.C.

American Relief Administration, Miscellaneous Papers and Documents, Herbert Hoover Presidential Library, West Branch Iowa.

American Relief Administration, Papers, Hoover Institution on War, Revolution and Peace, Stanford University

BAEF Papers, Herbert Hoover Presidential Library, West Branch Iowa

Babb, Nancy. Papers. Hoover Institution on War, Revolution and Peace, Stanford University

Bean, Joel. Papers. Friends Historical Library, Swarthmore.

Cadbury, Henry. Papers. Quaker Collection, Haverford College.

Detzer, Dorothy. Papers. Swarthmore Peace Collection, Swarthmore.

Evans, Charles. Papers. Quaker Collection, Haverford College.

Fisher, Harold H. Papers. Hoover Institution on War, Revolution and Peace Archives, Stanford University.

Fleming, Harold M. Papers. Hoover Institution on War, Revolution and Peace Archives, Stanford University.

Galpin, Perry. Papers. Hoover Institution on War, Revolution and Peace Archives, Stanford University.

Golder, Frank A.. Papers. Hoover Institution Archives on War, Revolution and Peace, Stanford University.

Goodrich, James P. Papers. Herbert Hoover Presidential Library, West Branch, Iowa.

Haskell, William N. Papers. Hoover Institution Archives, Stanford

Hobbs, Mary Mendenhall. Papers. Hobbs-Mendenhall Papers, Southern Historical Collection, University of North Carolina, Chapel Hill.

Hobbs, Mary Mendenhall. Papers. Hobbs-Mendenhall Papers. Friends Historical Library, Guilford College

Hoover, Herbert. Papers. Herbert Hoover Presidential Library West Branch, Iowa

Hutchinson, Lincoln. Papers. Hoover Institution on War, Revolution and Peace Archives, Stanford University.

Hull, Hannah Clothier. Papers. Swarthmore Peace Collection, Swarthmore.

Jay, Allen. Papers. Friends Historical Library, Guilford College.

Jay, Allen. Papers. Earlham College.

Jones, Rufus M. Papers. Quaker Collection, Haverford College.

Leffingwell, Russell. Papers. Library of Congress.

New England Yearly Meeting, Minutes. Providence RI

Pate, Maurice. Papers. Herbert Hoover Presidential Library, West Branch, Iowa.

Paul, Perry. Papers. Friends Historical Library, Swarthmore.

Rhoads, T. Edgar, 1883-1981. Family Papers, 1908-1920. Quaker Relief Worker, Germany. Friends Historical Library, Swarthmore.

Rhoads, Charles. Papers. Quaker Collection, Haverford College.

Rockefeller, John D., Jr, Papers. Rockefeller Archives, Tarrytown NY

Russell, Elbert. Papers. Earlham College, Richmond, Indiana.

Smith, Jessica, Papers. Hoover Institution on War, Revolution and Peace Archives, Stanford University

Thomas, Wilbur. Papers. Friends Historical Library, Swarthmore, PA

Thomas, Wilbur. Papers. Bowles-Thomas Family Papers, Monterey, MA

Thomas, Wilbur, Executive Secretary Special File, American Friends Service Committee Archives, Philadelphia.

U.S. Department of Justice, FBI Records. National Archives.

U.S. War Department, Records of the Department of Military Intelligence, 1919-1941, RG 165, National Archives.

Vail, Edwin H. Papers. Hoover Institution on War, Revolution and Peace Archives, Stanford

Wardwell, Allen. Papers. New York: Bakhmetev Archive, Columbia University

Wood, Carolena. Papers. Wood Family Papers, Braewold, Mt. Kisco, NY.

Wood, Hollingsworth. Papers. Quaker Collection. Haverford College.

Wood, James. Papers. Wood Family Papers, Friends Historical Library, Swarthmore.

World Student Christian Federation, Archives, Yale Divinity School.

YMCA Archives, University of Minnesota

INDEX

ABOUT THE AUTHORS

David McFadden, principal researcher and author, is a professor of history at Fairfield University in Connecticut where he focuses on Twentieth Century Russian-American relations. His previous book, *Alternative Paths, Soviets and Americans 1917 to 1920*, was published by Oxford University Press in 1983. He lives in Fairfield, Connecticut.

Claire Gorfinkel, writer and editor, is the author of *The Evacuation Diary of Hatsuye Egami* (1995) and *Much Remains to Be Done; Ruth Chance and California's 20th Century Movement for Social Change* (2003) both published by Intentional Productions. She lives in Altadena, California.

Both McFadden and Gorfinkel spent many years on the staff of the American Friends Service Committee, in Philadelphia, San Francisco and Pasadena.

Sergei Nikitin is a Russian Quaker and former staff of Friends House Moscow who has made a special project of visiting the sites where Quaker Service offered relief to Russians during the Great Famine.

THE COVER ARTWORK

The tapestry on the cover was stitched by a Russian peasant woman in the 1920s, presumably at one of Nancy Babb's cottage industries. It was presented to Rufus Jones, Clerk of the American Friends Service Committee from 1917 to 1928, as a thank you gift for the wheat that the AFSC sent to Russia during the famine. The base of the tapestry is a burlap bag in which the wheat was sent. Mary Hoxie Jones donated the tapestry to the AFSC in 1995, and it now hangs in the Rufus Jones Room at the AFSC headquarters in Philadelphia.